CRIME OF THE CENTURY
The Lindbergh Kidnapping Hoax

by

Gregory Ahlgren

&

Stephen Monier

BRANDEN BOOKS

Library of Congress Cataloging-in-Publication Data

Ahlgren, Gregory J., 1952-
    Crime of the century : the Lindbergh kidnapping hoax
/ by Gregory J. Ahlgren & Stephen R. Monier.
        p. cm.
    Includes bibliographical references and index.
    ISBN 0-8283-1971-5
    1. Kidnapping--New Jersey.
    2. Lindbergh, Charles A. (Charles Augustus), 1920-1974.
    I. Monier, Stephen R., 1952-   .
    II. Title.
HV6603.L5A43   1993
364.1'54'092--dc20   92-44191
[B]   CIP

(The entire text was produced with *Pages & Windows*
for DOS WordPerfect 5.1)

BRANDEN BOOKS
Branden Publishing Company, Inc
17 Station Street
Box 843 Brookline Village
Boston, MA 02147

CONTENTS

ACKNOWLEDGMENTS

The authors would like to thank all of those whose help, input and suggestions contributed to this project. A special thanks goes to Bill Lefebvre, Debbie Lajoie, Sheri Kelloway- Martin, Sue LeBel, Denise Roberge and Michael Theodosopoulos.

PREFACE

Colonel Charles A. Lindbergh was one of the central figures of the American twentieth century. His solo flight from New York to Paris in May of 1927 did more than rivet the attention of the world.

Technologically, it granted aviation a respect previously absent. Historically, it altered America's geo-political view. Never again could Americans feel safe behind an ocean which could be crossed by one man, alone, in 33 1/2 hours.

Lindbergh himself was transformed from a social misfit into America's greatest living hero. It mattered little that he was not the best pilot, nor that had he failed, others would have succeeded shortly thereafter. He had done it, and he would forever be "The Lone Eagle."

Accompanying his rise in social prominence was his rise in political stature. As the "Lone Eagle," Lindbergh was able to prevail in a clash with Franklin Roosevelt over issues concerning the federal regulation of airlines, and even for a time, over American foreign policy.

When in 1929, he married the young Anne Morrow, daughter of Ambassador Dwight Morrow, the press and the public treated the couple as the Europeans might royalty. They were hounded by paparazzi.

The 1932 disappearance of their infant son shocked and outraged the nation. When the child's body was discovered, other parents actually wrote to the Lindberghs offering their own children as substitutes.

Beyond the glitz and the grief, however, a darker side of Lindbergh was never exposed. His beliefs on racial superiority were not generally known by the adoring public. The cruel behaviors he often directed at those close to him, were given scant attention.

More than two years after the child's death Bruno Richard Hauptmann was arrested and convicted of the murder. In 1935, shortly before Hauptmann's scheduled execution, the New Jersey governor announced that several troubling aspects of the case compelled him to re-open the investigation. Lindbergh secretly slipped away to Europe with his family.

There he became openly pro-Nazi, often visiting Germany and even accepting an aviation award from Hermann Goering.

Upon his return to America in 1939 Lindbergh became politically outspoken. As the *de facto* leader of the America First Movement, he advocated total neutrality in World War II. He was openly pro-German and pro-Nazi, and in his speeches, made no effort to mask his strong anti-Semitism.

Recognizing the threat posed by a Nazi dominated Europe, President Franklin Roosevelt emerged as the leader of the internationalist forces; Lindbergh the spokesman for isolationism. Although his popularity declined, Lindbergh's position came close to prevailing. That it did not, was attributable to military developments beyond his control.

In the post-war euphoria, Lindbergh's *ante-bellum* stance was swept from the nation's consciousness. What remained were the twin images of "Lucky Lindy," crossing the Atlantic alone and brave, and, to a lesser extent, the tragedy of the loss of his first child. This book explores his role in that tragedy.

CHAPTER I

It is still the most spectacular kidnapping and murder case ever investigated. The disappearance of the 20 month old son of Colonel Charles and Anne Lindbergh from the nursery of their Hopewell, New Jersey home in the early evening of March 1, 1932 shocked the nation and the world. Later that evening Colonel Lindbergh claimed to find a ransom note on a nursery window sill, where Anne and other household staff had previously seen nothing. The note was assumed to be genuine, and the case was then, and has forever after, been treated as a kidnapping.

Colonel Lindbergh himself was allowed to head up the ensuing investigation. He specifically invited the kidnappers to negotiate with him, and a myriad of ransom demands dutifully arrived from various groups claiming to have the child, or the contacts to negotiate his safe return. The police chased after them all.

On May 12 of that year the badly decomposed body of the child was found less than three miles from the Colonel's home and the case was officially elevated to a murder. Two and one-half years later, an itinerant German carpenter named Bruno Richard Hauptmann was arrested, convicted and eventually executed for the crime. Public opinion was nearly unanimous in its belief in Hauptmann's guilt. However, doubt grew with the passage of time and the uncovering of further information. A legitimate school of thought has now developed that Hauptmann was innocent, a mere scapegoat for an embarrassed police force which had no real leads two years after the crime.

But that is not to say there were no suspects. When Betty Gow, the 27 year old Scottish nursemaid discovered the empty crib, her immediate thought was that Colonel Lindbergh, himself, had done it. Anne Lindbergh, upon entering the nursery, independently shared the same suspicion. Despite his image as an American Hero, Charles Lindbergh had a history of directing very cruel behaviors at anyone he perceived as a threat or whom he otherwise sought to control. Although his supporters have referred to this as his penchant for "practical jokes" there was nothing either practical or joking about them.

Just two months earlier he had hidden the baby in a closet and then dramatically announced that the child had been kidnapped. The whole household had been thrown into an uproar while a panic stricken Anne feared the worst. Lindbergh had allowed the ruse to continue for some 20 minutes before roaring heartily and admitting it was all a hoax.

And so, as Betty Gow and Anne Lindbergh stared at the empty crib shortly after 10:00 p.m. on March 1, 1932, they both inwardly suspected that the Colonel was again responsible. Yet that initial suspicion by both the mother and the nurse was the total extent of any investigation ever conducted into Charles Lindbergh's responsibility for this act. He claimed to have found the note, everyone believed the hero, and for 60 years his role in the disappearance and death of his child has gone unexplored.

But that says as much about Charles Lindbergh as it does about our own criminal justice system of 60 years ago. His public image did not accurately reflect the real character of the man the press reverently called "The Lone Eagle."

In many ways Charles Lindbergh's choice of 500 acres straddling the town lines of East Amwell and Hopewell, New Jersey as the site of his future home, was a direct reflection of his own personality. Situated on a hill it was isolated, remote and aloof from its surroundings. It was located in an almost unreachable spot on Featherbed Lane, a seldom used dirt road that left Lindbergh with his nearest neighbor a half mile away. During heavy rains the road would routinely wash out and become impassable.

Lindbergh had spotted the area from the air and it suited him perfectly. Before the post second World War boom in the American suburbs, when most of the population still worked and lived in major cities, Hopewell remained a desolate town in the middle of the depression riddled Sourland Mountains of Hunterdon County. It was agricultural, a mix of woodlands and hilly pastures dotted with ramshackle farms that could have as easily been situated in the Appalachians of Kentucky or West Virginia.

Yet the town was also close enough to New York City that Lindbergh could drive there with all that it offered: his job as a consultant with Trans-Continental Air Transport (later Transworld Airlines), his upper echelon social acquaintances in whose world he moved so easily, an intruding yet adoring public that never let him go, and the journalists and photographers who seemed to hound and record his every step since his epic flight.

The site was about one hour's drive from *Next Day Hill*, the Englewood, New Jersey country estate of wealthy Dwight and Elizabeth Cutter Morrow, Lindbergh's in-laws. Dwight Morrow had risen from an obscure law practice in Pittsburgh to become a partner of J.P. Morgan. He served as United States Ambassador to Mexico, and was often mentioned as a possible Republican nominee for president.

Shortly after purchasing the tract in September of 1930 Lindbergh began to personally supervise construction of his house. Personal supervision and direction dominated all of Charles Lindbergh's projects and his social stature prevented anyone from challenging him. To complete this project he and his wife Anne rented a farmhouse in nearby Mount Rose.

By November the Lindberghs and their five month old son Charles Augustus Lindbergh, Jr. had moved into the Mount Rose house with an English couple, Oliver and Elsie Whately, as butler and cook, and with a Miss Cummings as a nurse for the child.

Although located in the Town of Mount Rose, the rented farmhouse was just four miles from the Lindbergh tract and just a two hour train ride from New York City. Lindbergh commuted to the city on a regular basis.

The new house in Hopewell was a rambling two story whitewashed fieldstone structure built in the French Manor tradition. Set back from the dirt road by a half mile long winding driveway, it was further shrouded by dark woods of sassafras and dogwood.

In February of 1931, Ms. Cummings was replaced by Betty Gow. As his house neared completion, Charles planned a three month flight across the Pacific to the Orient and commanded Anne to accompany him. They left on July 29. Their son was sent with Betty Gow to the Morrow's summer home *Deacon Brown's Point* in North Haven, Maine, with the request from

Anne to "keep some kind of record of his actions and take a picture about once a month." On October 5, 1931, while in China, they received word of the death of Anne's father and returned home by sea. They were reunited with their son on October 27 in Englewood.

The Lindberghs then moved in with Mrs. Morrow and during the winter settled into a very regular pattern of behavior. During the week they would stay at Mrs. Morrow's estate and Charles would commute to New York. On weekends the Lindberghs, with their son and the Whatelys, would stay at their Hopewell house.

Although Betty Gow remained the child's nurse during the week, she did not accompany the Lindberghs on weekends. This was to give Anne Lindbergh a chance to be alone with and care for her child, and to give Betty Gow time off.

On the last weekend of February, 1932, Charles and Anne Lindbergh, with Charles, Jr., the Whatelys and the Lindbergh's English Terrier, *Wahgoosh*, traveled to the Hopewell house.

The three Lindberghs were all suffering from colds. The weather was raw and wet, and a sleeting rain had pulverized the area the whole weekend. The strict pattern had been that on Mondays Charles would leave for work in New York and on Monday afternoons Anne would pack up the household and travel back to Englewood. After work, Charles would join them.

On the morning of Monday, February 29, 1932, Charles left for work as usual. However, he later telephoned Anne and instructed her not to return to Englewood that day. The reason he later gave was that he had concerns about Charles, Jr.'s cold and felt that it was better if he did not make the one hour automobile ride to Englewood.

On Monday evening, Charles did not return home to Hopewell. Instead, he drove the shorter distance to Englewood and spent Monday night at *Next Day Hill*.

On Tuesday morning, March 1, 1932, the rain continued. From New York, Charles telephoned Anne and told her to stay over one more night, that it was still too raw for Charles, Jr. to be driven to Englewood. He further indicated that he would come home that night to Hopewell.

After speaking with Charles, Anne telephoned her mother's home in Englewood. Violette Sharpe, an English maid in the Morrow household, answered. Anne informed her that they would be staying yet another night in Hopewell and requested that Betty Gow be driven out to assist them. At about 1:30 p.m. the nursemaid was chauffeured over from Englewood.

After his solo Atlantic flight in May of 1927, Charles Lindbergh had emerged from obscurity to receive more accolades, awards and adulation from all corners of the globe, than had ever been received before, and has not been replicated since. Among the awards upon his return to America was, at age 25, his instant promotion by the Secretary of War to the rank of colonel in the Army reserves, although Lindbergh's earlier request in 1925 for a permanent commission in the Army had never even elicited a reply. He loved the title "Colonel" and used it constantly. He expected others to use it as well.

Because of his popularity, he was in demand as an after-- dinner speaker or head table guest at every fundraiser imaginable. Everyone recognized the magic which the name "Lindbergh" suddenly held. Despite his reputed contempt for the press he basked in the resultant publicity that accompanied his attendance at these events. On the evening of Tuesday, March 1, 1932, Colonel Lindbergh had such a social engagement in mid-town Manhattan, having accepted an invitation to be the guest speaker at a major fund raising banquet for New York University. The event had received wide publicity. Charles Lindbergh never attended.

In the evening the rain finally stopped, but the wind sprang up and the weather remained raw and cold. Shortly before 6:00 p.m., Betty took Charles, Jr. upstairs and fed him. Shortly after 7:00 p.m. Anne joined them and, together with Betty, prepared him for bed. Betty put Vick's Vapor Rub on his chest, decongestant drops in his nose and dressed him in a flannel shirt with blue silk thread which she had made herself.

They then put on him a sleeveless wool shirt, diapers and rubber pants and over everything a popular store bought "Doctor Denton's One-Piece Sleeping Suit." Over each thumb was placed a shiny metal cylinder which was pinned to his clothes and which was thought to discourage thumb sucking.

Not yet totally completed, the Hopewell house had no curtains, shades or drapes in any of the windows. Its remoteness in an otherwise desolate community was considered sufficient to assure privacy. However, all of the windows had exterior lattice shutters which swiveled in and, once closed, could be latched on the inside.

The child's bedroom was in the southeast corner of the home. Two windows faced east and bracketed a tile fireplace. One window faced south. This south window was located over a cement patio or walkway which ran along the back of the house. The ground below the two east windows was rough scrub as the landscaping had not yet begun.

Betty and Anne closed all three sets of shutters. However, the set of shutters on the east side just to the right of the fireplace were warped and although they could be swung shut, they would not latch. The two east windows were closed, but Betty opened the south window a crack behind its latched shutters to let in fresh air.

At 7:30 p.m. Betty and Anne put Charles, Jr. to bed and pinned his blankets to his sheets and mattress with two three inch safety pins at the head of the crib. They switched off the lights and left the room, closing his bedroom door behind them.

Anne went downstairs to work on her writing, while Betty began washing some of Charles, Jr.'s clothes in the bathroom adjacent to the nursery.

At approximately 7:50 p.m. Betty checked in on Charles, Jr. Finding him sleeping soundly, she descended to the staff sitting room for supper, leaving Charles, Jr. alone in that section of the house for the next two hours and ten minutes.

This was at the specific direction of Colonel Lindbergh, who had ordered that on that evening no one was to enter the nursery or otherwise disturb the child from the time he was put to bed until taken to the bathroom at approximately 10:00 p.m. The reason, the Colonel stated, was so that the child would not be unduly coddled. Like all of Colonel Lindbergh's commands, this one was dutifully obeyed.

Betty received a telephone call from her boyfriend Henry "Red" Johnson. Red was to have picked her up at the Englewood Estate for a date that evening. When she had been called out to Hopewell earlier in the day, she had attempted to telephone him to inform him of her sudden unavailability. As he was not at home, she left a message with his roommate. They talked briefly and she explained things directly.

At approximately 8:25 p.m. Charles Lindbergh arrived home. A slave to perfection, Lindbergh prided himself on his meticulous attention to detail and his devotion to accuracy. "Accuracy," he wrote, "means something to me. It's vital to my sense of values. I've learned not to trust people who are inaccurate. Every aviator knows that if mechanics are inaccurate, aircraft crash. If pilots are inaccurate, they get lost - sometimes killed. In my profession life itself depends on accuracy."[1] Yet he later told the police and others that he had gotten "mixed-up" as to the dates of his speaking engagement and so had missed it. When Lindbergh drove up the driveway at 8:25 p.m., he honked the horn and thereby alerted all of the household to his arrival. Despite the fact that he had ostensibly not seen his son since Monday morning, he did not enter the nursery or otherwise check in on him.

Instead, Charles Lindbergh ate in the dining room with Anne, finishing at approximately 9:10 p.m. Afterwards he and Anne went into the living room where they stayed for five to ten minutes. Outside the wind continued to howl. At one point Charles turned to Anne and asked, "Did you hear that?"

He later described the sound as a cracking sound like wooden slats of an orange crate falling off a chair in the kitchen. There is no evidence that Anne ever heard it.

Charles and Anne went upstairs where they talked for about ten minutes. Eventually Charles left to draw a bath while Anne remained in her bedroom reading. Although the bathroom was next to the nursery, he still did not enter or attempt to check on his son.

After his bath, Lindbergh returned to his study located on the first floor along the east wall directly beneath the second floor nursery. Anne remained in her second floor bedroom. Betty

Gow was upstairs with Elsie Whately in the latter's bedroom looking at her new dress. Ollie Whately was in the staff sitting room with the Lindbergh's Boston Terrier. A high strung dog, known to bark at the slightest provocation or approach of a stranger, *Wahgoosh* never barked that night or was otherwise disturbed.

At 10:00 p.m. Betty Gow went to the nursery to bring Charles, Jr. to the bathroom for one final trip that evening. Upon entering, she did not turn on the light for fear of startling him. She instead closed the south window which was as she had left it inside its latched shutters. She then turned on the electric heater to remove the chill from the room and momentarily stood over the heater warming her hands.

Without the electric light on she apparently could not see into the crib clearly for she sensed, rather than saw, that something was amiss. She could not hear his breathing and she feared that something had happened to him; perhaps he had become tangled in his blankets or his clothes had come over his head. What little light filtered through the doorway seemed to show an empty crib, but to be sure she felt all over the bed for him. He was gone.

Anne's room was immediately next door and connected by a passage. Anne had been in her room since leaving the dining room at approximately 9:20 p.m. Betty went in and, finding Anne preparing for bed, asked if she had the child.

Anne indicated that she did not and Betty suggested that perhaps the Colonel had him. Betty then went downstairs where she found the Colonel in his study directly below the nursery.

When asked if he had the baby, Colonel Lindbergh retorted that he did not and he raced upstairs. Entering the nursery from the corridor, he flicked on the electric light as Anne entered from the passageway.

"Do you have our baby?" Anne asked. The crib was empty. The two three inch safety pins were still in place. The undisturbed bed clothes and pillow still bore the indentation where the child had lain.

The Colonel did not respond to the question. Neither did he ask any questions of Betty or Anne nor conduct a search of the room or upstairs labyrinth of rooms for the location of a 20 month old toddler.

"Anne," he simply said in a calm voice, "they have stolen our baby."

Colonel Lindbergh instructed Ollie Whately to telephone the local Hopewell Police and then he went into his bedroom and loaded his rifle. Commanding everyone "don't touch anything", he rushed downstairs and out into the night and disappeared down the driveway.

Recovering from the impact of the Colonel's statement, Betty, Anne and Elsie now began a systematic search of all the rooms and closets in the house. After its fruitless completion they disconsolately assembled in the living room to await the Colonel's return.

Ollie Whately completed his call and then went outside to assist Lindbergh. He found the Colonel in his car and together they drove up and down the dirt road, shining headlights on either side. Finally Lindbergh told Whately to go into town and secure some flashlights while he returned to the house. Whately took Lindbergh's car and drove off towards town.

After re-entering the house, Lindbergh returned to the nursery by himself. Upon emerging he stated that there was an envelope on the radiator beneath the closed but unlocked east window to the right of the fireplace. This was the window with the warped shutter which would not latch. The right shutter of this window was open but the left one was shut. Despite the earlier search by Anne, Betty and Elsie, no one else had previously seen this envelope.

Instead of grabbing the envelope and ripping it open to learn of clues concerning the whereabouts of his child or the conditions for his safe return, Colonel Lindbergh calmly commanded that no one touch the envelope.

Colonel Lindbergh then made two telephone calls. The first was to his lawyer in New York City, Colonel Henry Breckinridge. After completing that call, he then telephoned the New Jersey State Police to report that his son had been kidnapped.

Ollie Whately encountered the Hopewell Police officers on the road. As they had flashlights with them he abandoned his quest into town and accompanied them back to the house. Present with Ollie Whately were Hopewell Police Chief Harry Wolfe and Assistant Chief Williamson.

Colonel Lindbergh adopted a pattern of behavior that he was not to relinquish in the coming days and months: he took charge of the investigation. He began by taking Chief Wolfe and Assistant Chief Williamson up to the nursery, showing them the note on the radiator under the window, pointing out clumps of yellow clay leading from the window to the crib, and telling them not to touch anything until a fingerprint expert arrived.

The local police officials were clearly in over their heads and were awed at actually being in the presence of Colonel Charles Lindbergh. They did not question his authority or challenge his commands. This initial mistake would ultimately be replicated by each succeeding level of police and prosecutorial authority throughout the case, and its effects would never be remedied.

Colonel Lindbergh took the two local police officers outside with their flashlights. In the soft mud just to the right of the nursery window with the warped shutters were two holes as if made by a ladder. Leading back from the holes were footprints which led to where the soft ground ended and scrub began.

The Colonel led the other two back along the footprint trail. At the edge of the scrub they found an obviously handmade extension ladder.

The ladder was unlike any other. It came in three sections and was designed so that each subsequent section would fit inside another, wherein it could be fastened by the insertion of a wooden dowel to hold that section in place. The rung slats were more like crosspieces, poorly notched into the side rails. The rungs were also very far apart. Whereas a standard ladder has rungs approximately twelve inches apart, these rungs were nineteen inches apart, making it appear to have been custom built by, and for, a very tall man with long legs. The top rung and adjoining side rail of the bottom section of the ladder had split.

When found, the bottom two sections were still together. The top section lay approximately twelve feet away. Also found in the mud under the window was a three-quarter inch Bucks chisel with a wooden handle. Later analysis revealed it to be at least thirty years old.

The three then trudged back inside the house and the Hopewell Police began to attempt an investigation. Assistant Chief Williamson later noted that the other members of the household were understandably nervous and agitated. Yet curiously, although his first and then only child had ostensibly just been kidnapped, Colonel Lindbergh appeared very calm and collected. The investigation made no progress and Williamson noted that no information was learned relative to the kidnapping. Before it could progress too far, officers from the New Jersey State Police began to arrive and the Hopewell Police were only too glad to step aside.

After Colonel Lindbergh's telephone call had been received by the New Jersey State Police, they had immediately put a call out on their wire. The flash was picked up by other departments and acted upon. New York City Police closed down the Washington Bridge as well as other bridge and tunnel connections from New Jersey to the city, searched all cars entering the city from New Jersey and recorded all license plates. The massive dragnet that was to sweep the nation in the coming weeks and months got off to a quick and thorough start that night.

The first State Troopers to arrive at the Lindbergh house were only the beginning of an unorganized horde of police and press people whose continued arrival progressed uninterrupted throughout the night. The New Jersey State Police had put out the word and the name "Lindbergh" prompted all who heard to converge without orders, and without organization. They simply came, and as their numbers swelled the chances of ever finding the truth decreased in direct proportion. Among the first were State Troopers Cain and Wolf from Lambertville; de Gaetano and Bornmann from Wilburtha, Captain Lamb, Lieutenant Keaton, Major Schoeffel and others. And as each rode up on his motorcycle and aimlessly tramped over the grounds he successfully helped grind every available physical clue deeper into the soft mud.

Each trooper was met personally by Colonel Lindbergh and, as was common with almost everyone who met "The Lone Eagle" in those heady days after May of 1927, each man, like Hopewell Officers Wolfe and Williamson, was awed at being in the Colonel's presence.

And the Colonel took advantage of their reaction. He commanded that no one touch the envelope until the fingerprint man arrived and no one did.

The troopers who tramped the grounds that night, obliterating every clue, were not the only arrivees. The initial State Police flash had been picked up by countless news reporters and radio journalists who routinely monitored all such calls. By 10:30 p.m., one half hour after the discovery by Betty Gow, radio stations were already broadcasting their first reports.

Shortly thereafter a steady stream of reporters began pilgrimages to the Hopewell house. As the troopers who arrived early were disorganized and without direction, no precautions were taken to limit the reporters' access to the house or grounds, nor were any precautions taken by the police to preserve the crime scene.

And curiously, Colonel Lindbergh himself, who supposedly was so calm and composed at the time (according to Assistant Chief Williamson), and who supposedly was the only one logical and cool enough to adamantly command that no one touch the envelope, did nothing to stop or stem the onslaught of reporters who added to the melee and trampled the soggy earth.

In fact, Colonel Lindbergh did the opposite. A man who hated the press and who often spoke bluntly and viciously of his feelings concerning what he considered to be its intrusion into his personal life, now acted atypically. As each reporter arrived Colonel Lindbergh met him personally at the door, invited him in, escorted him to the living room, made sure that Whately made sandwiches for everyone and that all had enough to eat, and thanked each one for the concern exhibited and for coming out on such a night. He was courteous, deferential and solicitous. He was not behaving in a manner consistent with his personality.

Eventually the head of the New Jersey State Police, Colonel Norman Schwarzkopf, arrived. A West Point graduate and World War I veteran, Colonel Schwarzkopf had since left the army. At one point he had sunk to being a store detective at Bamberger's

Department Store in New York before receiving the appointment by the Governor of New Jersey to head up the State Police, despite the lack of any previous police experience. A political appointee, Colonel Schwarzkopf, like the Hopewell officers and his own troopers before him, quickly deferred to the presence and commands of Colonel Lindbergh. Shortly after midnight the fingerprint expert, Trooper Frank Kelly, arrived. Only then was the envelope disturbed. Trooper Kelly put on a pair of gloves and dusted the envelope with black powder. There were no prints. He then slit open the envelope and dusted the inserted letter. There were no prints there either. The note was hand-written:

> Dear Sir! Have 50.000$ redy 25.000$ in 20$ bills 15.000 in 10$ bills and 10.000$ in 5$ bills. After 2-4 days we will inform you were to deliver the Mony. We warn you for making anyding public or for notify the Police the child is in gut care. Indication for all letters are singnature and 3 holes.

At the bottom of the note was a symbol of two interlocking circles whose overlap comprised an oval. The oval was colored red and the remainder of the circles blue. At the center of each geometric shape was a square hole.

Frank Kelly proceeded to dust the nursery for fingerprints. The popular significance given fingerprint analysis in movies, television and written fiction is greatly exaggerated. It is extraordinary how often television shows "solve" a crime by analyzing a forgotten fingerprint on cloth, clothing or even skin. In reality, fingerprints are not easily made and therefore not readily discoverable. The conditions have to be close to ideal: a hard, flat, clean surface and a distinct and clear pressure from a finger. The print is made when body oil from the finger is deposited on an appropriate surface sufficiently flat and clean so that it will record the ridged impression of human skin.

Fingerprints can rarely be made on cloth, skin, fabric, curtains, masonry, rugs or porous wood. They are useless if smudged. If the receptive surface is oily, greasy or wet they will not take. They are almost impossible to obtain from outdoor surfaces exposed to the elements for any length of time. Best results are obtained from a print on clear glass, flat metal or smooth surfaced wood.

Frank Kelly dusted the whole nursery. Good possibilities for expected fingerprint sources were the crib, rails and headboard, the radiator casing, the window, and perhaps the surfaces just inside the window such as the sill and sash. There was, of course, the risk that a careful kidnapper or gang of kidnappers would have worn gloves. If so, then the criminals would have removed the child from his crib and quickly left the room, leaving whatever residual fingerprints remained from Anne, Betty Gow, the Colonel and perhaps even the Whatelys. Yet the dusting by Frank Kelly revealed no fingerprints. None. Not even a stray print of an innocent household member was found anywhere: on the crib, the radiators, the windows, the walls or any other furniture. None. "I'm damned," said one trooper, "if I don't think somebody washed everything in that nursery before the printmen got there."2 Other cops nodded sagely, yet neither in that immediate investigation nor in the years since has anyone seemed to realize the import of that casual observation.

That evening, a massive investigation began that ultimately involved the total force of the New Jersey State Police, the New York State Police, the FBI and other law enforcement agencies on the State and Federal level. Every lead was tracked down. Thousands of witnesses and potential suspects were routinely picked up and questioned vigorously. In the face of such police interrogation two separate witness/suspects would eventually commit suicide rather than submit to additional police hounding. The reports and investigative notes of the New Jersey State Police alone would total over 100,000 pages.

Citizens got in the act. Reports of children vaguely resembling the Lindbergh child poured in from all over the country. In those years of heady police power before the Supreme Court put teeth into the constitutional protection to be free from unreasonable searches and seizures, countless parents in the company of their own young children were arrested, questioned and reluctantly released. One upstate New York couple was stopped so many times in their own town they began carrying a letter from their police chief stating that their child was theirs. They were still stopped. One motorist on a cross-country trip to California with New Jersey license plates was stopped and arrested twelve times as part of the Lindbergh investigation.

Yet despite the massive investment of police power, no trace of a kidnapping gang was ever found. No similar modus operandi were matched. No organized crime or underworld connection was uncovered. No lucky tip led to the inadvertent discovery of the kidnappers' den.

It was as if the kidnappers had appeared on the planet in the morning, kidnapped the child that night, and then immediately disappeared off the face of the earth, never to be heard from again.

On May 12, 1932 the body of Charles A. Lindbergh, Jr. was found in the woods just off a country road in Mount Rose, New Jersey, less than three miles from the Lindbergh home. In the initial cursory examination of the body, the coroner noted from the state of decomposition that it appeared that the child had been dead over two months and the police theorized the child was killed the night he disappeared. More certain data could not be obtained because, after Betty Gow and Colonel Lindbergh identified the body, the Colonel ordered the remains cremated immediately, before an autopsy or any pathological or toxicological tests could be performed. In compliance with his orders, the remains were cremated within the hour.

Some two years and six months after the kidnapping, an uneducated German immigrant carpenter by the name of Bruno Richard Hauptmann was arrested. In January and February of 1935 he was tried for the kidnapping and murder in a Flemington, New Jersey courthouse. Speaking only broken English, he was not afforded the opportunity of a translator at his trial. It is unknown if it would have mattered, because in any event the defense was never given the investigative notes in this case or otherwise apprised before the trial of the evidence that they would have to defend against. Hauptmann was convicted on extremely circumstantial evidence, and on April 3, 1936, maintaining his innocence to the end, was executed in the electric chair in

Trenton, New Jersey. With his death, the State officially closed their case.

Bruno Richard Hauptmann's conviction and execution troubled observers from the beginning. With the passage of time and the eventual release of police notes and other documents and exhibits, more and more doubt was cast on the sanctity of his conviction. His family has fought diligently to clear his name. What is now clear is that the Lindbergh baby was not kidnapped by either one person or a gang, but rather was killed negligently by his father who, facing the enormity of what he had done and its probable tarnishing of his public image, trumped up the kidnapping story as a cover.

For over sixty years it has worked.

CHAPTER II

Colonel Charles Lindbergh's grandfather, Ole Mansson, was born in Sweden in 1810. Despite his peasant origin, through hard work he became a land owner and, as such, was able to get elected to the Swedish Parliament at age 39. However, he developed so many political enemies that at age 50 he was forced, with his second wife and their newborn son Charles Augustus, to immigrate to the United States.

Ole changed the last name of his family to Lindbergh and settled in Minnesota where he resumed farming. When in 1862 he lost his right arm in a milling accident he reportedly never complained but merely, after a two year recovery, redesigned his tools for use with one arm.

The family homesteaded, and depended heavily on the hunting of wild game for their nutrition. Charles Augustus Lindbergh became proficient with a rifle and often solely shouldered the responsibility of securing game. During one winter hunting trip he brought down several ducks over a neighbor's pond. The water was so cold that the hunting spaniel retrieved only two mallards before refusing to re- enter the frigid pond. Lindbergh stripped off his coat and clothes and waded into the pond in the midst of the Minnesota winter to retrieve all the ducks.

Lindbergh eventually became a successful lawyer in Minnesota. He married and had two daughters, Eva and Lillian, before his first wife died of an intestinal tumor at age 31.

Three years later he married Evangeline Land, a school teacher from Detroit who was teaching in Little Falls. Her father was Dr. Charles Land, a dentist and inventor who held several patents.

Evangeline was shy and withdrawn and also 17 years younger than Lindbergh. On February 4, 1902 they had their only child, Charles A. Lindbergh, Jr.

The family settled on their farm on the west bank of the Mississippi near the town of Little Falls. In 1905 the farmhouse caught fire. A nursemaid rescued three year old Charles from a room in which he had been playing and carried him outside. Although she told him not to watch, he did anyway, hypnotically mesmerized as the family home disintegrated in flames before his eyes.

Disintegrating also was the marriage between Evangeline and Charles Augustus Lindbergh. Although they never divorced or even legally separated, thereafter they lived apart. When they did reside in the same house for appearances sake, they stayed in separate areas.

Appearances were important because in 1906 Charles A. Lindbergh, Sr. was elected to the United States Congress, a position he held for ten years. Thereafter he spent most of his time in Washington while Evangeline divided her time between D.C., the Minnesota farm, and her family's home in Detroit. The young Lindbergh also shuttled between three locales. While in Washington his father would indulge him by taking him onto the floor of the Congress. Although he later referred to Washington with a mixture of distaste and curiosity, he was also impressed by its historic nature.

In the spring he would move to Detroit, spending time with his mother and Dr. Land. He was fascinated by his grandfather's inventions and later would often refer to the hours spent in this laboratory.

After the short stay in Detroit, he and his mother would move west by train where they would open up the family farm in Minnesota for the season. During this period of constant migration, Charles attended eleven different schools and did well in none of them. He developed no close friendships. His half-sisters were significantly older and were out and living on their own while he was still a boy. His only constant companion was his mother.

Evangeline Lindbergh possessed a very negative image among the townspeople. She was considered aloof, pretentious, and patronizing. She often rode horseback alone through the area and few would even speak to her. On one occasion when riding through town with Charles, Jr. shots were actually fired at Mrs. Lindbergh by townspeople. They were aimed to frighten, not harm. Her young son grabbed his .22 rifle and fired back at those he believed had done the shooting. Although he did not hit anyone, his return shots came much closer than the original ones had to Mrs. Lindbergh.

Incidents such as these prevented anyone from attempting to develop a friendship with Charles, Jr. For her part Evangeline did not encourage him to develop relationships with anyone but herself and would quickly express her disapproval if he began to do so with other children his own age. Yet her own relationship with him was cold and somewhat formal. She would shake hands with him when they parted and when she put him to bed.

Discouraged or prevented from peer friendships, Charles, Jr. became fixated on machines. His autobiographical writings are filled with accounts of how he learned to drive an automobile at age 11, and of his subsequent love affair with a motorcycle. Conspicuously absent are tales of personal friendships. Nor is there any evidence that as he entered adolescence he had any interest in females.

Charles, Jr. invariably played alone on the Minnesota farm. He demonstrated a natural proclivity at an early age to construct items from wood. A raft by the river and a garden shed were two projects of which he was most proud.

When his father was home from Washington they occasionally hunted or swam together in the Mississippi River. During one such excursion, while playing on the riverbank at a spot where the current was especially swift, young Charles fell in. In order to teach him to be tough the elder Lindbergh refused any help to his son, thereby forcing him to learn to swim in order to avoid being swept downstream.

When Charles was ten his father bought their first automobile. Although neither of his parents were mechanically inclined, by age 11 Charles was driving it regularly.

During the summer of 1915 Congressman Lindbergh took a six week leave of absence to undertake an expedition on the Mississippi. He was to write a report following his journey on the efficacy of the system of dams then in existence. He took his 13 year old son with him.

It was a long and arduous journey. Traveling in a small boat powered by an outboard motor, they camped out along the way with Indians and farmers while contending with relentless insects. Despite the conditions young Charles held up well. To spend so much time with his father was an unusual experience which he revelled in. For his part the father took the occasion to talk of the great trials ahead for the nation, of the possibility of war, and of his own political ambitions.

Those ambitions were soon to be dashed because in 1916, after having announced his intention to give up his congressional seat to run for the United States Senate, Charles Lindbergh, Sr. was defeated in the primary. In the next two years the elder Lindbergh increased his opposition to the war and set his eyes on the Minnesota governorship. It was an ugly campaign filled with virulent attacks against Lindbergh, particularly for his stance on the war and for what was perceived to have been anti-Catholic sentiments expressed during the previous campaign. He lost the gubernatorial race, and this effectively marked the end of his political career.

During this period, Charles and his mother, along with her brother Charles Land of Detroit, decided to drive to California. In 1916 the roads which existed were hazardous and frequently subject to the whims of the weather. The trip, which was supposed to take two weeks, lasted forty days. Young Charles drove the entire distance himself in a recently purchased Saxon Six.

In California mother and son rented a cottage on Redondo Beach where Charles enrolled in High School. There he was little interested in school, made no new friends, and frequently was truant. He was arrested in California for driving while under age and without any headlights. When his mother appeared at the police station she let it be known that her husband was a Congressman, and when Charles appeared in Court with his mother, he was let go with a warning.

Evangeline received word that her mother was ill with cancer and they quickly returned to Detroit with Charles, underage or not, again driving the entire distance. Eventually Mrs. Land was brought back to the farm in Little Falls where her daughter looked after her until her death in 1919.

In the winter of 1916-17 Charles and his mother prepared to stay on the farm, a new experience for them. Charles reluctantly re-enrolled in school but his heart was not in it. Instead he actively prepared the house for winter habitation by installing storm windows, a wood furnace, a new well and plumbing. His father gave him permission to stock the farm with livestock and he set about this task with relish. He bought cattle, hogs, sheep, chickens and geese. A seventy year old retired lumberjack, Daniel Thompson, lived in the tenants' house and helped with odd jobs.

As he entered his senior year in high school he worried about the final examinations he would have to take to graduate. For the first time the realization that his low grades and lack of academic interest would be detrimental, troubled him. Fortuitously, the high school principal announced that anyone who wanted to work on their farm in lieu of attending school would be given full academic credit. Because of the war effort, and lack of farm laborers, the government had encouraged such a program to maintain food production.

Charles leaped at the opportunity and launched himself full time into the farming effort. The alternative program provided him not only with a chance to work on the farm but also to leave school where he had considered the other students, even those his own age, as "kids." He became a good and dedicated farmer, working from the crack of dawn until late at night, often in sub-zero weather. He also slept in the cold, preferring a bed on the screened porch piled high with blankets with only his dog as company.

Several years later he would write, "Farm work enabled me to combine my love of earth and animals with my interest in machinery. Each day was an adventure: taming cattle fresh from the range, breaking pasture for more cropland, dynamiting stone islands out of older fields."3

But he also found himself thinking of the future. "If war continued, I would soon become of military age, and soon afterward I would probably be in the Army. If peace came first, I would be faced with problems of college and examinations far more difficult than those I had avoided by farming in the war emergency."4 Neither was a happy prospect.

On November 11, 1918, word came by telephone at a farm auction he was attending that the war was over. Lindbergh continued farming for a few more months until, at his mother's urging, he enrolled at the University of Wisconsin at Madison. He was to study engineering. Never happy about this arrangement, he did so only because his parents, and in particular his mother, desired it. He never graduated and except for a few occasions, never again lived on the family farm in Little Falls.

During the one year he did spend in college, he made few friends. His mother secured a teaching job in the Madison area and rented an apartment close to the University where Charles continued to live with her. His academic difficulties continued. Rather than studying, he was much more likely to be found riding around the area on his motorcycle.

He also began to exhibit a tendency towards reckless endeavors. He delighted in racing through the woods and hills surrounding Madison on his motorcycle. When the two other motorcycle owners who were attending the University would join him, he would taunt them if they could not keep up. If they had to push their bikes over difficult terrain, he would turn and drive his motorcycle around them in a circle, all the while challenging their abilities to ride a bike.

Once, when these same acquaintances were standing at the bottom of a steep hill near the home of the college president, they told Lindbergh it was impossible to drive down the hill on a motorcycle at top speed and make the sharp turn at the bottom. Taking this as a challenge, Lindbergh assured them that not only could he do it but he could do it without brakes. When it became readily apparent that Lindbergh was quite serious they attempted, to no avail, to dissuade him.

Lindbergh drove his motorcycle to the top of the hill, put it in gear and, to their horror, drove at top speed down the hill. Approaching the bottom it was evident that he was not slowing, and as he came into the curve they could see he was not using any brakes. Although he leaned into the curve, he crashed into a fence. Bruised and battered, he picked himself up and, to their great discomfort, tried it again, this time successfully.

This was not the only odd behavior he began to regularly display. During a visit back to the farm one afternoon he was wandering through the house with a Colt .45 strapped to his hip. People who knew Lindbergh were aware of his fascination with guns and he often envisioned himself a "fast draw" expert. He regularly practiced shooting during the time he was in college. While going from room to room he would leap through entrance ways, practicing his "quick draw." Something went wrong during one of these quick draws and he shot a hole through the door between the kitchen and the hallway. Fortunately, no one was standing on the other side. Lindbergh's only reaction was disappointment in finding that the hole was too high to have killed the imaginary enemy.

He had returned to the farm that day because he was contemplating how to tell his parents, particularly his mother, that he was going to drop out of college after little more than one year. Had he not decided to leave school the University might well have made the decision for him. Because of his poor grades he had been placed on academic probation and it was only a matter of time before he flunked out.

Other students at the University recall that Lindbergh considered himself above the rules of the college, rebellious towards authority, and generally contradictory in his dealings with others. One classmate recalled Lindbergh complained to him that, "They treat you here as though you were a baby. Presumably a man comes to college because he wants an education. Why, then, all this taking of rolls, daily assignments, checks on your personal life, and so on?"5

He had also begun to think of learning to fly. When he expressed this to his mother she did little herself to dissuade him, although she did write to his father to ask that he discourage Charles from becoming a pilot. The senior Lindbergh sent his son a letter in which he pointed out that insurance companies would not insure pilots, even in peace time, because they considered the profession to have no future.

Charles had written a letter to the Nebraska Aircraft Company in Lincoln which made Lincoln Standard planes. They had advertised that they would give instructions to all potential buyers and Lindbergh wrote to them and said that although he was not yet in the market for a plane he would pay for the instruction. The cost for flight instruction, they wrote back, would be $500.00.

He decided that this was the opportunity he had been waiting for and so informed his mother. She replied simply that, "If you really want to fly, that's what you should do." Looking at him without emotion she said, "You must go. You must lead your own life. I mustn't hold you back. Only I can't see the time when we'll be together again."6

On March 22, 1922, he said good-bye to his mother in Madison and set out on his motorcycle for Lincoln, Nebraska, arriving alone on April 1. His mother moved out of the apartment and back to Detroit where she secured another teaching job in the high school, and where she remained for the rest of her life. Students at the Detroit High School would later nickname her "Stone Face."

In 1922 aviation was in its infancy in this country, limited primarily to military use, and "barnstorming," the equivalent of airborne circus rides, offered by lone pilots flying between rural fields. In many ways European aviation was well ahead of American - regular passenger routes had already been established between Amsterdam and London.

The planes "manufactured" by the Nebraska Aircraft Corporation were actually modified and rehabed surplus Army Aviation training bi-planes. They were converted for civilian use and equipped with a water-cooled V-8 engine which turned out approximately 150 horsepower. The company was owned by Ray Page, and the only regular student enrolled for flight instruction in 1922 was Charles Lindbergh. The company was about to be sold by Page. Lindbergh did not know this at the time he turned over the remainder of the $500.00 he owed for the flight instruction and which Page had quickly demanded upon his arrival.

Several people ended up giving lessons to Lindbergh while he was at the aircraft company, although his chief instructor was supposed to be Ira Biffle, a retired Army Air Corps instructor. Biffle, however, had lost his nerve after the flying death of a close friend, and gave many excuses why he could not take Lindbergh up on the days and times he had scheduled.

While at the school Lindbergh did form a friendship with a sixteen year old named Bud Gurney which lasted for several years. Gurney would hang around the mechanics who worked at the company, doing odd jobs, and hope that he also would be taught to fly. It was Gurney who began calling Lindbergh "Slim," a nickname which, like "The Lone Eagle," followed him for the remainder of his years. Lindbergh also spent many hours with the mechanics, learning how to service the planes, attach propellers, and complete repair work to the fragile wings covered with fabric stretched tight with rope.

Lindbergh began to develop a meticulous attitude towards all aspects of his life. He noticed how the better pilots tested and checked each part of a plane before flight, how each detail was analyzed and every contingency planned for before actually taking to the air. Though soon to be called "Daredevil Lindbergh" for his barnstorming stunts, he left little to chance and nothing unplanned. He expected perfection from himself, and certainly from those around him.

After more than eight weeks at Ray Page's, Lindbergh had little more than six or eight hours instruction in a plane. Moreover, he learned that Page was selling the training plane to a barnstormer named Erold Bahl. Lindbergh tried without success to convince Page to let him solo before the plane was sold. When Bahl arrived to pick up the plane (he was embarking on a month long barnstorming tour) Lindbergh asked if he could go along as an assistant. He even offered to pay his own way. Bahl eventually acquiesced.

Lindbergh did well as an assistant, and learned to "wing walk," to step out onto the wing as Bahl flew over town. A few days into the tour Bahl offered to pay for Lindbergh's expenses. After a month of touring, Lindbergh returned to the Lincoln Standard Factory. He received several more hours flight instruction there and in June, 1922 worked in the factory for fifteen dollars a week.

One day a husband and wife parachuting team visited Lincoln on their own barnstorming tour. The Hardins had been show-jumping at county fairs across the country to earn the modest fees and to market their own brand of parachutes.

Lindbergh was fascinated by the possibilities offered by a parachute and mesmerized by the demonstration put on by the Hardins. As he watched them practice an idea for a stunt occurred to him. He approached the Hardins with it.

At a fair one could jump from a plane and deploy his para-chute. After descending for a short period, the jumper could cut away the chute with a knife and plunge towards the horrified crowd below, who would assume that the chute had failed. The chutist would then deploy a second hidden parachute and safely float towards what would surely then be an adoring crowd.

The stunt had possibilities and the Hardins liked it. It was dangerous but they believed that an experienced chutist, if well prepared and well practiced, could pull it off. However, Lindbergh had different ideas. He wanted to attempt it by himself.

Both Hardins were aghast. Not only was there insufficient planning for such a stunt, Lindbergh had never made any parachute jumps. It was risky for someone with experience to attempt such a stunt; for a neophyte it was suicidal.

Lindbergh would not be deterred. He lied to the Hardins and told them that he was considering buying one of their parachutes and this would be the test. The Hardins finally agreed and Lindbergh, on his very first parachute jump, pulled off the double jump stunt. Although eventually Lindbergh did in fact acquire a Hardin parachute, it was not purchased from them but rather acquired as a settlement from Ray Page in payment for flying time owed to Lindbergh.

Shortly after, Lindbergh left the factory and went on a barnstorming tour with an excellent flyer named "Shorty" Lynch. Lynch took Lindbergh along as an assistant since he could wing walk and make parachute jumps from the plane. The publicity posters billed "Daredevil Lindbergh." The tour was successful, ending in October, and Lindbergh spent the next several months visiting first with his mother and then with his father on the farm in Little Falls.

In early 1923 Lindbergh read that the Army was selling surplus "Jennies," a nick name for the Curtis JN-4D, a bi-plane used to train pilots during the first World War. It was slow but reliable. With his father's assistance in the form of a loan guarantee, he raised enough money to buy one from Souther Field, Georgia, for five hundred dollars.

Lindbergh still had not soloed, and, since this was before pilot's licenses were required, no one asked him whether he was a pilot. Why else would he buy one?

Never having previously flown in a Jenny, he almost crashed on his first attempt to take off. An unknown pilot who had been watching, got in the plane and helped familiarize him with it. He spent the next week or so at Souther field, living alone by his new plane and practicing flying solo in the daylight. He finally left to begin a career of flying, determined to make his living from it.

Lindbergh headed into the central part of the country, setting down in farmers' fields, and offering rides wherever he could gather a crowd. He flew to Little Falls and landed on the family farm. He helped his father campaign for office by taking him up to distribute leaflets from the air. It was his father's first ride in an airplane.

His second one was not very successful. Lindbergh had taken off and was barely fifty feet in the air when the plane dove and crashed. Lindbergh's father bloodied his face and broke his glasses. The crash also damaged the plane. Lindbergh also gave his mother her first airplane ride during his barnstorming days. She seemed to enjoy being a passenger and later accompanied him on several of his mail routes.

While Lindbergh could earn up to $250.00 at one stop if the crowds were there, making a career from barnstorming was becoming more difficult as the market became flooded. Although many pilots began undercutting the unwritten rule of five dollars per ride, Lindbergh refused to reduce his price.

His existence during this period was spartan and devoid of much human contact. Those interactions he did have were with strangers such as the people to whom he gave rides. He usually slept with his plane in farmers' fields, sleeping in the open, or under the plane in a bedroll. He had no friends to speak of and struck up no relationships with women. Clearly, Lindbergh was more at ease with the machinations of man, than he was with man himself.

Lindbergh foresaw the demise of the barnstormer and so paid particular attention to a stranger's suggestion that he should join the Army Air Corps.   There, the stranger argued, he would further develop his piloting skills on more powerful machines cared for by Army mechanics.

He was attracted to the idea that the Army would broaden his skills as a pilot.   Certainly they offered the most extensive training available on some of the most modern machines, and even with the regimentation inherent in military life, Lindbergh reasoned that it was his best opportunity.   He wrote his letter of application, was interviewed at Fort Snelling, and took his entrance examination on January 1, 1924.   He was accepted in February and told to report to Brooks Field in San Antonio, Texas on March 15, 1924.

Graduates of the year long Army Aviation Program, commissioned as second lieutenants, were not required to serve a full three years. With two weeks notice they could resign and join the reserves. This also attracted Lindbergh. Flight training began in April and once again academics became an obstacle. He barely achieved a passing grade on his first examination. As a result, and perhaps for the first time in his life, he studied at night. He adapted much more quickly to the actual flying. Even though the Army had just installed left hand throttles in all their planes and Lindbergh had flown only right hand throttles, he showed great aptitude on the high powered military aircraft. By the end of June nearly half of his class of cadets had washed out.

Lindbergh did not adapt as easily to military life. He did not enjoy living in close quarters with others and he developed no personal relationships.   To those who offended him, or with whom he especially did not get along, Lindbergh did not hesitate to direct cruel behaviors, often without regard for his own personal safety.

A sergeant who offended him by snoring loudly found a dead skunk in his pillow case. The stench was so overwhelming in the entire barracks as well as in his bedroll that he had to sleep outside for the next two weeks. That was apparently not enough for Lindbergh. The sergeant returned home one night to find that Lindbergh had disassembled his bed, repeatedly climbed to the roof of the barracks carrying its components, and there reassembled it. For a person who would hang from an airborne plane by his teeth, climbing to the roof was no obstacle at all.

However, Lindbergh could not take it as well as he could dish it out. When a group of five cadets attempted to throw him into a pond he became sullen and began plotting. Four of the five cadets soon found that all their underwear had been laced with itching powder, and the fifth, known to be deathly afraid of snakes, found himself in bed with one. He asked afterwards, "It wasn't venomous, was it?" Lindbergh reportedly replied, "Yes, but not fatally so."7

Lindbergh may have demonstrated superior flying skills during his Army training, and by graduation was actually second in his class, but he was not well liked. During his off hours, he continued to give lessons to students and rides to the public at a nearby commercial field.

While Lindbergh was enrolled in the Army Aviation Program his father died of an inoperable brain tumor.

Lindbergh requested a permanent U.S. Army commission. When he had not received a response by the time of his graduation, he decided to resign from active service and automatically became a member of the reserve corps. On March 25, 1925 he re-entered civilian life.

Lindbergh began flying U.S. Mail as part of a fledgling effort being run out of St. Louis by two brothers named Robertson, who were ex-army air pilots from the war. Major Bill Robertson offered Lindbergh the position of chief pilot. During this time Lindbergh met up again with Bud Gurney who hired on with Phil Love and Thomas Nelson as the other pilots with the airline. This group pioneered the St. Louis to Chicago Air Mail route on a shoe string. The planes were old, and navigational and safety equipment was scarce. Only one flare was allowed per plane for night landings or bad weather.

Solitary as usual, Lindbergh put all his energies into the development of the mail route, and he openly resented it whenever the other pilots expressed interest in any outside activities. When Phil Love tried to talk on the telephone with his girlfriends, Lindbergh would make rude and loud noises in the background, finally causing Love to sneak away to make the calls. When Love returned from a date he would crawl into bed to find it filled with lizards, frogs or snakes. If he did not wake immediately when the alarm sounded, Lindbergh would rip back the covers and throw a bucket of ice water on him.

But the "joke" which had the most serious consequence, and displayed a sadistic bent on the part of Lindbergh, very nearly cost Bud Gurney his life. Lindbergh did not smoke, drink coffee or liquor, nor did he socialize or dance with young women. He scoffed at those who did and derided them for their lack of "productivity." He claimed that he avoided these vices as he believed that they would impair his reflexes. He tried to force the other pilots to similarly refrain.

One night Bud Gurney returned from an evening out enjoying the company of others. Thirsty from the heat and alcohol, Gurney took up the jug of what he thought was ice water and poured it down his throat. However, Lindbergh had replaced the ice water with kerosene. Gurney was rushed to the hospital, suffered serious throat, stomach and intestinal burns, and nearly died from the ingestion.

Nelson, Love and Gurney had all in turn shared a room with Lindbergh. They all moved out. Love did so after he and his girlfriend had rigged up Lindbergh's bed and caused it to collapse when he got into it. Lindbergh said nothing to them that night but the next day told Love to move out.

There was an element of danger to the early air mail routes. But despite the lack of safety equipment most pilots attempted to operate in as safe and prudent a manner as the existing technology would allow.

Not so with Lindbergh. He would routinely set off on a mail run in weather conditions in which there was little doubt that his destination would be completely fogged in. Twice he flew into blizzards over Chicago and simply grabbed the mail pouch and parachuted out, leaving his plane to crash wherever it might end up. Upon reaching the ground he hopped a train with his pouch to continue his run.

However, not every flight posed a hazard. On clear days, when weather was not a factor, the flights provided ample opportunity for Lindbergh to contemplate his future. It was during such a flight that he first got the idea that not only were transcontinental flights possible but so too was a transatlantic one. Lindbergh increasingly dwelled on this idea. In September of 1926 he watched a news reel which had a clip about the Orteig Prize.

Raymond Orteig, a Frenchman who operated several hotels in New York, had offered $25,000 to the first flyer or group of flyers "who shall cross the Atlantic in a land or water aircraft (heavier than air) from Paris or the shores of France to New York, or from New York to Paris or the shores of France, without stop."

The offer had first been made in 1919 and stipulated that the flight must take place within five years. This was beyond the capabilities of any plane then built and although two people had successfully crossed the Atlantic already by making several stops, the prize was re-offered by Orteig at the urging of a French newspaper.

Lindbergh decided that he would attempt the flight. Several had already perished in the process. The French ace Rene Fonck had put together significant financial backing for he and a crew of three others to fly from New York to Paris in a mammoth tri-motored plane built by Sikorsky. They crashed on take off from Roosevelt Field, and two of the crew members died in the ensuing flames.

Lindbergh knew that planes must be made lighter and more streamlined for such a trip, not heavier and saddled with excess weight and crew members. He convinced a group of St. Louis businessmen to put up $10,000 to have a plane designed, built and delivered to New York in time for him to be the first to cross the Atlantic. He would do it alone. It would be a monoplane, equipped with a single powerful engine, stripped of all unnecessary weight. The gas tank would be in front of the cockpit, to cushion the possibility of injury in a crash. It would be fast, and designed for endurance.

The plane was built by a group of young, enthusiastic, bright and dedicated men at the Ryan Aircraft Company in San Diego, California. Lindbergh lived there and worked with them during construction. They felt the pressure to get the plane completed because several others had been planning the trip, including the popular Commander Byrd in a joint venture with the great Anthony J. Fokker. They were planning to fly in a tri-motored plane. It crashed during a test flight.

The nation and the world took a great deal of interest in the attempts to cross the Atlantic. When another team, Captains Nungesser and Francois Coli, departed Paris on the 8th of May in a bi-plane, news organizations around the world tracked their progress. Radio stations interrupted their programming to give reports of sightings; all of which turned out to be false. The pilots disappeared and were never heard from again.

On May 10, 1927 Lindbergh took off from San Diego, headed for New York in his new plane, the *Spirit of St. Louis.* He made record time to St. Louis where he was to make a breakfast and dinner appearance with his benefactors. Lindbergh pointed out that time was of the essence, however, and left the same day for Curtis Field on Long Island.

He was unprepared for the media who awaited his arrival and astonished at how they pushed and pulled each other, how they shouted instructions to him on how to pose with the plane, and to his mind, asked him ridiculous and irrelevant questions.

It was here that Lindbergh began his long and enduring "love-hate" relationship with the press. "The press," Lindbergh wrote, "would increase my personal influence and earning capacity. I found it exhilarating to see my name in print on the front pages of America's greatest newspapers, and I enjoyed reading the words of praise about my transcontinental flight... But I was shocked by the inaccuracy and sensationalism of many of the articles resulting from my interviews... Much the papers printed seemed not only baseless but also useless."8

When his mother came to New York to join him before his flight she and Lindbergh posed together for the press. But as

Lindbergh would report it, they refused to take the "maudlin position some of them had asked for."9 He was outraged the next day to see that through composite photography they ran such a picture anyway. The "maudlin" position they refused to take was Lindbergh giving his mother a kiss on the cheek.

This love-hate relationship with the media continued throughout Lindbergh's life. When he needed or wanted the press he was friendly with reporters. When they wrote complimentary or positive pieces about him, he would cooperate. But if he did not want them to ask questions, or if the press were the least bit critical, they were pariahs and "distasteful."

Yet, Lindbergh never hesitated to use the press whenever he felt it would further one of his objectives. At such times he was courteous, polite and even solicitous.

Very early on the morning on May 20, 1927, the weather was finally breaking over the north Atlantic. Lindbergh had the *Spirit of St. Louis* towed from Curtis to Roosevelt Field for takeoff. In a light drizzle, weighing 5,250 pounds, Lindbergh and machine lifted into the sky bound for Paris. It was a flight which would forever change the nature of aviation. No longer would winged transportation be bound by the borders of the country. Shortly after, continents and people were linked by a method of travel many saw then only as a form of amusement and which insurance companies, only four years earlier, had believed had no future. While Lindbergh may have been prepared to usher in the age of aviation, he was vastly unprepared for the attention his flight received.

CHAPTER III

The flight of the *Spirit of St. Louis* has been forever imprinted in the American psyche. An event which now seems commonplace was wondrous and daring in 1927. After 33 and one-half hours in the air, Lindbergh touched down at Le Bourget field in Paris. The flight shrunk the oceans and all of humanity and it coalesced American pride in its emerging technological power.

In 1990, "Dear Abby" devoted a special column to people who remembered the Lindbergh landing. "I was a student at the Sorbonne," a reader wrote, "when the radio announced that Lindbergh had been sighted over Ireland and would be landing in Paris in a few hours. A classmate and I took a bus to the airport. We were among the thousands of spectators restrained behind a wire fence. When Lindbergh landed, the crowd pushed the fence over and ran out on the field. The police had to rescue him from his enthusiastic admirers."

Another wrote, "I was at the theater when an announcement was made at intermission that Lindy had landed safely in Paris. Everyone cheered and left the theater to join a wild celebration in the streets, dancing and hugging strangers! The next day, Lindy was honored with a huge parade down the Champs-Elysees. It was one of the highlights of my life. I am 93 now, and an American citizen living in New Jersey."10

His reception throughout France, Europe and particularly upon his return to the United States was no less enthusiastic. His first night in Paris, Lindbergh slept at the home of the United States Ambassador to France. Soon after, he met the President of France, addressed the French Assembly, was received by King George V of England, and given accolades the world over for his feat.

To get him home, and America wanted him home fast, President Calvin Coolidge dispatched the United States cruiser *Memphis* under the command of Admiral Guy Burrage to Cherbourg where it picked up Lindbergh and his plane. The

Secretary of War, Dwight F. Davis, had already arranged to promote Lindbergh to the rank of Colonel in the Air Corps Reserve, a title Lindbergh would cling to in the ensuing years.

He was exceedingly tall, and his height seemed to amplify his solitary nature. He captured the imagination of a nation with his stoical and fearless nature, and he appeared bright, even if he was somewhat aloof and lonely. He was quiet and reserved, not given to boastful behavior. He was, in short, a person whom everyone could romanticize as the adventurer, who embodied all that we wanted him to embody. He became an American Hero.

The country could forgive him his idiosyncrasies. It would shower him with admiration, pridefully boast to the world of his name, and, in his presence, defer to him. This would later include law enforcement officers who were involved in the investigation into the disappearance of his first born son. As America's Hero he quickly became acclimated to deferential treatment.

When he stepped off the ship at Alexandria, he was met by his mother. She had been brought to Washington as the guest of President and Mrs. Coolidge. From there he joined a parade which led him to a huge stage erected at the Washington Monument. Waiting on the stage was the President of the United States, who gave a long speech extolling the virtues of a young man who, only a few days earlier, had been a virtual unknown.

Lindbergh responded with these words. "On the evening of May 21, I arrived at Le Bourget, France. I was in Paris for one week, in Belgium for a day and was in London and in England for several days. Everywhere I went, at every meeting I attended, I was requested to bring home a message to you. Always the message was the same. 'You have seen,' the message was, 'the affection of the peoples of France for the people of America demonstrated to you. When you return to America take back that message to the people of the United States from the people of France and of Europe.' I thank you." And Lindbergh sat down. It is the shortest known response ever given to a Presidential speech.

Lindbergh was awarded the Distinguished Flying Cross, and for the first time in an action unconnected with war, the Congressional Medal of Honor, the United States' highest award for bravery for a person serving in the Armed Forces. The French presented him with the French Legion of Honor, and the British with the Air Force Cross. He received thousands of offers to endorse products, lucrative job offers, gifts, proposals for marriage, and several million letters, telegrams and cables.

On June 13th he traveled to New York City and was given a parade attended by what is still believed to be the largest crowd in New York City history. Some four and one half million people turned out to see him in the motorcade. In a speech at City Hall, Mayor James J. Walker looked up from his script at the end of his long discourse and said, "Colonel Lindbergh, New York City is yours - I give it to you. You won it."

The Wright Aeronautical Corporation had assigned a corporate public relations specialist named Dick Blythe, along with an assistant, Harry Bruno, to handle the Colonel's public relations, and to help sort through the offers which were pouring in. Lindbergh had signed contracts with Mobile Oil, Vacuum Oil, AC Spark plugs, and Wright before departing. Each contract averaged $6,000 and the companies were now cashing in. Each could have afforded to pay him much more after the flight, and many more wanted his endorsement. On June 16, 1927 he was awarded the Orteig Prize and given the $25,000 at a small ceremony. Interestingly enough, Raymond Orteig's committee had to bend the rules to present the money. The published rules had stated that in order to qualify, sixty days had to lapse between the time the entry was received and the time the flight took place. It had not. Even though the rules had been well publicized in advance everyone had agreed that they could overlook it "in this case." After all, Lindbergh was special.

He wrote an account of his flight called *We*, which earned him $100,000 in royalties. In the summer of 1927 he was also paid to take a cross-country tour. Flying the *Spirit of St. Louis* he made stops in all 48 states, flying through all weather conditions and missing only one date in Portland, Maine. In every location he was mobbed, particularly by women. He was, after all, perceived to be the most eligible bachelor in the world, though anyone who took the time to inquire further found that Lindbergh held most women in disdain.

Harry Guggenheim, who had established the Foundation for Aeronautical Research, was the financial backer of Lindbergh's cross-country flight. Known as "Captain Harry," Guggenheim was a wealthy philanthropist who was more than willing to provide Lindbergh a safe haven from the crowds and press by offering him a permanent room at his mansion on the north shore of Long Island. There Lindbergh rubbed elbows on a regular basis with influential people such as Thomas Lamont, John D. Rockefeller, Jr. the publisher George Palmer Putnam, Herbert Hoover, Theodore Roosevelt, Jr., and a banker named Dwight Morrow.

These were the power elite of society - mostly Republicans. Dwight Morrow was also the Ambassador to Mexico and a prominent Republican whose name was already being touted as a possible Presidential nominee. When Ambassador Morrow invited Lindbergh to come to his home in New Jersey and later to Mexico, Lindbergh readily accepted.

Morrow's New Jersey home was a sprawling manorial mansion in Englewood. He was married, and the father of a son and three daughters, one of whom was Anne Spencer Morrow.

Lindbergh used the invitation to Mexico to promote a South American tour, and to begin it, announced that he would fly non-stop from Washington to Mexico City in December of 1927.

Upon arrival Lindbergh found that Morrow had arranged a greeting by the President of Mexico and he was widely feted wherever he went. He stayed at the Ambassador's home during the Christmas holiday with his mother, who had also been invited by the Morrows, and who had reluctantly come.

While staying there he spent time with the three daughters. It was reported that he got along very well with Constance, who was younger than Anne and still attending an exclusive boarding school, Milton Academy, in Milton, Massachusetts.

Anne arrived from Smith College shortly after Lindbergh's arrival. In 1927 she was twenty-one years old. She was intelligent and sensitive but also extremely shy and introverted. Although she was not quite sure of herself around Lindbergh, she was definitely attracted to him.

In her diaries, Anne wondered whether Lindbergh would be more attracted to her older sister Elisabeth, or her younger sister Constance, with whom he seemed more at ease and able to engage in conversation. The pair seemed to have developed a natural rapport.

Dwight Morrow invited him to spend more time with them at their summer home off the coast of Maine. Later that year Lindbergh quietly began courting Anne Morrow. He asked her to go flying with him and this became his regular method for seeing her. Anne's diaries reveal mixed emotions about Charles Lindbergh and she wrote that he was "terribly young and crude in many small ways."11

Lindbergh maintained his tumultuous relationship with the press. He responded angrily at several newspaper accounts which reported that he was "getting a swelled head," and in a huff declared that henceforth he would only see reporters when it had to do with aviation.

Unless of course it furthered his own interests, as it did on October 3, 1928 when he released to the press a telegram he had sent to Herbert C. Hoover, then the Republican nominee for President:

> The more I see of your campaign the more strongly I feel that your election is of supreme importance to the country. Your qualities as a man and what you stand for, regardless of party, make me feel that the problems which will come before the country during the next four years will best be solved by your leadership.

The newspapers continued to track Lindbergh's activities, reporting on his flights to further causes in aviation. They also tracked the possible link between Charles and the Morrow daughters. At the end of April, 1929, the *New York Times* had daily stories on the fact that Mrs. Morrow and her daughter Anne were on their way north by train, traveling from Mexico to New Jersey. What did not receive much attention however, is that Constance Morrow had received a letter at the Milton Academy threatening violence against her unless a ransom was paid. She was also instructed not to tell the police. The amount demanded as payment was $50,000 - the same amount which, almost three years later to the day, would be asked for the Lindbergh baby. The official records of the Milton, Massachusetts Police Department reveal that on April 24, 1929 at 10:20 p.m. "A.H. Weed, 150 School Street brought to station a letter received by Constance Morrow, Milton Academy, demanding money under threats of violence. Miss Morrow lives at Hathaway House. Sergeant Shields sent to detail Officer Lee guard Hathaway House tonight. Mr. Weed will bring letters to station tomorrow after he had had a copy of it made."12

Two weeks later a follow-up letter arrived instructing her to put the $50,000 in a certain size box and to place it in the hole in the wall behind a nearby estate. By this time the police were involved and the whole Morrow family, including future in-law Lindbergh, knew of their involvement. An actress placed an empty box in the designated hole and the police staked it out. No one picked up the box.

Charles Lindbergh and Anne Spencer Morrow were married May 27, 1929 in a small ceremony at the Englewood, New Jersey home of the Morrows. They left for what they had hoped would be a quiet honeymoon on a yacht moored off the east coast. But Charles Lindbergh was the most famous man in America, and now there was a Mrs. Lindbergh. The media attention focused on the couple. Anne's diaries are particularly revealing about their relationship.

Although there is no doubt she was infatuated, there are many indications that she considered Charles her intellectual inferior. She expressed disgust with his "school boy pranks," which he continued to pull on a regular basis. She also chafed at the role of his faithful companion, there only to service his needs. It did not go unnoticed that Anne was expected to learn new skills in order to fly with Lindbergh and that she was the one carrying equipment from the plane when they landed while he remained the focus of attention.

Lindbergh himself certainly had a strange way of describing his courtship, marriage and relationship with Anne, the person with whom he had decided to spend the rest of his life. In his autobiography he wrote:

> On May 27, 1929, I married Anne Spencer Morrow. From the standpoint of both individual and species, mating involves the most important choice of life, for it shapes our future as the past has shaped us. It impacts upon all values obviously and subtly in an infinite number of ways.
>   One mates not only with an individual but also with that individual's environment and ancestry. These were concepts I comprehended before I was married and confirmed in my observations over the years that followed. 13

This rather clinical description of "finding a mate," contrasts markedly with Anne's poetic descriptions of life, her trials, aspirations, hopes and dreams for the world. Anne Morrow was a deeply sensitive and caring person, who experienced and suffered much in her life.

After their brief honeymoon, Charles and Anne went to work promoting aviation. Charles taught Anne to fly. She also took courses on navigation, learned how to operate a wireless from a plane, and flew with him on many cross-country flights. Harry Guggenheim announced that he had placed Lindbergh on a retainer for $25,000 for the Guggenheim Aeronautical Foundation so that Lindbergh could promote air travel as a safe, efficient, and effective means of transportation.

In the fall of 1929 Anne's suspected pregnancy was confirmed by her doctor. Nevertheless, Charles expected Anne to continue to accompany him on flights around the country. Lindbergh had announced to the press, with whom he had grown aloof and curt, that he and Anne would break the record for a transcontinental flight between Los Angeles and New York. He had a new plane specially built in California, which he and Anne picked up. They named the plane *Sirius*, after the bright star in our galaxy.

While in Los Angeles, he introduced Anne to Amelia Earhart at the home of Mary Pickford. Ever since her flight across the

Atlantic in 1928 Amelia Earhart's fame as an aviatrix had grown. Newspapers had given her the nickname of "Lady Lindy," a title which she later confided to Anne she did not care for.

Nor, frankly, did she seem to care that much for Charles Lindbergh. After spending about four days with him and Anne, she told her soon to be husband, George Putnam, that Lindbergh was an "odd character." In Putnam's 1930 biography of Earhart, *Soaring Wings: A Biography of Amelia Earhart*, Putnam recounts Amelia's story about socializing with Anne and Charles that week at the Hollywood home of Jack Maddux.

> Anne, the Colonel and AE (Amelia Earhart) were fellow guests at the home of Jack Maddux in Hollywood. One night they were sitting around close to the icebox. Anne and AE were drinking buttermilk. Lindbergh, standing behind his wife munching a tomato sandwich, had the sudden impulse to let drops of water fall in a stream on his wife's shoulder from a glass in his hand.

> Anne was wearing a sweet dress of pale blue silk. Water spots silk. AE observed a growing unhappiness on Anne's part - but no move toward rebellion, not even any murmur of complaint. AE often said that Anne Lindbergh is the best sport in the world.

> Then Anne rose and stood by the door, with her back to the others, and her head resting on her arm. AE thought, with horror, that the impossible had come to pass, and that Anne was crying. But Anne was thinking out a solution to her problem, and the instant she thought it out, she acted upon it. At once - and with surprising thoroughness.

> With one comprehensive movement she swung around and - quite simply - threw the contents of her glass of buttermilk straight over the Colonel's blue serge suit. It made a simply marvelous mess!

Odd indeed. Imagine yourself in such a scene with your spouse. What would your reaction be to such a cruel and embarrassing moment, in front of virtual strangers, in someone else's home? Such were the manifestations of Charles Lindbergh's "practical jokes."

It fitted a typical behavior pattern inherent in all of his "jokes." Lindbergh used his "jokes" to control people whose behavior he wished to alter. He did not want the sergeant to bother him, the cadets to harass him, Love to socialize with women or Gurney to drink alcohol. He performed his jokes to punish them for their behaviors.

It is unknown what prompted him to dump a glass of water on his wife's head in front of Amelia Earhart. But it is known that Lindbergh had an extremely sexist view (even by 1929 standards) of women and accorded them little respect. Anne Lindbergh was not only very bright, she was extremely well educated and clearly his intellectual superior.

Amelia Earhart was more than an accomplished flyer. She was a leading American feminist who promoted her political beliefs by demonstrating that women could perform equally to men.

Anne and Amelia were engaged in an intense discussion. If Lindbergh perceived Anne becoming swayed by Amelia's political belief on women, then the water dumping fits a classic pattern.

Shortly thereafter the new plane was completed, and Anne and Charles left for their return flight across the country. Charles was determined to set the new cross-country speed record in *Sirius*. A storm system gathered almost immediately after their departure from California, forcing Lindbergh to fly extremely high over the Rockies and throughout the flight. They had no oxygen with them. Anne was seven months pregnant.

At several points during the flight Anne thought that she would plead with Lindbergh to land the plane, but did not. It was the worst flight she had yet endured with her husband and it caused her to be so sick that when they landed in New York she had to be carried from the plane by stretcher and rushed to the hospital.

Since the press was waiting for Lindbergh at the airport to report on his efforts to break the cross country speed record, Anne's apparent sickness was reported the next day in the newspapers. Lindbergh angrily denied that Anne had been ill, and his office castigated the press for reporting such. However, years later Anne herself admitted in *Hour of Gold, Hour of Lead* that the flight had caused her great misery, particularly in her condition. Today any physician would strongly advise against an expectant mother, seven months pregnant, flying without oxygen for a prolonged period. Oxygen deprivation to a near full term fetus is quite dangerous.

In May of 1930 Anne moved in with her parents at Englewood to await the birth of their first child. The country, and most certainly the press, was greatly interested in the arrival of the first born of Charles Lindbergh. Several newspaper accounts drew a parallel between awaiting the arrival of the Lindberghs' baby and the British anticipating the arrival of an heir to the throne.

But when the baby, Charles Augustus Lindbergh, III, was born on June 22, 1930 (which was Anne's 24th birthday), the world was kept waiting two weeks before Colonel Lindbergh would release either the name or photographs of the baby. The family reported that both mother and child were doing very well, and that the baby was "normal" in all respects. Later it was disclosed that the child had two overlapping toes on one of his feet, but other than that was "healthy and normal." This description of the baby as "healthy and normal" appears often in published accounts of the baby's birth, during the time of the kidnapping, and of his death. It was often rumored, though never established, that there was something "wrong" with the Lindbergh baby.

Colonel Lindbergh developed a pattern during the beginning of his marriage, and after the birth of his son, which he followed for most of his life. He would travel frequently, spending little time at home. In July of 1930, his business affairs were growing, and he was placed on the "preferred customer" listing at J.P. Morgan's Bank, which enabled him to buy choice stock at below market value. Since his interest in a number of airline companies was growing, a family friend of the Morrows, Manhattan lawyer Colonel Henry C. Breckinridge, became Lindbergh's advisor.

He also struck up an association with Dr. Alexis Carrel, a Nobel scientist and French doctor who was working at the Rockefeller Institute in New York. Lindbergh often joined Carrell at the Institute and helped him develop a perfusion pump to keep organs alive. Its designs were studied later during the development of the artificial heart. Carrel was a strange individual who wore a black hooded robe in the laboratory and insisted that all of his lab assistants do the same. He had won the Nobel Prize in 1912 for his work on suturing blood vessels during surgery instead of destroying them. But as he grew older, his views became more radical, and he wrote papers and published articles on subject matter well beyond his expertise.

In a published book entitled, *Man, the Unknown*, Carrel postulated that "dark skinned people" were part of the "lesser races" because of their high exposure to sun light, as opposed to the Scandinavian races which did not get exposed to as much light. Lindbergh was fascinated with Carrel's views on these and other subjects, and after he and Anne fled to Europe following the trial of Hauptmann, lived for a time near Carrel's island home off the coast of France.

In the spring and summer of 1931, the Lindberghs prepared for a northern surveying flight to the Orient. It was hoped that by doing so a commercial air route could be developed since this seemed to be the shortest route. For this trip the *Sirius* was equipped with retractable landing gear and pontoons as most of the landings would be on water.

It was also a route filled with hazards. Water landings, even under the best of circumstances, could be extremely dangerous. Lindbergh was widely criticized for the route he had charted. Several prominent explorers and experts on the Arctic advised him that his "straight line between two points" approach to his charted course was filled with unnecessary risk taking, and that by slightly altering his course he would avoid many of the more extreme hazards. He refused. Risk taking was welcomed by Colonel Lindbergh. Hadn't he, after all, piloted in all sorts of weather, crossed the Atlantic alone, wing walked, completed a double parachute jump on his first leap from an airplane, and survived several crashes? One of the scientists reminded Lindbergh, however, that this time he was taking his wife on the trip.

Of the many dangers encountered several could have been avoided. After departing Point Barrow, Alaska, the northern most point of the trip, he was forced to land due to a fuel shortage. He did so at an inlet called Shishmaref near Nome, and had greatly miscalculated the time of sunset. He set down in near darkness with fog approaching, an extremely dangerous combination for water landings. Not carefully tracking the hours of sunset near the Arctic Circle was a mistake commonly made by inexperienced pilots. Later the Arctic expert and flyer John Grierson publicly criticized Lindbergh in a letter for taking this kind of a risk. He asked why he hadn't checked sunset time at Nome before leaving Barrow. Lindbergh defended himself, but was not convincing in his arguments.

While flying south from the Soviet Union to Japan, Lindbergh had to land between very jagged mountainous peaks in dense fog. For Anne, it was the most terrifying landing she had ever experienced, describing it as "a knife going down the side of a pie tin, between fog and mountain." She wondered whether her husband would then say "It was nothing at all."[14]

There were three forced landings of this kind during their trip which effectively ended in China. The Lindberghs had been gone since July 31, 1931. Anne missed her baby, who was being cared for by her parents and their staff. When the plane was damaged in China at the beginning of October, she was frustrated and homesick, and wanted to return as quickly as possible. When a cable arrived in Shanghai on October 5, 1931 telling her that her father had died from a brain hemorrhage, Lindbergh canceled the flight, ordered the plane shipped back to San Francisco, and booked passage on the first ship home. They were reunited with their son on October 27th. When Anne Morrow Lindbergh's account of this journey was published in her first book entitled *North to the Orient*, she established herself as a first rate author. She would go on to become well published.

Dwight Morrow's death at 58 was a shock to his family. Anne wanted to stay with her mother, to be close to the family during

a very difficult period. While Anne enjoyed a very close relationship with her mother, this was not the case between Charles and
Mrs. Morrow. During his later anti-war and pro-Nazi activities,
Anne's mother publicly criticized her son-in-law for his "un-Amer-
ican" behavior. Dwight Morrow had once remarked, "what do we
know about this young man Lindbergh?"15

Though liveable, their new home in Hopewell, New Jersey
was not complete. On weekends, the Lindberghs would stay
there, along with the Whatelys and the Lindbergh dog. Betty
Gow would not accompany them to Hopewell. This was her time
off, and it gave Anne a chance to have time alone with the baby.

Lindbergh settled into a routine of traveling into New York
City on Monday mornings for his work with the airline. Later in
the day Anne and the baby would return to Englewood. Colonel
Lindbergh had found that when he stuck to a regular pattern, the
press was far less likely to bother him. He closely guarded, and
kept secret, any variation in his schedule.

Such was not the case, however, on Monday, February 29,
1932. Charles' telephone call to Anne, instructing her to stay
over an extra day, reflected a clear deviation from their usual
pattern.

The Colonel himself stayed over Monday night in Englewood.
On Tuesday morning he telephoned Anne and told her to stay
over in Hopewell one more night, again citing the weather and
the baby's cold. He left other specific instructions about the
baby, and said that he would drive home to Hopewell from work
that evening. According to Anne's testimony at the Hauptmann
trial, Charles honked his horn in the driveway upon his arrival at
8:25 p.m. that evening. In a letter the next day to her mother--
in-law Anne wrote that, "C was late in coming home."16 The
arrival was approximately 35 minutes after Betty Gow had last
checked the child.

Lindbergh never explained why he had arrived home late that
evening. At the trial he explained his occupation as "aviation"
and made vague reference to having been in New York that day
on business. No further details or explanation were ever offered
by him or elicited on cross-examination concerning his own
actions that day.

The situation in Hopewell was ripe for a Charles Lindbergh "practical joke" against Anne. She was alone, cut-off from her mother, family and the other staff at *Next Day Hill*. Even Betty Gow was not with her. During weekends she alone was responsible for the care of the child.

If Lindbergh had kept to his usual schedule he would have arrived home at approximately 7:45 p.m. That would have allowed him plenty of time to pull in the driveway approximately 100 yards from the road, (but still out of sight of the home) and park his car. Since he was the owner of the house and discovery of his "prank" at that time would not have been damaging to him, and since he knew that no one else was expected, there was no need to park along the road and forsake the easier access the driveway afforded. He would have had plenty of time to remove the child through the window with the warped shutters in preparation for some sort of later dramatic presentation of the child. Perhaps he planned a front door arrival with the announcement, "Look who I had with me in New York all day."

For a person who had made a career of wing walking and hanging from airplanes by his teeth, who was unfazed by a double jump on his first parachute drop, climbing a ladder at night was nothing. For a person who would carry a bed up to a roof at night, carrying a child down a ladder would be easy.

But unlike with the sergeant's bed, this time Lindbergh miscalculated. The ladder broke and the child was dropped to the granite ledge below. The impact crushed his skull, causing instant death.

Lindbergh would have immediately grasped his quandary.

To reveal the truth, to go to the front door and tell his wife, "I was taking our 20 month old child out of his second floor window over my shoulder and down a ladder in a windstorm at night as a joke and I dropped him and here's your dead baby," was unthinkable. He would be a fool, not only in front of his wife and in-laws but in the eyes of the whole world. All he had accomplished for his own reputation would be gone. In one instant he would be transformed from the American Hero to the American Buffoon. Charles Lindbergh would never allow it.

He had begun this prank as a kidnapping and he would see it through as such. There were enough ransom kidnappings that this one would be plausible. He had lived in Mount Rose while supervising the construction of the Hopewell house and knew the woods there. He would drive there, leave the body, and return to play out the role of the father as victim in a real kidnapping.

Lindbergh could have gathered up the body, retreated down the driveway, bundled the body into the rear of the car, backed out of the driveway, and driven off. Once in Mount Rose he would have to leave the body hurriedly. He could not take a chance on any delay which would be occasioned by digging a grave. Nor, since he had not planned on having to dig one, would he have had any shovel or similar implement with him. He could not go too far, as he would want to minimize his own tardiness in arriving home. A half hour delay would be tolerable.

The spot where the body was found was less than three miles *south* of Hopewell, in the opposite direction from New York City. Lindbergh parked by the side of the road and brought the body a short distance into the woods where he lay the child in a depression on top of the ground.

He could easily return by 8:25 p.m., when he would honk his horn as he drove up the driveway to assure that everyone in the household would notice *this* arrival.

Lindbergh now merely had to do five things. First, he had to make sure that *he* did not find the empty crib, for if he did, his past history of pranks and in particular his having previously hidden the child would focus suspicion right on him. This would mean he could not enter the nursery until the child was discovered missing by someone else.

Two, he had to set the time of the "kidnap" so that it occurred when he had an alibi with the person most likely to suspect him: Anne herself.

Three, to complete the kidnap scenario he had to get a ransom note into the nursery. This would be especially hazardous since he could not afford to risk entering the nursery until after the baby was discovered missing.

Four, he had to do something about the "fingerprint problem" once the police were involved. Since the prank had never been intended to go this far he would not have bothered to wear gloves during his initial window entrance to the nursery. But now that the child was dead and he was going to continue with a kidnap story the police would be involved. Lindbergh knew that the first thing they would do would be to dust the note and nursery for fingerprints. He had to make sure that his prints were not on the note he would write, a task he could easily accomplish.

However, the problem with the nursery was more difficult. A dusting of that room would not only reveal the lack of any stranger's prints but would also reveal Lindbergh's on surfaces where they would not ordinarily be expected including the window, windowsill, sash, etc. All such traces would have to be removed. The room would have to be wiped before the police arrived.

Five, he had to consistently play the role of the father as victim and make sure that suspicion focused anywhere but on him.

If he followed those five steps faithfully he would be all right. He had pulled off the other stunts, he had flown blind into blizzards over Chicago and parachuted to safety, he had cut his engine and skimmed the Mississippi before restarting, he had flown solo across the Atlantic, in what, by contemporary standards, was not much more than a motorized hang glider. He could pull this one off too.

The first step, to avoid finding the empty crib, was easy. Upon re-entering the house shortly after 8:25 p.m. he immediately realized that the disappearance had not yet been discovered. He went upstairs and washed up. However, even though the bathroom was adjacent to the nursery he did not enter it to "check" on his child.

He returned downstairs where he and Anne ate supper. Afterwards he steered Anne into his study directly under the child's nursery.

It was here at approximately 9:15 p.m., while the wind continued to blow outside, that Charles interrupted the conversation by asking, "What was that?" Anne had not heard anything. The Whatelys never heard anything. Betty Gow never heard anything. The high strung terrier Wahgoosh never barked.

Only Charles Lindbergh claimed to have heard something, a sound he later described alternately as a snapping sound or as wooden crates falling. He knew the wooden ladder lay outside in the mud with a broken rail. He needed to establish the time of the break to a moment when he had an alibi. He did, and the second part of his plan was complete. At approximately 9:20 p.m., Anne and Charles went upstairs where they spoke briefly in Anne's bedroom. Charles left and drew a bath in the upstairs bathroom. Again he did not use the occasion to enter the adjacent nursery. Anne remained in her bedroom writing.

The bath was important for Charles. It allowed him to assure that any remaining tell tale evidence was removed from his person and also gave him additional time to collect his thoughts.

After his bath, Charles descended to his study where he remained alone with his pens, his writing paper and his envelopes. He had to complete the third part: the ransom note. Yet he was in a tough situation because he dared not risk planting the note until after the disappearance was discovered.

At Hauptmann's trial the chief handwriting expert for the prosecution, Albert Osborne, testified that the original nursery note had been written in a disguised hand. Lindbergh wrote the note, disguising his handwriting all the while.

South Jersey was heavily populated by German immigrants. To draw attention away from his household, Lindbergh attempted to make it appear that the note had been written by one. He used some simple German words ("gut" for "good") and phonetically spelled other English words as he believed a German immigrant might pronounce them. A German struggling with the English language often says "d" instead of "th" as the "th" sound does not exist in German. For instance, the English definite article "the" in German is "Der", "Die" or "Das", depending on the gender of the following noun. In conformity with this, the note used the word "anyding" instead of "anything." What is patently false is that the use of a "d" sound instead of the English "th" is an enunciation problem. A German would not spell a word with a "d" instead of a "th"; it is not the case that he thinks that the word is spelled with a "d"; rather he knows it is spelled with a "th" but he simply can not pronounce the "th." The writing of "anyding" is simply the attempt of one trying to imitate a German immigrant's speech.

The European method of placing the monetary symbol "$" after the numerals was also employed. And lastly, Lindbergh used the plural "we" to make it appear that the kidnapping was the work of a gang.

Lindbergh then sealed the envelope, after making sure his prints were not on it or the note, and awaited his opportunity to begin his role as the victim. That opportunity arrived with Betty Gow's 10:00 p.m. entrance to his study asking if he had the child.

It must have been nerve racking, waiting for the knock on the door he knew would come. When it did he sprang into action almost too quickly and thereby almost made a fatal mistake. Fortunately for him, no one at the time noticed.

He quickly bounded up the stairs to the child's room, the note safely hidden on his person. His wife and Betty Gow looked at the empty crib. He knew that it was time to get everyone immediately focused on an outside kidnapping.

At Hauptmann's trial two and one-half years later Betty Gow remembered, and testified, as to the Colonel's exact first words. "Anne," he said, "they have stolen our baby."

At that point the note had not been placed, let alone discovered or read. Its contents were known only to its author. The note referred to a kidnap gang and specifically used the plural "we." However, Lindbergh's use of the plural "they" before he supposedly found the note never raised any police suspicions.

Lindbergh dashed outside with a loaded rifle to look for the kidnappers. Anne and Elsie searched for the child. Oliver Whately eventually went outside to help and was dispatched into town. By the time Lindbergh came back inside Betty, Elsie and Anne had completed their search and had assembled in the downstairs living room.

It was here that Charles Lindbergh re-entered the nursery where he remained alone. The room could be hurriedly wiped down with a handkerchief in less than sixty seconds while Anne, Betty and the Whatelys remained downstairs. Until this point no one else had seen a note, despite the search by Anne, Elsie and Betty Gow. It was here, upon emerging from the nursery, that

Colonel Lindbergh called to Betty to come upstairs. She did, whereupon the Colonel showed her an envelope on the sill of the southeast window. At Hauptmann's trial she specifically testified that she had not seen that envelope earlier. The Colonel asked her to go to the kitchen to get a knife and she obliged.

Lindbergh needed someone to see that envelope, and recalling Betty upstairs so that he could tell her to go downstairs to get a knife to open the envelope served that purpose. For reasons of logic, it served no other.

With that one act Charles Lindbergh was home free. The child was gone, the time of the kidnap had been established with Anne as an alibi for Charles, the fingerprints were wiped away, and the ransom note verifying this as a kidnap was written and planted.

All that now remained was to play out the role of the victim, to let events take their course come what may. Lindbergh would become the central power of the investigation, tracking its course and ensuring it did not come back to him. An analysis of the subsequent events reveals that he accomplished this fifth and last goal very well indeed.

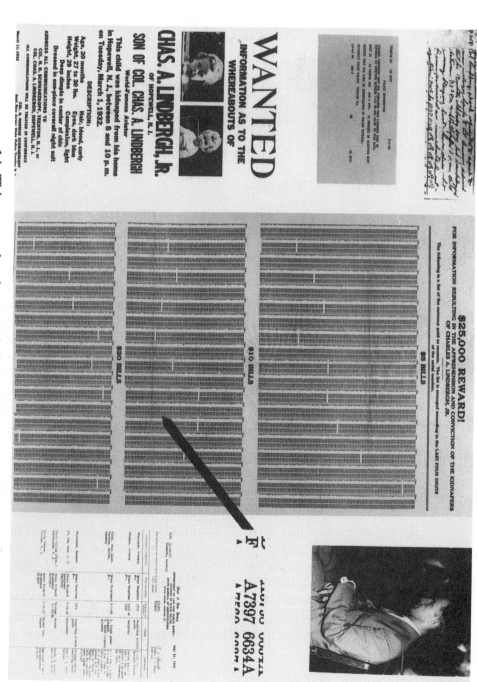

1A. This composite photograph, from the New Jersey State Police archives, displays several items from the "Crime of the Century" (courtesy New Jersey State Police Museum).

CHAPTER IV

Many of the investigations and journalistic analysis of the Lindbergh case completed after the fact have been critical of Colonel Norman Schwarzkopf. Although he did not have prior police experience, and although much of the investigation was sorely deficient by contemporary standards, the total castigation of his efforts is unjustified.

Colonel Schwarzkopf's immediate instincts concerning the case were good. In hindsight, we can postulate that he may have been on the right track although waiting for the wrong train. Those leads he wanted to follow, if they had been pursued, would have, at least early on, eliminated many of the false leads whose time consuming pursuit prevented the case from being solved. The obstacle to Colonel Schwarzkopf's solution of the crime, in those anguished days immediately after March 1, was the same obstacle that dogged the investigation for its duration: Colonel Charles A. Lindbergh.

From the beginning Charles Lindbergh took personal control of the case. He instructed Colonel Schwarzkopf that the paramount concern was the return of the child and no effort should be directed to solving the kidnapping or apprehending those responsible.

This contrasted sharply with Colonel Schwarzkopf's perception of his obligation as a police officer to catch criminals and solve crimes. The conflict was resolved rather abruptly.

The day after the baby disappeared, Colonel Lindbergh called in his own assistants for help in the kidnapping. Arriving at his request were Colonel Breckinridge (the lawyer he had first telephoned before calling the State Police on the previous evening) and Colonel William "Wild Bill" Donovan.

In addition to being a lawyer in private practice in New York City and Lindbergh's lawyer/advisor and confidant, Colonel Breckinridge had been the United States Assistant Secretary of

War (now Department of Defense) from 1913 to 1916. He was, to say the least, a person of considerable political clout.

Colonel "Wild Bill" Donovan was a political heavyweight in New York, who was then planning to run for Governor of the State. Colonel Lindbergh put himself at the head of these four colonels. He just assumed command; no one challenged him and he enforced his command. "C. now a General," Anne was compelled to write to her mother-in-law, "managing his forces with terrific discipline."17

The original suspicion by the police was that the ladder might be a red herring placed where it was to confuse the investigation and might not have been either an avenue of entry to, or escape from, the house.

They based this supposition on several factors. There was only one nursery window which had the outside shutters which could not be latched. At the other two windows the shutters were still latched when the child was discovered missing. Since the shutters could not be latched from the outside, entry through a window had to have been through that southernmost one on the east side.

This theory was reinforced by the impression in the soft earth just to the right (from the outside) of that window. The base portion of the ladder fit into these two holes perfectly. A cursory conclusion would be that the ladder had been placed here for the ascent to, and descent from, the window with the defective shutters.

The police were skeptical. How did the kidnappers know which room was Charles, Jr.'s? The footprints and holes in the earth seemed to indicate that there had been only one attempt at entry. But how did the perpetrators know which room? And more significantly, how had they known which window had the defective shutters which could not be latched from inside? Since all the shutters swung shut, that could not have been determined by surveillance of the house from the woods.

Compounding their quandary were problems inherent in the ladder itself. It was not a typical modern extension ladder whose length could be adjusted. As each section was added its length was then fixed. When all three sections of the ladder were attached and placed against the house the top rested too far up for a person to be able to reach over, swing back the shutters, open the window and gain entrance. Exiting would be even more difficult.

If only two sections were utilized, the top of the second section rested about thirty inches below and to the right of the bottom of the window sill. It would be theoretically possible for the person to stand on the top rung of the ladder in the howling wind with nothing to hold onto for support, reach over and swing back the shutters, and then, with one hand on the sill for balance, force up the window. One could have then shimmied up over the sill and tumbled into the room. But exiting the room and closing the window after oneself (at 10:00 p.m. the window was found closed) would be very difficult if one were carrying a thirty pound baby.

The police did not accept it. The kidnapper or kidnappers could not have entered and exited the window using that ladder without some athletic ability.

The ladder itself was an enigma. Aside from the problems of its length, its construction was not logical. It was obviously handmade, yet why would someone go to the trouble to make a three-section extension ladder and place the rungs nineteen inches apart as opposed to the usual twelve inches? When assembled, the police discovered that it was extremely difficult for anyone except a very tall man to climb the ladder. Descending such a ladder, especially with a thirty pound bundle, was almost impossible.

There was also the problem of the time of the child's disappearance. If Colonel Lindbergh's statement about the cracking wood was accurate, the time of the disappearance could be set at approximately 9:15 p.m. which the police readily did. If Betty Gow were telling the truth about looking in at the child at 7:50 p.m. then the time could be set at a minimum of between 7:50 p.m. and 10:00 p.m. when the whole household could confirm the absence of the baby. And if, for whatever reason, Betty Gow was lying or otherwise incorrect about visiting the child at 7:50 p.m. then there was still the confirmed bedtime of 7:30 p.m. when Anne and Betty together had put the child to bed.

Thus, at the very outside, the time of the kidnapping could be set between 7:30 p.m. and 10:00 p.m.

Yet during this period the household members were awake and moving about. Lights were on throughout the house. Betty Gow was in the second floor bathroom adjacent to the nursery until 7:50 p.m. with the light on. Anne was in her bedroom adjacent to the child's bedroom writing from approximately 9:20 p.m. until 10:00 p.m. Charles Lindbergh drove up the driveway at 8:25 p.m., a fact reinforced by his having deliberately honked his horn. He was eating dinner in the dining room and later conversing with Anne in the living room downstairs with the lights on until 9:15 or 9:20 p.m., in the upstairs bedroom with Anne with the light on until approximately 9:25 or 9:30, taking a bath upstairs until 9:40 or so, and then was in his study directly under the nursery with that light on until 10:00 p.m. Why would the kidnappers seek entry when lights were on throughout that section of the house and all of the household members were up and moving about? It would have made much more sense to wait until the early hours of the morning when all household members were asleep and their reaction time, if startled awake, would be the slowest. That, after all, is the reason that police execute most no-knock search warrants early in the morning. It is also when most surprise military attacks occur.

Not only would an early evening kidnapping risk detection, but even assuming the kidnappers were able to remove the child, their lead time to escape before their act was discovered was limited. On the other hand, a successful entry and removal after midnight could give them a five or six hour solid head start on any pursuit.

And there was the problem of the dog. Wahgoosh had never barked the whole evening, which he certainly would have done had there been a stranger in the house. In a letter to her mother-in-law written during the investigation Anne herself noted this and very troublingly added, "He has been barking ever since."18

No, Colonel Schwarzkopf and his staff reasoned, the scenario of a stranger coming through the window in the early evening simply did not make any sense. They reasoned that the kidnapping could not have been carried out solely by an outsider. It must have been an inside job carried out with the help of one of the staff. They theorized that perhaps the child had been removed from the nursery by a household conspirator and carried down the staircase where he was handed over to another kidnapper at the door. The note was then left and the ladder placed in the scrub to give the appearance of an outside job. Since the staff would have known of the defective shutter, the ladder holes were placed next to that window to reinforce the impression of the outside entry and thereby explain how latched shutters had been breached.

Colonel Schwarzkopf's initial instincts were good. Almost all of the later reviewers and investigators who have researched the Lindbergh case have also been troubled by these same facts. Yet having shown good instinctual first judgement in suspecting that someone inside the household had to have been involved, the police then made a fatal mistake. They limited their subsequent investigation to Betty Gow, Elsie and Ollie Whately, and Mrs. Morrow's household staff members. The Lindberghs were never considered suspects and were never investigated.

Certainly if the report made on March 1, 1932 were made to a police agency today the parents would be at the top of the suspect list. The files of welfare agencies and criminal courts are filled with instances in which parents have abused, maimed and even killed their children, either with intent or through neglect, and then manufactured a story to the police which sought to blame some anonymous third party.

Although many criminal perpetrators seek to cover their acts by blaming others, the ones which involve assaults or other crimes against children seem to offer a more fertile ground in which these "cover stores" can be cultivated.

The reasons are many. A man who loses control and strikes his wife or girlfriend can not credibly allege that a stranger did it because the wife or girlfriend is available to contradict it. A child, on the other hand, because of its age, is not always able to refute that a stranger abused him or her, or that he or she did not fall off the high chair by accident.

Compounding the problem is the fact, as any parent will attest, that children and especially toddlers do injure themselves in bizarre fashions, receiving oddly placed bruises. These are the nemesis of any pediatrician who can never know for certain whether the child was clumsy or was victimized. And so cover stories with regard to injuries to children remain a component of protective service and police investigation. In November of 1984 a Pawtucket, Rhode Island couple alleged that someone had kidnapped their infant from their second story window. A passionate plea by the mother was broadcast for its safe return.

Two days later, the child's body was found in a culvert in a nearby alley. The police determined that the child had died as a result of abuse and that the kidnapping had been fabricated.

On February 2, 1990 in the upstate New York town of Lansing a young mother, Christine Lane, reported her 23 month old daughter Aliza May Bush as kidnapped. She told police that she had arrived home and left Aliza in the living room while she went to the bathroom. When she exited the bathroom Aliza was gone. Thinking that the child had wandered outside she searched the grounds but found only one mitten. She telephoned the police and the case received widespread notoriety. The authorities publicly speculated that the child had wandered outside where a passing motorist had impulsively snatched her.

We live in a society that deeply protects and fears for our children. When Christine Lane made her report, regardless of the illogical aspects, she was believed and a massive and well publicized child search commenced. People believed it because Christine Lane had kindled one of our deepest embers of fear. The specter of a stranger suddenly snatching an innocent child is a fear which, at some level, haunts all parents.

But this was 1990 and Christine Lane was an unmarried mother, not America's hero. As the police pursued their investigation she was administered a lie detector test. She passed. However, an internal FBI memorandum indicated that she might be a suspect.

Lane played the part. She cried in front of television cameras and pleaded for her daughter's safe return. Hundreds of volunteers combed the area. Dozens of concerned citizens telephoned tips to a special toll free hot line. Aliza's picture was printed on over one million milk cartons.

Five days after the kidnapping Christine Lane received Aliza's other pink mitten in the mail. Back on television she went to talk of the renewed hope the mail had brought: that Aliza was alive and in the hands of kidnappers who wanted the mother to know that she was alive. "Please return my baby," she tearfully pleaded. The local district attorney promised leniency for the kidnappers if they would just return the child.

The package in which the mitten had arrived was postmarked in a nearby small town. A witness remembered the person who had mailed it. The description fit. The witness identified the mailer of the package as Christine Lane.

Faced with a new round of questioning, she confessed and then led the police to a wooded area near her apartment where she had hidden the body, wrapped in plastic bags and placed under a pile of brush. Christine Lane said the child had died naturally in her crib (sudden infant death) but that she had panicked that no one would believe her and so had invented the cover story. She admitted to mailing the mitten to herself and addressing the package with her left hand so as to disguise the handwriting.

On November 8, 1990, after a nearly month long trial, a Thompkins County, New York jury did not in fact believe Christine Lane. Although originally voting nine to three for conviction of first degree murder, they eventually convicted her of manslaughter.

These are but examples. Any police investigator, any protective services social worker, any criminal defense lawyer, has wrestled with hundreds of such reports, perhaps not as notorious as Christine Lane's, but certainly just as difficult to decipher as to whether they were true or a cover story. Stories are so often greeted with skepticism now that any criminal defense lawyer, sworn to protect his client, can cite at least one instance when he or she did not believe his or her client's "cover story," only to have it turn out, usually to the great embarrassment of the lawyer, that the defendant was in fact telling the truth all along. In the Christine Lane case the police, quite properly, listed her as a suspect from the beginning. The successful lie detector test result did not remove her from that list. There is no evidence that either of the Lindberghs were ever considered suspects.

It is too simplistic to attribute the New Jersey State Police failure to do so to "back then." For even today police often fail to investigate exceedingly respectable members of the community who claim to have been victims, regardless of how suspicious their own stories are.

Just a few months before Christine Lane fooled all of upstate New York, the Boston Police Department experienced its most embarrassing moment when they immediately believed Charles Stuart's "I am a victim" story. Despite the improbabilities, coincidences and inconsistencies in his statement, Charles Stuart played on deep seated racial fears in his cover story that a black man had jumped into his expensive car, shot and killed his pregnant wife, and wounded him. It was unquestioningly believed and the investigation proceeded accordingly, an investigation which came very close to using twisted evidence and coerced testimony to convict an innocent Willie Bennett.

The response to the Lindbergh kidnap report can not be simply attributed to the attitudes of the 1930's. It was more than that. Lindbergh was a giant, an imposing figure both in physical stature and social prominence.

But even if he had not been Lindbergh, it is doubtful that the Colonel would have been investigated or considered a suspect. Child abuse, whether intentional or neglectful, did not raise the social conscience in the same way as it does today. Children who made such allegations were not believed in 1932. Social services designed to detect and prevent abuse and neglect were non-existent. Crimes against children by their parents simply didn't happen.

The agencies which did exist were not equipped. In 1932 the mandate of the police was strictly para-military: arrest bootleggers, capture gangsters, stop bank robberies. The concept of a police officer as a social worker, one trained to recognize, investigate and intervene in domestic crisis of alcoholism, child abuse, spouse abuse and incest, was a concept that still lay some fifty years in the future. Colonel Lindbergh's son had been reported kidnapped and they would find the child and arrest the kidnappers.

That initial mistake was neither limited to the police nor confined to the early days of the investigation. The possibility that a kidnapping had never occurred was a viable defense which could have been advanced at Hauptmann's trial by his lawyers. It was not because they, like everyone else, could not conceive of it.

One defense which was advanced by Hauptmann's chief lawyer, Edward J. Reilly, was that this kidnapping could have been an inside job done with the cooperation of Gow or the Whatelys. His questions to witnesses were often designed to raise this as a possibility in the jurors' minds. At one point during Riley's cross-examination of New Jersey State Police Detective Bornmann, he tried to get him to admit that the police had suspected Gow and the Whatleys. However, his questions reveal his own limitations of thought.

"Wasn't everybody in the house that night," he asked Bornmann, "with the exception of Colonel Lindbergh and his wife, under suspicion?"

The question produced an immediate objection by Attorney General David Wilentz, who claimed that there was no evidence that Gow or the Whatelys were involved. In defending his question, Reilly reiterated the mistake that everyone, including Hauptmann's own defense team, had made. "I say," he told the Judge, "that in a case of such monumental importance as it occurred that night, this officer knew the minute he arrived, as a trained detective, and as every detective knows, that excluding the father and mother of that child, everybody that night should have been under suspicion."

Reilly was right. Bornmann, Schwarzkopf and the rest of the New Jersey State Police put under suspicion everyone, except the parents. And sixty years after the event the disappearance of the child is considered by most to remain unsolved.

We know better today. The FBI National Crime statistics indicate that in 1989 and 1990 there were 1,452 homicides in the United States of children aged 0 to 9 years. Of these, over 70% were committed by one or both of the parents. Yet in 1932, neither Lindbergh was ever considered a suspect or otherwise investigated. And so Colonel Schwarzkopf made two mistakes: he did not consider the Lindberghs suspects and he allowed Colonel Lindbergh to establish himself as head of the investigation. Once the latter mistake was solidified the first mistake was irreparable.

CHAPTER V

Colonel Lindbergh moved swiftly to consolidate his power as chief investigator of his own son's kidnapping. He was so imposing, and invoked such awe, that when he spoke people just complied. With his two advisors, Colonels Donovan and Breckinridge, Lindbergh spent much of March 2 with Colonel Schwarzkopf. The four agreed on a strategy.

That Colonel Schwarzkopf allowed the parent of the victim to not only be a part of the investigation but to actually head it up, was absolutely violative of good police practice. Regardless of Colonel Schwarzkopf's lack of police experience, he was the head of the New Jersey State Police and should have exerted his authority accordingly. Why he didn't is not perfectly clear, but four possibilities exist.

One, he may have been so much in awe of Lindbergh that he simply deferred to the great man as others had.

Two, he may have believed there was nothing else he could do. Being a gubernatorial appointee, he certainly had the political savvy to realize that if he tried to challenge Lindbergh's authority by making unilateral decisions about the course of the investigation, Lindbergh simply could have gone over his head.

Because of Lindbergh, any of Schwarzkopf's political superiors would willingly pressure the state police head. If Schwarzkopf resisted further he may very well have believed that he would lose his position. If he did believe that, he may actually have been right. Lindbergh probably was that powerful. There were times during the investigation when he crossed swords with other investigators and threatened to have them removed. Inevitably the others backed down.

A third possibility is that Schwarzkopf, not possessing a police background, may have lacked self-confidence with regard to his investigative methods and simply believed that Lindbergh would do a better job.

The fourth and last possibility is that Schwarzkopf may have been so astute that he realized that if Lindbergh headed the investigation he, Schwarzkopf, could not be blamed by Lindbergh or anyone else for its failure if the child were not returned home safely and/or the kidnappers not apprehended.

The last possibility is not likely. Had Schwarzkopf allowed Lindbergh to lead in order to avoid personal failure he would not have challenged Lindbergh at all. But the evidence is that he did offer some token resistance. From the beginning, he suggested that the focus of the investigation should be solution of the crime, and the apprehension of those who did it.

Colonel Lindbergh over-rode this goal and his over-ride was allowed to stand. Instead, he insisted that the police goal should not be the discovery of what had happened or the apprehension of the kidnappers. Rather, their only goal should be the safe return of the child. All police efforts were to be directed towards successfully negotiating with the kidnappers. He, Lindbergh, would direct such efforts.

This remained the source of quiet tension between Schwarz-kopf and Lindbergh until the body of the child was discovered on May 12. That event seemed to awaken in Schwarzkopf a recognition of his proper role, for he immediately announced that the game was now different and he would lead the investigation to discover who had done this. At that point Schwarzkopf did begin to exercise his control and Lindbergh's role shrunk. But by that time it was too late.

It is similarly unlikely that Lindbergh was allowed control in those early days because of any lack of confidence Schwarzkopf had in his own investigative abilities. Even though he had little police background, as Colonel of the state police he was an administrator with professional investigators better trained than Colonel Lindbergh to conduct a police investigation.

The reasons for Colonel Schwarzkopf's abdication of authority to "the council of four colonels" probably lies in a cross between the first two theories suggested: Schwarzkopf's awe of Lindbergh and his recognition of Lindbergh's considerable social and political stature.

And so, for whatever reasons, Colonel Lindbergh established his council of four colonels, including the two who were advisors to him, and he put himself at its head. The first thing he did was threaten to personally shoot any police officer who made a move without his fore-knowledge and approval.

He should have been arrested for such action and charged with criminal threatening. But he was not. Colonel Schwarzkopf should not have allowed the parent (a person who today would be routinely considered a suspect) to be involved in the police process. But he did.

The fact that Lindbergh was chief investigator of his own son's kidnapping has been much discussed but never criticized. It should be. The first great failure of the Lindbergh investigation was simply allowed to happen. Someone should have belled the cat, but this cat was just too big.

Once he took control, Colonel Lindbergh directed the case. He had a plan, and others simply adhered to it. Colonel Schwarzkopf's initial suspicions about the case were brushed aside.

Instead, Colonel Lindbergh began his investigation by attempting to enlist New York underworld figures to act on behalf of his family in negotiating with the kidnappers. The plan made no sense for two reasons.

First, there was nothing in the nursery note to suggest that underworld figures were involved. In fact the kidnapping seemed to be the type of crime that would so enrage the public (which it did) that the underworld would not want to risk the increased police attention which would inevitably result.

Second, there was nothing in the note or the circumstances of the child's disappearance to support the proposition that the perpetrators were from New York as opposed to Newark, Philadelphia or Washington, D.C.

But Colonel Lindbergh's command was dutifully obeyed. Colonel Breckinridge had in his law firm a young lawyer by the name of Robert Thayer. Thayer did then what a lot of young people do: he went to bars. But in 1932, prohibition was on and people who frequented illegal speakeasies rubbed shoulders with a class of people generally characterized as "underworld types."

Through Attorney Thayer contact was made with a character straight out of a Damon Runyon story: Mickey Rossner. Lindbergh stated that since the underworld was involved, an "underworld intermediary" was necessary to make contact. Colonel Lindbergh was an intelligent man and any explanation which rests on the contention that he did not know better, is flawed.

The "underworld" is not a monolithic corporate octopus where communication with one tentacle will be eventually received by the brain. There is no Doctor Moriarity of Sherlock Holmes' delusions who controls all crime. Choosing Mickey Rossner as liaison was no more likely to be successful than choosing any individual picked at random. Yet no one objected. Under Colonel Lindbergh's direction the investigation of a very serious crime was off to an almost farcical, circus-like beginning.

Mickey Rossner, through Thayer, was summoned to the Hopewell home on March 3, the situation was explained to him and his help was sought. He agreed to help but on certain conditions: he wanted $2,500.00 up front in cash, the absolute right to unquestioned activity without interference, and the commitment that he would not be followed by any police. Lindbergh agreed. No one objected.

It is unclear from the evidence now available whether Mickey Rossner was actually given a copy of the nursery note. There is some evidence to suggest that he was, and that he immediately took it to New York City on March 3 where he showed it to an Owney Madden, another underworld friend of Rossner's.

The evidence on this is uncertain and it may be that Rossner was actually only shown the original kidnap note with the "secret symbol," but not given a copy.

However, it is apparent that copies of the original note were soon circulating among the press and among criminal circles in New York City. Some journalists have revealed that copies were circulating as far west as the Rocky Mountains. Even without a leak by Rossner, members of the press corps had been able to purchase copies of the original note from bribable members of the New Jersey State Police.

The security of the investigation was becoming abysmal. That there were members of the New Jersey State Police who were willing to give or sell copies of the note to the press was certainly not Lindbergh's fault. However, the involvement of Lindbergh and his personal advisors, as well as junior attorneys and staff at the law firm of one of those advisors, and the granting of access to the note to an underworld client of one of the lawyers, made any type of security surrounding the investigation a forlorn hope.

On March 4, Charles issued a statement to the press from himself and Anne jointly. It read:

> Mrs. Lindbergh and I desire to make a personal contact with the kidnappers of our child....We urge those who have the child to select any representative that they may desire to meet a representative of ours who will be suitable to them at any time and at any place that they may designate. If this is accepted, we promise that we will keep whatever arrangements that may be made by their representative and ours strictly confidential and we further pledge ourselves that we will not try to injure in any way those connected with the return of the child.

The statement was, of course, published universally.

On March 5 a second kidnap note arrived at the Lindbergh's house in Hopewell. It was postmarked at 9:00 p.m. on the evening before and had been mailed in Brooklyn.

The letter was written in a somewhat illegible script similar to that of the original nursery note. It read:

> Dear Sir: We have warned you note to make anyding Public also notify the Police now you have to take the consequences. This means we will holt the baby until everding is quiet.... We are interested to send him back in gut health. ouer ransom was made aus for 50.000$ but now we have to take another person to it and probable have to keep the baby for a longer time as we expected So the mount will be 70.000$....

Although the evidence regarding Mickey Rossner's access to the nursery note is uncertain, it is clear that this second letter was immediately taken by him to New York. On the morning of March 5 Rossner met with Colonel Breckinridge at his law office. Also present were Owney Madden and two other underworld characters, Salvy Spitale and Irving Bitz. All had access to the note there. However it happened, it appears that within a very short time copies of that letter, too, were in general circulation among underworld figures.

The two new characters, Spitale and Bitz, were present at Rossner's invitation. And characters they were. Spitale had worked his way up from night club bouncer in a Williamsburg dance club to owning his own speakeasy and being a bootlegger. Bitz had done time in prison for sale of a controlled drug, had become a bootlegger, and was currently the boss of a speakeasy.

The next day, Sunday, March 6, 1932, Rossner took Spitale and Bitz out to Hopewell and introduced them to Lindbergh. For reasons that have been lost in history, Rossner asked Lindbergh to officially appoint them both as Rossner's assistant intermediaries. Charles Lindbergh readily agreed and quickly issued a public statement to that effect.

By this point Colonel Schwarzkopf and the New Jersey State Police were not vetoing or even objecting to Lindbergh's actions. This had become Colonel Lindbergh's case; Colonel Schwarzkopf and the New Jersey State Police were working for him.

However, actions which did not elicit any response from the New Jersey authorities were eliciting responses across the nation. Ministers, newspaper columnists and police officials in other jurisdictions were universally appalled at the way this case involving the son of America's hero was progressing, and they spoke out against it.

A Michigan priest who appeared regularly on a syndicated radio show which reached millions (the fore-runner of today's televangelists), Father Charles E. Coughlin, asked rhetorically, "Do you know who these men are? They are unlawful. They are racketeers. They are the new Almighty we have in the United States . . . the bootleggers, the gamblers, the thugs. Such are the people Colonel Lindbergh felt it necessary to appoint."

The press also criticized the selectees, if not the selection itself. Numerous articles about the past dealings of the three were researched and published, including the fact that Rossner was currently under indictment for grand larceny in a stock selling promotion in which he had swindled victims out of more than two million dollars.

New York Police Commissioner Ed Mulrooney was perhaps the most stunned by the developments. In his position he was well aware of the backgrounds and reputations of Rossner, Spitale and Bitz, whom Lindbergh was designating to play the central role in this, The Crime Of The Century.

It was also in Mulrooney's city, in his jurisdiction, that the second ransom note had been mailed. It did not strike him, or anyone else, strange that New York City should be linked to this Sourland Mountains' kidnapping only after New York City criminals were purposely brought in by the victim's father, or that such involvement constituted in any way a self-fulfilling prophecy. "Involve people from New York," the case seemed to be saying, "and that is where the answer will lie."

Colonel Lindbergh had brought into this case people from the underworld, and people from New York where he worked, and sure enough, clues began pointing to the New York under-world.

Commissioner Mulrooney did not seem to wonder about that, or if he wondered he did not comment upon it. He only knew that a second ransom demand had arrived in Hopewell, and that it had been mailed from his jurisdiction.

Mulrooney was an experienced police commissioner. He thought like a policeman. He was logical. He was not under the direct personal spell of Charles Lindbergh. He knew what would be the logical thing to do to solve this quickly.

The plan he formulated was simple, and as he explained to Lindbergh in Hopewell, was based on good solid police experience. If the kidnappers mailed a ransom letter they were probably mailing it from a place to which they had easy access. They either lived or worked in Brooklyn. The contents of this second note and the status of the negotiations had at that point mandated that the kidnappers would have to write again. They were probably inexperienced and over confident in the anonymity of the mailing process. They would probably mail again in the same neighborhood, if not at the same mailbox.

There were only a finite number of mailboxes from which the letter could have been mailed to receive the postmark it had. Mulrooney suggested that all such mailboxes be staked out and equipped with a device to hold each mailed letter just inside the slot. After each letter was deposited and the sender had departed a detective could retrieve the letter. If it were innocent it would be thrown back into the box. However, if it were addressed to Lindbergh, Schwarzkopf, or to the Hopewell house the mailer could be followed and his identity and whereabouts quickly learned.

The plan had little risk. The twenty month old infant could not identify the kidnappers, let alone ever be able to testify against them. At that time kidnapping was not a capital offense for which they could be executed. If, even by mistake, the tailing police officer were spotted and stumbled into the den of the kidnappers, there was no reason to fear that the kidnappers would then harm or kill the child, thereby elevating their crime to a capital offense.

The plan as presented to Lindbergh was solid. It was the only logical one in the works. It probably would have worked too. However, when it was presented to Lindbergh he flew into a rage and immediately vetoed it. Too risky for the child, he stated.

Mulrooney was a tough, realistic cop who knew the plan was sound and further that Lindbergh had no jurisdiction over him. Mulrooney repeatedly explained that the plan was safe. Lindbergh would not budge. He finally told Commissioner Ed Mulrooney flat out that if he went ahead with the plan he, Colonel Lindbergh, would use every ounce of political power to see that Mulrooney was broken. Mulrooney backed down.

The next day a third ransom letter was mailed from one of those very mailboxes.

CHAPTER VI

This is not to say that during the early days of the Lindbergh investigation the New Jersey State Police were doing nothing on their own. They had their original suspicion of the inside job and despite their instructions from Lindbergh that this was not their primary function, they pursued and investigated, if not all of the household members, at least those they were allowed to by the prevailing American caste system of 1932.

In the last scene at the airport in the 1941 movie classic *Casablanca*, Humphrey Bogart's character Richard Blaine shoots and kills the Nazi Major Strasser in front of the (up until then) French collaborationist Captain Renault. Troops rush in and there is a moment of uncertainty. Captain Renault announces, "Major Strasser's been shot," and pauses. "Round up the usual suspects!" The soldiers rush out to, we assume, dutifully arrest and interrogate countless innocents until someone confesses.

The scene was not far removed from American police practice of 60 years ago or, embarrassingly, sometimes today. The technique is sufficiently successful that it remains a police tool. The New Jersey State Police of 1932 used this technique and thus began their investigation of "the usual suspects." The problem is the police did not consider any of the unusual ones. If a household staff member were involved he or she would have had the assistance of an outside conspirator. The one fact which most stood out about the commission of this crime was the availability of the target. The Lindberghs never stayed in Hopewell during the week. If the kidnapping had been conducted by a group without inside help their intelligence could have been generated by possible surveillance of the house over an extended period of time.

Yet surveillance would not have indicated that on February 29 and March 1 the Lindberghs would decide to stay over an additional day. Since the decision to stay over the second day had only been made on March 1 this could only have been learned from an inside source. The police were initially convinced that a source inside the Lindbergh household *had* to have been involved. And the number one inside source seemed to be Betty Gow.

Betty was 27 years old and single. Like many, if not most, of the domestic help in the 1930's for the privileged American families, Betty was an immigrant, in her case having arrived from Scotland.

The decision to stay the extra day had been made by the Colonel in the morning and then communicated by Anne to Englewood by telephone. It was that call that had prompted Betty Gow's arrival in Hopewell.

The police also learned that Betty had telephoned her boyfriend "Red" Johnson to tell him about the change in plans and to cancel their planned date for that evening.

The police immediately placed Red Johnson near the top of their list. Their initial investigation of Red looked promising. He was either a Swedish or Norwegian immigrant (depending on whose report and investigation you believe) who worked as a sailor on the private yacht of Thomas Lamont, a business partner of Dwight Morrow's. In fact, it was when the Lamont yacht had docked in Maine during a Lindbergh family visit to the Morrow's summer home that Johnson and Gow had met. They had been dating since.

In order to be nearer his fiance' Johnson had recently taken an apartment in Englewood. When the police heard this they placed Johnson a notch higher on the suspect list.

After his telephone call to Betty at about 8:30 p.m., Red had left for his brother's house in Hartford, Connecticut. At the request of the New Jersey State Police bulletin local police in Hartford located Red there early the next morning. Although there was no legal justification to do either, they arrested Red and searched his car. As Americans we often get upset when we learn of human rights violations in other countries: people routinely picked up by the police, arrested, held in jail for no other reason than for "investigation" or for "questioning." Few realize that in the 1930's, 40's and 50's, before the Supreme Court curbed unbridled police power, such intrusions were common-place.

Red Johnson was about to find this out first hand. The search of his car revealed an empty milk bottle. The police immediately believed they had the right man; after all, wasn't the milk bottle proof that a baby was in the area? Johnson's explanation that he liked to drink milk and toss the empties in the back seat was not believed by the police as it didn't fit their theory. Besides, they reasoned, it is not milk that sailors drink.

Johnson was held in jail for 18 days without a trial, without bail being set, and without any formal charges being brought against him to which he could answer. He was simply held on "suspicion in the Lindbergh case." During the 18 days he was constantly questioned, sometimes rather vigorously, while outside, the police scurried around to see what else they could find out about Red.

In the end they found nothing except that he was here illegally. All their investigative sources led them to reluctantly conclude that Johnson had nothing to do with the kidnapping or the baby. He was, in fact, a milk drinker.

But he was here illegally. So after 18 days of incarceration they put him on a boat and shipped him to Norway where he was never heard from again.

The police investigated Betty Gow. In the days immediately following the kidnapping she came in for some pretty rough questioning. "Rough questioning" seems to have been the order of the day. In the case of Betty Gow even Anne Lindbergh, who we can assume would support any tactic to promote her child's safe return, took note of it. In a letter to her mother-in-law she thanked her for her encouraging note to Betty adding that, "She has had so much grilling and criticism, and is such a loyal girl."[19]

After a lengthy investigation Trooper Bornmann of the New Jersey State Police concluded that Betty Gow was, "a highly sensitive girl of good morals . . . above being in any way connected with the persons responsible for the kidnapping of the baby."[20]

The police also investigated Ollie and Elsie Whately. They had been in the country for approximately two years since immigrating from England. Contrary to claims made by Ollie

Whately at the time of his hiring by Lindbergh through a New York employment agency, it turned out that he was not a person who had a long history of domestic service but had been in turn a jeweler, a munitions worker and a mechanic. Despite these revelations nothing was discovered to link the Whatelys, either jointly or individually, with the crime.

Finishing, as they thought, with any possible suspects in the Hopewell house, the police turned their attention to the staff at Englewood. After Anne's call in the morning the whole staff at Englewood was aware of the change in plans, that Betty was being dispatched to Hopewell and that the Lindberghs would be staying an extra night. Each one of the twenty-nine household staff members was investigated.

Anne's original telephone call had been answered by Violet Sharpe, a 28 year old single house maid and immigrant from England.

When questioned, her original story to the police was that on the night of March 1 she had been to a movie. However, she could not name the movie, describe the plot or tell who any of the actors had been. She was also vague about whom she had attended the movie with. The police found her to be cold and defiant, and they believed she was hiding something about her movements on the evening in question.

One of the classic mistakes police make - one of the great investigative pitfalls - is that when they catch a witness lying, or trying to hide facts, they invariably assume that the person is therefore connected with the crime and is lying to protect their involvement. They have historically failed to realize that people in general have all sorts of reasons to lie, to withhold facts or conceal their movements on a particular day, and that such prevarication often has nothing to do with the incident under investigation. People have affairs, gamble on sporting events, use too much alcohol or illicit drugs, skip school to go to the beach, call in sick at work to attend a baseball game, pad their expense account or do any one of several deceptive acts which, while being performed, may somehow inadvertently overlap with an independent criminal act. During the course of the subsequent investigation, if the police find evidence of a witness covering up, they often leap to the wrong conclusions.

The reason is that the police tend to over estimate the importance to others of the investigation they are conducting. They assume that all witnesses will tell the truth when questioned about an incident not involving them. They fail to realize that the office worker would prefer that a burglary in her apartment complex go unsolved rather than have it be known that she was home at the time having an affair with a fellow co-worker. Even if the magnitude of the criminal investigation impresses the witness, he or she may still believe that relevant information can be given while embarrassing facts are being withheld.

With Violet Sharpe, the police again believed that they were zeroing in on the truth. Under continued questioning she changed her story. She had not gone to the movies but rather dancing at a roadside cafe. Another couple had accompanied them. She did not know who the other couple was because they were friends of her date and she did not know that they would be going until she had got into her date's car. She could not remember her date's name. She had met him on her day off and never got his name. And so it went.

During the investigation into her background, she claimed to have been married briefly in 1929 in England to a George Payne. She had had an abortion in the United States after an affair with the Morrow's butler. Apparently she was still in love with him although it was unclear if he felt the same. Her inability, or unwillingness, to provide either corroborating details or a consistent story put Violet Sharpe at the top of the suspect list. However, her placement there was more by default than deduction, because despite her hostile nature there was no tangible evidence that she was involved in any kidnap conspiracy. The police probed and dug but could uncover nothing further to link Violet Sharpe. However, they kept her in mind.

Each member of the Morrow's staff was painstakingly questioned and their backgrounds exposed. Each of the 130 workmen who had worked on the construction of the Hopewell house was similarly scrutinized. Every neighbor in a five mile radius was questioned, re-questioned and questioned again. Tips, anonymous and not, poured in from all over the country. Each and every one was carefully and meticulously checked out. There was no shortage of police manpower available for this case, for this family.

Searches were conducted all across the United States. Boats in harbors, abandoned warehouses, empty sheds in back yards, garages, automobiles with "suspicious" characters or characteristics (such as out of state license plates) were all routinely, arbitrarily and thoroughly searched. Some of these searches may have been legal; most were not, but it mattered little. Back in 1932 the nation was outraged. If Lindbergh had become an American God then his only son also had a certain preeminence, and someone had had the audacity to take him.

But despite the massive rounding up, arresting and searching of all of "the usual suspects" there were no good leads. The sheer volume of the investigation led to many tips but there were no good ones. When pursued, each and every one fizzled.

The police did not resort to only the usual methods of investigation. A number of psychics were called in, or volunteered their help, and many, many hours of police investigation were expended in driving around a number of these clairvoyants in an effort to sense the location of the child. All failed.

The fact that there were no arrests made or good leads developed in those early days after the child's disappearance was certainly not due to lack of effort. The effort was massive, and was, as indicated, not confined to New Jersey. There simply was no evidence of any kidnap conspiracy, of any kidnapping group, or of any kidnapper.

CHAPTER VII

Rossner, Bitz, Spitale and the other characters who paraded through this case in the days immediately following the child's disappearance were bizarre and colorful, but they pale in comparison with Dr. John F. Condon, the main intervenor in the most celebrated crime in the world.

Condon was a 72 year old long-winded bore who resided in the Bronx. His personal history until then had been unremarkable. He had played football for Fordham University in 1883, served as a teacher and principal in the public schools and lectured in education at Fordham. He also styled himself a physical fitness enthusiast.

When not lecturing or exercising, Dr. Condon had written numerous essays, poems and letters to the editor for the *Bronx Home News*, a neighborhood newspaper with a general circulation of 150,000. He would often sign his letters with pseudonyms tailored to his topic such as P.A. Triot, for the patriotic letter, L.O. Nestar or J.U. Stice, etc.

Whenever the editors at the *Home News* wanted an outside opinion on some topic they would send a reporter to Condon. The professor could always be counted upon to give some garrulous quote on any topic. He loved to see his name in print and fancied himself an expert on everything.

The Lindbergh baby's disappearance and the way the subsequent investigation was progressing seemed tailor made for the involvement of people like Dr. Condon. He was pompous and totally devoid of any information or talents which would be helpful to the solution of this crime.

On the evening of March 9 Dr. Condon telephoned the Lindbergh household and asked for the Colonel. He instead got Robert Thayer. Believing that he had Colonel Lindbergh on the line Condon told his story. He related that he had been upset at the kidnapping and desired to help in the return of the child. Earlier he had, on March 6, written a letter to the *Bronx Home*

News in which he had offered to serve as intermediary between the Lindberghs and the kidnappers. This offer had been in response to Colonel Lindbergh's March 4 published request for intermediaries.

The *Bronx Home News* had written a story about Condon's offer and featured it on their front page. After all, Dr. Condon was well known to the newspaper and its readers. In his letter he had offered an additional $1,000.00 of his own money to sweeten the pot for the child's safe return.

Condon further related to Thayer that he had on that evening, upon returning home, found an envelope addressed to him in a crude script. Opening it, he had found another sealed envelope and a note. The note read:

Dear Sir: If you are willing to act as go-between in Lindbergh case follow strictly instruction. Handel inclosed letter personally to Mr. Lindbergh...After you gets the money from Mr. Lindbergh put them words in New York American. Money is ready. After notice we will give you further instructions.

Don't be afrait we are not out for your 1,000$. Keep it only act strictly. Be at haus every night between 6-12 by this time you will hear from us.

Dr. Condon read the note to the listener at the other end of the telephone line in Hopewell. The voice asked him to open the envelope and share its contents. Dr. Condon did so. The second note read:

Dear sire, Mr. Condon may act as go-between you may give him the 70,000$ make one packet, the size will be about ...[and here the extortionist drew a box, six by seven by fourteen inches]. We have notify you allredy in what kind of bills.

We warn you not to set a trapp in any way ... after we have the mony in hand we will tell you where to find your boy...

The voice asked Condon if there was anything else in the note. Condon replied that there was no signature but that there were secantal circles and holes.

At this point another voice came on the line, identified himself as Colonel Lindbergh and indicated that he would send a car for the doctor. Condon declined, responding that the Colonel was much too busy, but that he would come up to Hopewell.

Approximately three hours later Condon arrived at the Lindbergh home, having been driven out by a Milton Gaglio and accompanied by a Maxie Rosenhein. Condon explained that upon receiving the note he had not known what to do with it and so had gone to Maxie Rosenhein's restaurant to seek the advice from Mr. Rosenhein as well as other regular patrons including Al Reich, a retired heavyweight boxer and friend with whom he often shared a midnight snack at Rosenhein's. As Mr. Reich had not yet arrived Condon had laid out the situation to Rosenhein and Gaglio, another patron, and they suggested that Condon telephone Lindbergh.

The notes were reviewed by those at the Hopewell house including Lindbergh and Breckinridge. Colonel Lindbergh then announced that the notes were from the real kidnappers. Lindbergh cited the consistency of the March 4 ransom letter (in which the demand had been increased to $70,000.00 coupled with the fact that the contents of that letter had not been released to the general public) with the demand in the Condon letter of $70,000.00. Also, the Condon letter contained a reasonable facsimile of the previously used secret signature. The undisputed fact that the March 4 letter, although not released to the general public, had nevertheless been taken by Rossner and copies of it were in general circulation amongst small time hustlers in New York City, was either not known by Lindbergh or else purposely ignored by him.

Lindbergh immediately appointed Condon his new and latest intermediary and signed an official letter of appointment to that effect.

The hour was late and Condon was invited to spend the night in the Hopewell house. As the other guest rooms were not yet completed, he was put up on a cot in the nursery from which the child had been taken.

Dr. Condon later described a very maudlin scene in which he knelt by the child's crib before going to bed and prayed for his safe return. Perhaps inspired by the prayer he came up with the idea of removing the two safety pins which still fastened the bed clothes to the mattress and taking them with him to confront the kidnappers. His plan was that they could be used to verify that the persons with whom he was dealing were in fact the real kidnappers.

At breakfast the next morning there was some discussion as to the necessity of Dr. Condon having a secret code name. As his initials were J.F.C. he suggested the acronym "Jafsie" and this was agreed upon by all.

In the book he later wrote which purported to accurately describe his role in all this, *Jafsie Tells All*, Condon maintained that while in the nursery he had observed a smudged handprint on the edge of the window frame, ostensibly left by the kidnapper when exiting out the window. Despite the fact that Condon had absolutely no law enforcement experience or training he claimed in his book that upon glancing at the handprint he could discern a "prominent and well-defined mark left by the ball of the thumb ... there is evidence of muscular development there ... the print might have been left by a painter, a carpenter, a mechanic."[21]

That claim is absurd for two reasons. First and foremost, the police had found no prints at all in the nursery, so how could Condon have seen this?

Second, there is no fingerprint expert in the world who would say that one can ascertain a person's profession by a fingerprint or handprint and this certainly could not have been done by an amateur blowhard like Condon. The real relevance of the claim is that it shows Condon to be a self- impressed, pompous oaf who was willing to lie in order to make himself look like a Sherlock Holmes. Later journalists and other students of the crime who have relied on Condon's book for information, rather than on records of witnesses' actual statements, may not be getting an accurate or reliable picture. It must be remembered that Condon's book was written after the arrest of the German born carpenter, and after Condon's testimony had helped to convict and execute Hauptmann.

Lindbergh did not trust him and indicated to others that Jafsie might be part of an extortion plot. Lindbergh wanted him watched. Accordingly, when Jafsie returned to the Bronx that day he was accompanied to his Decatur Avenue home by Colonel Breckinridge who proceeded to move in. It was explained to Jafsie that since his home might soon become the ransom negotiating center Breckinridge, as Lindbergh's advisor, needed to be there. Jafsie agreed.

On March 12 Jafsie returned home to be informed by his wife that he had received a telephone call from a man with a German accent who had said he would call back.

At approximately 7:00 p.m. Condon received a telephone call from a man who inquired if he had received a letter with the sign. When Condon responded positively the caller instructed him to remain at home every night that week from 6:00 to midnight to await a further message.

And then the caller asked, "Do you write sometimes pieces for the papers?" When Condon responded that he did, it appeared to him that the caller turned away from the mouthpiece and spoke to another, "He say sometimes he writes pieces for the papers."

The caller returned to the business at hand and told Condon to remain at home and act as instructed. The doctor agreed.

Condon then heard another voice in the background shout in Italian, "*Statte Citti!*" Condon spoke the language and recognized the Italian equivalent of "Shut up!" The caller said he would be in touch again and hung up.

At approximately 8:30 that evening a man came to Condon's door. He was Joseph Perrone, a cab driver, and he delivered another sealed envelope to Dr. Condon.

Perrone told Condon and Breckinridge that he had been driving along Gun Hill Road, not too far away, when he had been flagged down by a man who approached the passenger side of the motor vehicle and asked Perrone if he were aware of the location of Decatur Avenue. When Perrone indicated that he was, the man asked if he knew where 2974 Decatur Avenue was. When

Perrone again replied affirmatively the man reached into his overcoat and extracted a sealed envelope and a one dollar bill.

The envelope had Dr. Condon's name and address written on the outside. Perrone described the person he had encountered as having a long and narrow face, blue eyes, high cheek bones and a heavy German accent. Breckinridge and Condon took down Perrone's name and let him go.

Inside the envelope was yet another note. It instructed Condon to bring the ransom money with him and drive to the last subway stop on the Jerome Avenue Line. About one hundred feet before the stop was an empty hot dog stand with a large porch. Underneath a stone on the porch Condon would find another note.

Condon persuaded Breckinridge to remain at Condon's home while he negotiated with the kidnapper. He then telephoned his friend Al Reich and requested that he accompany him to the meeting. For what happened after that we have only the statement of Dr. John F. Condon as later told to the police, as testified to at Hauptmann's trial, and as contained in his book. There is no outside corroboration for Condon's version of what happened that evening other than Reich's brief trial testimony.

According to Condon, he and Reich arrived at the porch and found the note. This one ordered Condon to cross the street to the fence surrounding Woodlawn Cemetery and to proceed on foot towards 233rd Street.

Reich drove Condon across the street and parked. Condon stepped outside and waited for approximately 15 minutes before the cold forced him to re-enter Reich's car to warm up for a few minutes. He eventually exited and began walking as instructed. As he proceeded along the sidewalk outside of the cemetery, he saw a hand holding a white handkerchief through the bars of the wrought iron cemetery fence.

Condon yelled, "I see you," and broke into a trot. The man responded, "Not so fast," and climbed up and over the nine foot fence, landing next to Condon on the sidewalk.

"The Police!" the man shouted, and ran off towards Van Cortland Park. Apparently a night watchman alerted by the suspicious actions had come to investigate. Condon claimed he was able to mollify the guard by simply telling him that the man who had just fled on foot was not worthy of further investigation because he was with Condon.

Condon then ran after the man and caught up to him in the park where they sat down together on the park bench. The man was shivering and Condon offered to give him his own overcoat. The man declined.

Condon asked for some proof that he was in fact dealing with the kidnapper. The man responded that Condon had received the note with the secret signature which was the same as that on the original note left in the baby's crib.

The problem, of course, is that the note was not left in the crib, but rather on the window sill. According to Condon the two spoke for over one hour on the park bench. However, in that time, the discrepancy about the note was never pursued or explored by Condon.

There are two possible explanations for this, both of which are inconsistent with the Hauptmann as kidnapper theory. The most obvious is that the person with whom Condon was dealing was a fraud. Copies of the "secret signature" in the original nursery note, as well as in the March 4 letter, were in general circulation among underworld types and newspaper reporters. The whole response to Dr. Condon's letter in the *Bronx Home News* could have been an attempted extortion by a person who had not taken the child and therefore did not know where the original ransom note had been left. Since the location of the nursery note had not been publicized, the fraudulent extortionist could have just assumed that it had been left in a logical place, like the crib, for instance.

Second, it is possible that Condon himself was part of some sort of fraudulent extortion plan and that this whole meeting never happened or, if it did, that its details were manufactured by Condon. If so, Condon might not have himself known where the original note had been left and therefore manufactured a conversation which he assumed to be consistent with the facts.

It is unclear whether Condon actually knew where the note had been left. In his book he later claimed that he did and tried to explain away the discrepancy. However, as Breckinridge and

Lindbergh had not trusted him from the beginning and suspected him to be part of an extortion plot, it is doubtful that such information would have been shared with him.

In *Jafsie Tells All*, Condon theorized that the note had in fact been left in the crib but in all the excitement had inadvertently been removed to the sill by a household member before being rediscovered by Lindbergh. Although totally implausible, it was the only theory which would protect Condon and explain why, if he knew of the note's true location, he had not asked about that in the park.

The authors of this book are themselves divided on whether the evidence suggests that Condon was an extortionist or merely the unwitting dupe of other extortionists.

Condon and the man spoke for over one hour. Condon described the man as having a "German accent" and was certain his was the same voice he had heard on the telephone. The man himself claimed to be a Scandinavian sailor by the name of "John." Thereafter he was always referred to as "Cemetery John."

John claimed that there were four men and two women in the kidnap gang and that the baby was safe on a boat. Attempting to verify the man's authenticity, Condon pulled from his pockets the two safety pins and asked the man to identify them. "Yes, those pins fastened the blanket to the mattress in the baby's crib, near the top, near the pillow."

Condon later wrote, and argued to the authorities, that this proved Cemetery John was the real kidnapper and therefore entitled to the ransom money. Obviously Condon knew the source of the pins since he himself had disconnected them from the mattress. If he were part of the extortion plot or even if, like the story about his observation of the handprint, he created the pin story to bolster his own role, he could have created Cemetery John's response in order to add to his authenticity.

Condon later claimed that, suspecting the man was German, he tried to trap him by asking him in that language if he were one. *"Bist du Deutsche?"* elicited no reply. The pair continued talking. Condon tried to negotiate the price down to $50,000.00 but John refused, indicating that the gang's leader would never allow such a reduction.

At the conclusion of the meeting Cemetery John informed Condon that when he had the money he should place an ad to that effect in the *Bronx Home News*. John would then mail to Condon his next set of instructions along with the sleeping suit the child was wearing when he was taken. That would serve as proof that the gang actually had him.

Condon indicated that he would place the ad the next morning and the pair rose and shook hands. Condon later claimed that upon shaking hands he felt the hard lump of muscle he had expected to feel at the base of the man's thumb.

Again, like the handprint observation, this is merely self-serving manufactured recollection. Although no one has previously challenged Condon's observations in this instance, we would challenge the reader to conduct his or her own test. Blindfold yourself, shake hands with several individuals of different professions, and identify which ones are the painter, the mechanic, the carpenter, the doctor, the college professor or the lawyer. This is great fiction and nothing more.

Upon returning to his home that night, Condon informed Breckinridge that in his opinion Cemetery John was authentic and should be paid the ransom.

Thereafter events became muddled. Although Jafsie inserted a series of confirmatory responses into the *Bronx Home News* no arrangements for payment were immediately made.

A few days later, a very common number two Dr. Denton sleeping suit arrived via mail at Condon's home. Although there was no marking of any kind to distinguish it from the thousands of other store bought Dr. Denton sleeping suits then in circulation, several writers have maintained that Lindbergh positively identified it right then as the one his son was wearing the night he disappeared. However, according to Lindbergh, he had not seen his son since February 29, 1932. It is, therefore, somewhat perplexing as to how he could have identified which number two Dr. Denton sleeping suit the baby was wearing on March 1.

Regardless of that problem, a review of the primary sources and actual statements by the various witnesses in this case does not substantiate that Colonel Lindbergh (or anyone else) in fact did identify right then and there the sleeping suit which arrived at Condon's house as the one the baby was wearing on the night of March 1.

At Hauptmann's trial Anne Lindbergh identified the sleeping suit received by Condon as the one Charles, Jr. was wearing on March 1, but there is no evidence that it was ever shown to her until the time of the trial.

Condon testified that he had received it in the mail and showed it to Colonel Lindbergh. He was never asked at the trial if Lindbergh had identified it as his son's at the time Condon received it.

Lindbergh himself merely testified that the sleeping suit came in the mail to Condon but not that he had identified it at that time as the sleeping suit. This leaves open several possibilities.

Since the prosecution never elicited any testimony that the suit had been identified by anyone at the time it was received by Condon as the one the baby was wearing, perhaps it was because no one had so identified it. The suit was simply that common.

At the trial only Anne and the Colonel identified the suit as the one the child had been wearing when put to bed on the night he disappeared. As the Colonel supposedly had not seen the child on March 1 we certainly can discount his testimony to that effect. The only way he could have known for certain was if he were the person responsible for his son's death.

This leaves only Anne Lindbergh as a competent identifier of the suit. But how reliable is her identification? When she testified on January 3, 1935 there was no evidence that she had seen the suit since March 1, 1932, almost three years earlier. There was no evidence that there were any unique characteristics, flaws or marks in that suit. There was no evidence that she had had any reason to pay special attention to that suit three years earlier. There was no evidence that it was anything other than a very common store bought product.

The tendency for any witness in that situation is to testify about the item in a way he or she assumes is correct. Having been shown a sleeping suit that the kidnapper supposedly sent after removing it from her child, it's very understandable why Anne testified at the trial that it was the sleeping suit of her child.

Interestingly, although Betty Gow was questioned extensively by the prosecutor about the other clothes the child was wearing, and was asked to identify them piece by piece, she was never asked to identify the sleeping suit. Was it because the prosecutor knew that she believed that the sleeping suit received by Condon was *not* the one worn by the baby? If so, the defense team should have picked up on this but never did.

The sleeping suit sent to Condon was devoid of any blood stains. If it had been worn when the child received the extensive head injury the suit would have been soaked with blood. The prosecution explained that the absence of blood was the result of the kidnapper having laundered the suit prior to sending it to Condon. This is unlikely.

What is more likely is that the sleeping suit sent to Condon was the same type and style that the baby was wearing but not the same suit. Anne Lindbergh's identification of it at the trial occurred nearly three years after she had helped place it on her son. Without any foundation for that opinion having been laid, very little, if any, reliability can be attached to that in-court identification.

If the sleeping suit was not the one the child was wearing then the two possibilities cited earlier (Jafsie as extortionist or Jafsie as a dupe of extortionists) still remain.

As discussed in subsequent chapters, other extortion groups whose members claimed to be able to return the child also had in their possession details regarding the March 1 sleeping suit. Those details had not been released to the general public. We therefore know that details regarding the child's sleeping suit, like copies of the ransom notes, had come into the possession of criminal extortionists.

Following the receipt of the sleeping suit, Condon continued to place ads in New York newspapers designed to initiate a swap. More ransom notes arrived.

Lindbergh was given $70,000.00 in cash from the Morgan Bank. The Colonel noted that the police were recording the serial numbers. He became enraged and ordered them to stop. He claimed that this might jeopardize the safe return of the child. Since the swap of the money for the child was supposed to be a simultaneous transfer it is difficult to perceive how it would have threatened the child.

Lindbergh's tirade was witnessed by Elmer Irey of the Treasury Department who had been ordered by President Herbert Hoover to assist Lindbergh. Although this technically made Irey one of Lindbergh's assistants, his loyalty was to the Treasury Department and President Hoover, and he did not cower to the Colonel as others did in this case. Unfazed by the tirade, he strolled into the dispute and ordered that the serial numbers be recorded. It was the only occasion in this whole case where Lindbergh backed down and allowed a wiser course of action.

Fifty thousand dollars in bills were wedged into a wooden box of the specifications set forth in the earlier ransom note. The money barely fit and in fact Lindbergh had to kneel on it to get the lid to close. When he did the force of his weight split the wood of the box. Although this was the second time in the case that a person's weight had caused wood to split, the irony of that act escaped the attention of its observers.

The "kidnappers" had upped their demand to $70,000.00. The additional $20,000.00 could not fit into the box and so 400 fifty dollar bills were bundled into a brown paper package.

Meanwhile Condon waited for definite news. According to him, his life began to assume a sort of spy-like aura.

On March 19 Condon was working at a charity bazaar to raise money for the construction of a chapel. As the owner of a number of violins he had decided to donate some for sale with the proceeds going to the charity. He was manning the violin booth himself.

According to Jafsie, late that afternoon he was approached by a nervous middle-aged Italian woman who claimed to be interested in his violins. As he began describing them to her she appeared not to be listening and instead leaned close to him and furtively whispered, "Nothing can be done until the excitement is over. There is too much publicity. Meet me at the depot at Tuckahoe, Wednesday at 5:00 in the afternoon. I will have a message for you."

Condon then watched her leave but attempted neither to follow her nor to alert any authorities in the immediate vicinity.

As only Lindbergh's close circle of advisors and supposedly Cemetery John himself knew that Condon was Jafsie, Condon claimed that this overture had to be authentic.

Although the woman's instructions were faithfully followed, she did not show up nor was there any further instruction or contact at Tuckahoe Depot.

On April 2 Condon received another message at his home via taxi driver. Lindbergh was present and had with him the $70,000.00. Lindbergh and his associates had been anticipating this note.

The New Jersey State Police had made the logical suggestion that when it arrived they should be in position to follow Colonel Lindbergh and Jafsie to the pay-off spot and stake it out. Lindbergh had vehemently vetoed that proposal, stating that such might jeopardize the child's safety. Lindbergh was adamant on this point. The suggestion of several New Jersey officers was rejected and any tailing or stake-out forbidden.

Colonel Lindbergh apparently did not trust the New Jersey police to fully obey this command. After securing the money from the Morgan Bank and packing it away he set off alone to New York with the cash to await the final note. Even if the New Jersey Police officers had been inclined to disobey Lindbergh, they were without sufficient information to act. Nor were other police agencies alerted.

Pursuant to Colonel Lindbergh's orders, Ed Mulrooney and the New York City Police were not even informed that a ransom pay-off in this, The Crime of the Century, was about to be made in their jurisdiction. Like some press people and others in New York they had noticed the anonymously placed Jafsie ads in the newspapers, but had no further information and had not been told about the first cemetery meeting between John and Jafsie.

The only agency not under Lindbergh's control was the FBI. Although kidnapping was not a federal offense in 1932 (the so-called "Lindbergh Law" passed as the result of this case), J. Edgar Hoover had been persuaded by the President himself to render assistance. He had accordingly and dutifully dispatched agents to Hopewell. However, Lindbergh had been cold and openly hostile and would provide no information. It was clear to

Special Agents Merrick and E.J. Connelley, who interviewed Lindbergh, that the Colonel was intentionally holding back information. Since they had no jurisdiction, there was nothing they could do to force themselves into this case.

The FBI had become aware of Condon's identity however, and despite Lindbergh's rebuff, J. Edgar Hoover ordered the bureau to stand by to render assistance if necessary or finally asked. Condon's home on Decatur Avenue was put under surveillance, but the FBI could only sit by helplessly and watch. Thus, Lindbergh insured that the only ones present for this final chapter in the Condon/Cemetery John pay-off were Lindbergh, Colonel Breckinridge, Al Reich and Dr. Condon. As in other crucial junctures throughout the case, law enforcement was excluded.

The four individuals at Condon's house examined the note which had been delivered and listened to Lindbergh's instructions. Colonel Lindbergh laid down the plan of attack. None among the other three would dare challenge him no matter what he proposed, and Lindbergh most certainly was aware of that.

This note instructed them to drive to a florist shop across the street from St. Raymond's Cemetery; under a rock on a bench they would find another note. Condon, accompanied by only Lindbergh armed with a shoulder holstered revolver, set off with the money. Al Reich and Colonel Breckinridge remained behind.

There on the bench they found the subsequent note. It commanded Condon to follow Whittemore Avenue south on foot. Condon left the car, telling Lindbergh that he first wanted to speak with Cemetery John alone. Charles Lindbergh remained behind with the money.

After Condon began walking a voice shouted, "Hey, Doctor!" Both Condon and Lindbergh heard the voice.

A man was standing in the cemetery behind a tombstone; upon approaching, Condon recognized him as Cemetery John. John asked if Condon had the money and was told it was in the car. John asked who else was in the car and upon learning that it was Lindbergh himself asked if he were armed. Condon lied and said no.

John said that the baby could not be returned for six to eight hours. Condon pleaded with John to immediately deliver the child or to allow Condon to see him. When told that this was impossible, Condon demanded a receipt in the form of a note revealing the child's location. John indicated that he did not have such a thing with him. Condon demanded that he produce one.

Condon attempted to negotiate John down to the original $50,000.00 with arguments concerning the economic hard times and the fact that the Lindberghs were not wealthy.

John agreed to both the lower figure of $50,000.00 and to the production of a receipt. He said that it would take him ten minutes to get the receipt and he stood up and strode off. Condon checked his watch to time the length of his absence in order to estimate how far John had travelled.

Condon then hurried back to the car, told Lindbergh of the developments and took the box back to the hedge. Condon never looked inside the box. John walked back through the cemetery. According to Condon's watch, Cemetary John had been gone thirteen minutes.

They exchanged the note for the box. John put the box on the ground and indicated that he wanted to count the money. Condon assured him that it was all there. John opened the box anyway, and using a flashlight shrouded by his hand, quickly thumbed through the bills. "I guess they are all right," he said. He then closed the box. There is no evidence that, at this point, John had any trouble doing so.

John told Condon that it was the opinion of everyone in his gang that Condon's work had been perfect and that the baby was all right and on a boat, *Nelly*, as indicated in the note. He then warned Condon not to open the note for six hours to which Condon agreed. They shook hands and parted.

When the note was opened it read:

The boy is on boad Nelly. It is a small boad 28 feet long, two persons are onboad. They are innocent. You will find the boad between Horsenecks Beach and Gay Head over Elizabeth Island.

The bay was the same Buzzards Bay area off the coast of Massachusetts where Lindbergh had honeymooned less than three years earlier. Lindbergh made some telephone preparations and then, with Breckinridge and Condon, drove to Bridgeport, Connecticut where the three of them, together with a federal officer, departed in an amphibious aircraft to search the area.

While they searched from the air, arrangements had been made to have a Coast Guard cutter patrol the area. For two days they flew over the area from dawn to dusk. For two days the coast guard cutter patrolled the waters. There was no boat *Nelly,* nor any evidence that there had ever been one.

CHAPTER VIII

When the Buzzards Bay area turned up empty, the police quite naturally began to shift suspicion onto Condon, and he became the subject of quiet police investigation. That suspicion never lifted until Hauptmann's trial.

But Condon's negotiations with John, his evening excursions into New York City cemeteries, and his claims of having heard the Italian language on the other end of the telephone line and having encounters with Italian looking women, were not the only developments in this case.

While Lindbergh and Condon were in New York City trying to figure out how to hand over a box of money in a New York Cemetery under Lindbergh's gaze, the police continued their watch in Hopewell. They had occupied a gatehouse at the entrance to Lindbergh's driveway to check any visitors.

One afternoon Elsie Whately and Betty Gow were strolling back up the driveway to the house after delivering sandwiches to the officers manning the gatehouse. They had progressed approximately one hundred yards when they saw a shiny object at the edge of the gravel driveway. Although they both saw it at about the same time, it was Betty who stooped first and retrieved it. It was the shiny thumbguard cylinder that Charles, Jr. had been put to bed wearing on the fateful night. Although at the trial neither Betty nor Elsie recalled the exact day they found it, they estimated it to be around the end of March.

During this period, the Condon dealings in New York were not the only ongoing negotiations being directed by Lindbergh for the supposed safe return of his child. He had received telephone calls and a letter from Admiral Guy Burrage of Norfolk, Virginia. The Admiral was the Commander of the navy ship that had returned Lindbergh and *The Spirit of St. Louis* to New York after his Paris flight in 1927. Admiral Burrage had been approached by two men who claimed to have information about the kidnapping and the return of the child. Lindbergh responded by letter,inviting Burrage and the two men up to Hopewell for a meeting on Tuesday, March 22.

Accompanying Burrage was Commodore John Hughes Curtis, president of a Norfolk boat building company, and Dean H. Dobson Peacock, Dean of Norfolk's Christ Episcopal Church, and an acquaintance of Anne Morrow Lindbergh and her mother.

It was Curtis' story. He claimed to have been approached by a man he only knew as Sam, a bootlegger who made his living in that prohibition era by smuggling rum on his boat. Although Commodore Curtis did not know Sam socially, he had once repaired a boat for him. No one bothered to ask why, if Curtis had repaired a boat for him, he wouldn't know or at least have recorded Sam's last name.

According to Curtis, Sam claimed that the kidnappers had approached him and asked for his assistance to help them return the Lindbergh baby. They had suggested that Commodore Curtis form a committee of prominent Norfolk citizens to act as intermediaries. The March 4th published Lindbergh request for representatives of the kidnappers to contact his representatives was certainly achieving the desired results.

Curtis claimed that at first he had doubted Sam's story and had originally intended to do nothing. However, after tossing and turning one sleepless night he settled on running the idea past Dean Peacock, whom he knew to be an acquaintance of the Morrow family.

On March 10 Curtis had told his story to the Dean who, like almost everyone else touched by this case, was more than eager to become involved. However, the Dean's prompt telephone call to Hopewell was answered by Mickey Rossner, who was now calling himself Lindbergh's secretary. Rossner had been basically uncommunicative during the conversation and the two in Norfolk had finally hung up discouraged.

Not knowing at first what to do, Dean Peacock eventually thought of another prominent Norfolk citizen, Admiral Guy Burrage, and of his connection with the Lone Eagle. It was Burrage's involvement which produced the March 22 meeting.

Curtis further told Lindbergh that Sam said that he knew Lindbergh was negotiating with another member of the same gang "up here" who would deliver the baby for $50,000.00 or even $100,000.00, but that Sam could deliver for $25,000.00.

Lindbergh immediately stated that he was very impressed and authorized them to continue with their negotiations. He cited several factors as a basis for his pronouncement that Curtis was dealing with the real kidnappers. First, the fact that he had been involved with Condon and through him with Cemetery John in New York was supposedly not known by the press. Thus, Sam's claim to know of the negotiations "up here" generated a great deal of credibility. According to Lindbergh, so did the fact that the Virginian claimants apparently knew the amount of the demand in the ransom notes.

Many of the recent Hauptmann defenders and other critics of this investigation have pointed to the Curtis overture as evidence that the real kidnappers could have been from Virginia. What they fail to realize is what the investigators at the time failed to realize, not only about Curtis but about Condon as well. Copies of the original ransom note as well as the March 4 follow-up note were in circulation among all sorts of purveyors of fraud and the fact that ransom overtures contained accurate details did not attach reliability to those overtures.

Encouraged, Curtis pressed forward. He asked Lindbergh for $25,000.00 to be placed in a bank account in Virginia under Curtis' control. The money would be used by Curtis at the appropriate time as ransom money. Lindbergh's enthusiasm for Curtis' ability to assure his child's safe return apparently did not extend so far when it came to spending money. Lindbergh refused to transfer the money.

However, Colonel Lindbergh encouraged Curtis to continue his negotiations with Sam and his contacts. In turn, the Commodore described to Lindbergh how he and Sam had driven to Newark where Sam had introduced him to four Scandinavian men who claimed to be the kidnappers. They in turn drove him to Cape May, New Jersey where he met the wife of one of the Scandinavians who told him the child was on board a boat called the *Mary B. Moss*, then cruising off the coast of New Jersey. As proof of their authenticity they had Curtis present Lindbergh with a previously unpublished detailed map of the interior of the

Hopewell home together with an explanation of how the kidnapping had been executed.

Curtis told Lindbergh that he had been told that the ladder had been used for entrance only and the kidnappers had then made their way through the house with the child.

Lindbergh indicated that he believed this, as it was the theory which made the most sense to him and therefore he was inclined to attach more credibility to Curtis and his group. Overlooked in this endorsement was the fact that Lindbergh claimed to have heard a snapping sound which police theorized was the breaking of the ladder under the added weight of the child.

Although Condon and Curtis were two of the more famous characters in the drama known as the Lindbergh case, they were not the only ones claiming to be in touch with the real kidnappers.

Gaston Bullock Means was a small time political hack and general swindler. Although originally from South Carolina he had settled in Chevy Chase, Maryland. He had worked for the Department of Justice and had also been a "fund raiser" in various shady political deals during the Warren G. Harding administration.

One day, out of the blue, he received a telephone call from Mrs. Evalyn Walsh McLean, a wealthy, albeit eccentric, Washington, D.C. socialite who invited him to her house. Upon his arrival Mrs. McLean told Gaston Means that although she had done much in her life she would now like to do something really dramatic, such as returning the Lindbergh baby. She was aware of his shady connections and thought that perhaps he might know something about the case. Never one to miss an opportunity, Means indicated that by pure coincidence some of his "underworld contacts" had just recently approached him to ask his assistance in returning the Lindbergh baby.

Mrs. McLean was intrigued, but skeptical, and demanded some proof that Means was in touch with the real kidnappers. Means responded that the New Jersey State Police had released a description of the sleeping suit that the child had been wearing, but that the published description was inaccurate. The real suit did *not* have a flap in the rear.

Mrs. McLean then telephoned Admiral Emory S. Land of the United States Navy, who also happened to be a relative of Colonel Lindbergh. His mother had been a Land. The Admiral later went on to become head of the United States Maritime Commission.

Mrs. McLean convinced Admiral Land to intercede on her behalf with Lindbergh. Land used both his rank and family tie to Lindbergh to eventually secure a personal audience with the Lone Eagle for himself, Mrs. McLean, and Gaston Means.

Means made his pitch to Lindbergh and included the information about the sleeping suit with no flap. Colonel Lindbergh immediately announced that he was very impressed with Gaston Means, as the description of the suit released to the press had in fact been purposely erroneous to eliminate false tips. Colonel Lindbergh decreed that he was convinced that Gaston Means was dealing with the real kidnappers and he authorized him to proceed accordingly. Means also told Lindbergh that the gang he was dealing with had authorized Mrs. McLean to be their official intermediary in their efforts to return the child. Why any of these supposed gangs, who could so easily steal a child from his house, would need intermediaries to return him, is a question no one bothered to ask.

Means also said that the gang had jumped the demand to $100,000.00 and that he needed the cash up front to be ready to present it to them on short notice.

As with Curtis, Lindbergh's enthusiasm for, and belief in, the authenticity of these various gangs seemed to wane when it came to putting up his own money for his son's safe return. However, Mrs. McLean did not want to miss out on her chance for publicity. Although she did not have the money in cash she did raise it herself by borrowing against substantial real estate holdings she had in Washington, D.C.

Means told Mrs. McLean that the kidnappers with whom he was dealing would only hand the child over to a Catholic priest. Mrs. McLean thereupon enlisted the help of Reverend Francis J. Hurney. The four principals, Means, Land, Hurney and McLean, gathered in the latter's house the evening the cash finally arrived. It was delivered in two large boxes filled with five, ten and twenty dollar bills. Reverend Hurney said a prayer for the project's success and then Gaston Means left with the cash stuffed into two suitcases.

The very next day Means telephoned McLean and asked for some money for himself to help defray the expenses he was incurring in securing the return of the Lindbergh baby. At his request Mrs. McLean gave him another $4,000.00 of her own money.

Means claimed that the return of the child would occur at the deserted summer country home Mrs. McLean owned in Maryland. At his suggestion Mrs. McLean, together with Reverend Hurney, Admiral Land and a butler and a maid from the McLean household, occupied the house and waited to hear from Gaston Means, who supposedly was finalizing arrangements for the transfer.

The Lindbergh case had many bizarre twists, but what occurred at the McLean summer retreat surpassed them all. Some years before one of the male inhabitants of Mrs. McLean's summer home had killed his girlfriend by striking her over the head. While the McLean entourage waited for word from Means one night, the maid awoke screaming and complained that the sheets had been yanked off her bed and inanimate objects had flown about the room. This had all occurred while nobody else was in the room and the door was locked from the inside.

The rest of the household was quick to ascribe this to the maid's over-active imagination. To prove their point, on the next night the butler occupied the same bedroom alone. He also claimed to have been awoken when his sheets were yanked off and articles flew about the room. On the third night Mrs. McLean herself agreed to occupy the room. The episode was again repeated and in fact, she claimed to have been almost struck by a book which flew off a bookshelf.

Eventually Means returned with information from the kidnappers. The child was safe on board a boat off the coast of Norfolk, Virginia. He suggested that the group travel to Mrs McLeans' Aiken, South Carolina home to await further developments. Dutifully, they packed up and traveled to Aiken.

There, Means would sporadically appear and offer various explanations as to why the child had not yet been returned. On one occasion he returned to the Aiken house with an individual whom he introduced simply as "The Fox," who, supposedly, was a member of the kidnap gang. The Fox did not say one single word; instead, he prowled around the house wearing gloves and checking for hidden microphones before departing. Means told them the return of the child was imminent.

When the child was not returned Means blamed it on the publicity that John Curtis was getting, that this had somehow upset the real kidnappers with whom he was dealing. He then told Mrs. McLeans's entourage that the child had been taken to Juarez, Mexico and that the group should reconvene just across the border in El Paso. Again the group complied.

Day after day in Juarez, and with Lindbergh's encouragement, they waited to be contacted by supposed kidnappers anxious to relieve themselves of the child. As the days passed the group fell apart. Mrs. McLean returned to her Washington social world and Means returned to Chevy Chase. When Mrs. McLean asked for the return of her $100,000.00, Means told her that he no longer had it.

Meanwhile the Curtis group began to splinter. In many ways Dean Peacock was like Dr. Condon - he loved being in the newspapers. While in New York City to have some publicity photos taken of himself, he was approached in the Cumberland Hotel by a group of individuals who claimed that *they* were in contact with the real kidnappers. Pursuant to Lindbergh's March four invitation, they would act as the gang's intermediaries if the Dean would act as Lindbergh's and assist in returning the child. The March four invitation was succeeding beyond expectations.

This group told Peacock that the child was being held by the real gang in upstate New York. His hair had been dyed red and he was being passed off as a girl. Peacock latched onto this story also (although just in case, he stayed in touch with Curtis) and arranged for these small time racketeers to be brought to Lindbergh. The Colonel listened to their story and indicated that he was impressed. He authorized them to form the nucleus of a fourth group that now had his authority to deal with the kidnappers.

There would have been other groups and teams of negotiators invited into the case by Lindbergh but time, space or, occasionally, common sense, would not allow it.

Perhaps because of the publicized involvement of characters like Rossner, Bitz, and Spitale, and perhaps because of Lindbergh's March 4 invitation, it seemed as if hoodlums, conmen and racketeers from all over the country wanted to be involved.

In 1932 Al Capone was doing time for income tax evasion, having been successfully prosecuted by the Treasury Department. However, he claimed to be so touched by the tragedy of the Lindberghs that he volunteered his services and suggested that he be let out of prison in order to re-establish his underworld contacts. He assured everyone who would listen that he could use his connections to secure the return of the child.

In prison Capone was interviewed by Arthur Brisbane of the *Hearst Press*. Brisbane endorsed the Capone plan in print and suggested that Capone be freed, deputized and allowed to work on his own.

Lindbergh announced that he was impressed with the idea and tried to get Capone involved. He immediately telephoned Ogden Mills, the United States Secretary of the Treasury, who was responsible for Capone's prosecution. Mills seriously contemplated deferring to Lindbergh on this before his own investigators convinced him that Capone could not be of assistance.

Stymied in his efforts to bring in further negotiators, Lindbergh continued working with the groups he had created. Pursuing the line offered by the Virginians, Lindbergh and Curtis took to the air and began searching the Atlantic for the *Mary B. Moss*. When that failed, Lindbergh borrowed a yacht and attempted a sea search with Curtis.

He was at sea with the Commodore on May 12, 1932 when a truck driver named William Allen stopped his truck in Mount Rose, New Jersey along some woods to go to the bathroom. The spot was less than three miles south of the Lindbergh house in Hopewell. In fact, the spot where he entered the woods was within sight of the Lindbergh home. The site was also less than one mile from the house in Mount Rose in which the Lindberghs had stayed while the Colonel had supervised the Hopewell construction. The only nearby structure was St. Michaels, a Catholic orphanage, located on the other side of the road. Going into the woods approximately 75 feet, Allen came upon a decomposing corpse of a young child laying face down.

The body lay in a shallow depression and the remains were covered with vermin and leaves. There was no evidence that the shallow area had been dug out and no digging instrument was found nearby. From all the evidence it appeared the baby had simply been placed face down in the depression and hurriedly covered with leaves. The only other object nearby was an empty burlap bag.

Some of the clothing on the child was brought to Betty Gow who identified it. In addition, samples of the cloth used to make the child's night shirt were brought to the scene and compared by Jersey City police officer Harry W. Walsh with the fabric remnants found on the body. In his opinion they matched.

The county coroner, Dr. Charles H. Mitchell, went to the scene and directed that the remains be removed to the county morgue at Trenton. He then ordered the police to get him a picture of the Lindbergh baby. One was produced that evening.

Although the body was in an extensive state of decomposition the facial muscles had not deteriorated, and he was able to compare the facial features of the corpse with the photograph in front of him. He concluded that the body was that of Charles Lindbergh, Jr.

His "autopsy" consisted of a brief and superficial review of the remains. Dr. Mitchell noticed a small pencil size hole in the skull and at first speculated that perhaps it might have been caused by a bullet. However, no bullet was found and Officer Walsh admitted that he had turned the body over with a stick and when doing so had inadvertently punched the hole in the child's skull.

There was also an extensive skull fracture which ran from behind the back of the head three or four inches around the left side to the front of the skull. It was so extensive that death would have had to have occurred either instantaneously or very shortly after the impact. The existence of a blood clot at the edge of the fracture confirmed that the fracture had indeed occurred while the child was still alive and the circulatory system operating.

Within one and one-half hours after first seeing the body in the woods Dr. Mitchell had reached his conclusion on the cause of death. The state of decomposition led him to conclude that the child had died and been in the woods at least two months and the police thereafter theorized that the child died the night he disappeared.

Betty Gow was summoned to the morgue and after looking at the remains for approximately a minute and one-half identified them as those of the Lindbergh baby.

The authorities attempted without success to reach Lindbergh on the yacht where he was still cruising the Atlantic with Curtis. Two of Lindbergh's assistants met the yacht when it docked that evening at Atlantic City and informed him of his son's death. Ironically, as the radio had been broadcasting the news across the country all afternoon and evening, Colonel Lindbergh was actually one of the last individuals to learn of the discovery.

The next afternoon Lindbergh was driven to the morgue. He was inside the morgue for less than ninety seconds where he viewed the remains. He made a show of counting the teeth of the tiny corpse. He turned away and walked out. Upon emerging he was asked by the local prosecutor if he could identify the body. "I am perfectly satisfied that is my child," he responded.

He then ordered that no toxicological or pathological examinations be conducted and that there should be no further autopsy. The child was to be cremated immediately without delay.

The case was now one of murder. It is axiomatic that in any murder case the single most important piece of evidence is the body. A careful forensic examination is important not only to determine the exact time and manner of death, but also because such an examination very often will reveal physical clues regarding other circumstances of the incident.

If this crime occurred today many aspects of it would be different. The Lindberghs certainly would be suspects. But the most radical difference would actually be the autopsy and the forensic, toxicological and pathological testing to which the remains would be subjected. A parent's order for immediate cremation would be ignored.

But the parent here was Colonel Charles A. Lindbergh and that made all the difference. Less than an hour after he had identified the remains they were cremated.

The discovery and identification of the body has generated much controversy over the years. One of the many interesting side stories to the Lindbergh case centered on an aging and scrappy New Jersey country detective named Ellis Parker. Known as the "Old Fox," he had an ability to solve cases other detectives could not. Parker was chief of detectives in Burlington County.

He had built quite a reputation and was proud of the fact that larger city departments had often called upon him for assistance. Parker actually had no jurisdiction in the Lindbergh case as the child's disappearance had occurred in Hunterdon County, while the body had been discovered across the line in Mercer County. But Parker was intrigued by the case and kept tapping his sources in the State Police to keep abreast of developments.

Parker had his theories and suspicions and one of them was that it was uncertain that the body discovered was actually Charles, Jr. Information released at the time of the baby's disappearance seemed to list his height as 29 inches. He had had a physical examination by Dr. Philip Van Ingen in New York City just two weeks before he disappeared and it was the measurements taken at that appointment which provided the source for the information.

The length of the corpse was 33 1/2 inches long. If death had indeed occurred on March 1, Parker reasoned that there was no way that a child could have grown four and one-half inches in two weeks. Inaccuracies might account for a one-half inch discrepancy but anything beyond that was a problem. Parker also believed that the extent of the decomposition of the Mount Rose corpse was inconsistent with it having been exposed in the woods for only 72 days, especially when the actual average temperatures in New Jersey for that March and April were considered.

Parker considered the ninety second identifications by Gow and Lindbergh to be the product of mere psychological tricks. They had entered the morgue in Trenton expecting to see Charles Lindbergh, Jr. They viewed a horribly decomposed young corpse which had been found in the woods less than three miles from the Lindbergh house and which they had been told had already been identified from clothing and by Dr. Mitchell as the baby. They each viewed the remains for less than ninety seconds. Under these circumstances Parker suspected that they would have identified any child's body as that of Charles, Jr.

Dr. Van Ingen had been called to Trenton and after looking at the body for a long time, said, "If someone were to come in here and offer me ten million dollars I simply wouldn't be able to identify these remains."

Parker also believed that the spot where the child had been found had been combed by searchers shortly after the disappearance and no body had been found then.

Various alternative theories were suggested. The best was that the road on which the body was discovered was an oft used avenue for bootleggers heading north into New York City. The child's disappearance had caused the police to increase their patrols, increase their road blocks, and step up the occurrence of randomly stopping and searching motor vehicles, including trucks, in that area. Those searches, though fruitless with regard to the Lindbergh case, were too frequently turning up cargoes of bootleg whiskey. To put an end to the desperate police searches, perhaps bootleggers had dug up another corpse and planted it in the Mount Rose woods. Some post-trial critics of the jury verdict have challenged the identification of the corpse.

However, a reasonable review of the evidence supports the contention that the body found was that of Charles, Jr. First, the information which indicated a height of 29" was incorrect. The report should have had the foot abbreviation after the numeral "2" so that it should have read 2'9". That was in fact the measurement obtained by Dr. Van Ingen and contained in his office records. That height, of 33", is sufficiently close to 33 1/2 inches of the corpse that the half inch discrepancy can be explained by inaccuracies in measuring an active child and the loosening of skeletal frame caused by the decomposition of the muscle structure.

Although the pictorial comparison made by Dr. Mitchell is certainly not at all reliable, there was a better identification made not only by Lindbergh himself (which we could discount if our theory were true) but also by Betty Gow who appears throughout this case as collected, intelligent and very observant.

The assessments regarding the extent of decomposition were not scientifically verified. Parker never saw the corpse and so had no reliable data to support his postulation that the Mount Rose corpse was "too decomposed."

Dr. Van Ingen, as the child's pediatrician, was only a casual observer of Charles, Jr. and therefore his initial reaction is certainly not as reliable as that of Lindbergh or Gow who were in daily contact with the child. Besides, despite Dr. Van Ingen's original statement, he did ultimately give an opinion that the remains of the child were those of the Lindbergh baby. The statements given to Parker that the area where the child was found had been extensively searched were in fact inaccurate. There had been some searches in the woods but they had been confined to the Lindbergh property and the area immediately adjacent and had not extended into Mount Rose.

No other child meeting the general description had been reported missing. Finally, the bits of fabric found on the body matched exactly the unique fabric and thread at the house from which the child's shirt had been made. Although there was no forensic testing to prove identification absolutely, these factors lead one to conclude that the identification of the body, at least, was correct.

CHAPTER IX

William Allen, the 46 year old black truck driver who discovered the Lindbergh baby, told the *New York Times* that night, "I just hope they get the man that did it. Nothing would be too bad to do to him."

Colonel Schwarzkopf and the American public couldn't have agreed more. Schwarzkopf announced that "all restraints" which had been in place to ensure that the child would be safely returned, "were now lifted," and he boldly predicted that the "group of people" responsible, would soon be in custody. He did not specify just who this "group" was, but with every pronouncement, the press and the public clamored for more.

The New Jersey authorities remained very interested in the activities of Dr. Condon and John Curtis. Even as Condon was being summoned to police headquarters for interrogation - there were many questions about his involvement and contacts with "Cemetery John" - the truth about Curtis was discovered. From start to finish, Curtis' "contacts" with the kidnappers, and information about the child's location, were pure fabrication. Curtis signed a full confession admitting that he had led Lindbergh on fruitless journeys to rendezvous with non-existent people.

He did this, he said, as a result of a "distorted mind," and he apologized for any inconvenience he had caused the Lindberghs. The State of New Jersey was unwilling to let it go at that. On June 28, 1932, he was found guilty in a Flemington, New Jersey Court, of the vague charge of "obstruction of justice." He was sentenced to a year in jail and a $1,000.00 fine. The sentence was later reduced to just the fine, which he happily paid. Curtis' trial received banner coverage in the press.

Condon, too, was immediately suspected following the discovery of the child. Did he have any ties with the kidnapper? How could an obscure and elderly man from the Bronx have been chosen to act as a go between for the kidnappers? After all, the response he claimed to have gotten from his first ad in the *Bronx Home News* was immediate. (Neither a copy of the ad, nor the paper itself, was ever produced at the time of Hauptmann's trial.)

At Colonel Breckinridge's urging, however, Lindbergh wrote a letter to Condon thanking him for the "great assistance" he had rendered, and for his courage and cooperation. The letter was released to the press for publication. The publication of the letter caused the police to stop their intense questioning and investigation of Condon.

By this time both Lindberghs felt that it was impossible to stay in Hopewell. This was particularly true for Anne. They moved to *Next Day Hill*. There Anne felt more secure, and sheltered from both the glare of the press and the constant public interest in her ordeal. Betty Morrow had to place guards around *Next Day Hill* to keep out the countless sightseers.

Lindbergh himself initially continued to participate in the investigation. A few days after the discovery of the body, he watched silently as the police had an exact duplicate of the ladder constructed, and reenacted the descent from the nursery window. They placed a bundle in the crib weighing about the same as the baby. Then, at Schwarzkopf's direction, they sent an officer up the ladder to retrieve the bundle. The officer repeatedly placed the bundle into the same burlap bag found near the body. Each time that he started down the ladder with the bag, he slipped and dropped the bundle onto the ledge below. They also noted that a rung near the top of the ladder broke with the weight of an individual weighing 185 pounds carrying the 30 pound bundle.

After watching this reenactment, Lindbergh actively participated in the discussion which followed. The police concluded that the child's death had been caused by dropping him onto the ledge below, and that once this was discovered, he had been left in the first remote spot that could be found.

Anne wanted no part of this sort of postmortem analysis, and was uncomfortable with her husband's intense interest in it. She later wrote in her diary that Lindbergh "works on it incessantly."[22] She was trying desperately to look forward, and she focused her energies on the birth of her second child.

Jon Lindbergh was born on August 16, 1932 in Betty Morrow's apartment on East Sixty-Sixth Street in New York City. It was two months before the baby was named. The Lindberghs released a statement to the press which they hoped would quell for a time the intense interest in their family life. The statement issued by Charles Lindbergh read:

> Mrs. Lindbergh and I have made our home in New Jersey. It is natural that we should wish to continue to live there near our friends and interests. Obviously, however, it is impossible for us to subject the life of our second son to the publicity which we feel was in large measure responsible for the death of our first. We feel that our children have the right to grow up normally with other children. Continued publicity will make this impossible. I am appealing to the Press to permit our children to live the lives of normal Americans.

But of course, the Lindberghs were not, in any stretch of the imagination, a "normal" American family. It was naive for Charles Lindbergh to believe that newspapers would discontinue writing about them. To the contrary, newspaper circulation had increased approximately 20% across the country following the kidnapping and murder of little Charles, and interest in the case remained high.

Friends of Lindbergh tried to persuade him to adopt a more cooperative attitude with the press. Even Harry Guggenheim argued that it was better to develop a relationship with the newspapers, since Lindbergh's fame made him a public figure. Lindbergh resented this advice and refused. Why should he have to deal with an intrusive and demanding press corps?

Except for occasional visits back to Hopewell, the Lindberghs never returned to the home they had attempted to build there. Anne could not even imagine ever again living there. Instead, they took up permanent residence at *Next Day Hill*, and Anne immersed herself in her mother's many charitable and social activities. Besides taking care of her newborn son, she also began writing *North to the Orient* while living at her mother's. As there were no immediate developments in the investigation, Lindbergh returned to his work with the airlines, and with Dr. Carrell, travelling to New York almost daily. In the spring of 1933, he and Anne took off on another transcontinental flight for Transcontinental Air Transport, to check on a route for their new cargo plane service.

They also prepared for a second international air route survey for Pan American. The purpose of the flight was to study three alternative routes for the prospect of regular passenger and freight service. He was to provide data to Pan American on whether flying boats could be successfully used on transoceanic routes.

The journey, which began in Flushing Bay, New York, on July 9, 1933, took them first to Copenhagen by way of Newfoundland and Labrador. Anne worked the radios during the flight. Jon was left with Mrs. Morrow at the summer home in North Haven.

From Scandinavia they flew to Russia and then Britain, before turning south to Spain, to West Africa, back across the Atlantic to Brazil, and then on to the Caribbean. After a short stay they flew to Miami and back to New York. The trip took five and one half months, covered twenty nine thousand miles, and was another milestone in the aviation career of Charles Lindbergh. In the air, it seemed, Charles Lindbergh could do no wrong. His fame grew.

The plane which was flown on this journey was the same *Sirius* which had been used on the China trip, but it was now outfitted with a new and more powerful engine and the latest in electronics. Following the flight, the plane was placed on exhibit in New York City, then moved in 1955 to the Air Force Museum at Wright-Patterson Air Force Base.

Almost immediately upon his return to the United States, Lindbergh became embroiled in a conflict with the Roosevelt Administration over the awarding of air mail contracts to the large airlines. Just before Franklin Roosevelt took office, a Hearst reporter by the name of Fulton Lewis, Jr. had uncovered evidence of dealings between these airlines and members of the Hoover Administration which were designed to squeeze the smaller airlines out of the lucrative air mail contracts. This evidence was turned over to a Senate Committee looking into the U.S. mail contracts.

Lindbergh's name came up during the Senate hearings. He had strong ties to the big airlines, and was being paid considerable sums of money, either in the form of retainers or in stock options. While there was no evidence of his having directly influenced the awarding of the postal contracts, he did, nevertheless, turn over his financial statements to the Committee at the urging of Colonel Breckinridge.

The Senate Committee concluded that secret meetings had been held between the Postal Department, under the Hoover Administration, and several of the large airlines. They also discovered that contracts for certain routes had been awarded at three times the rate of some bids offered by smaller companies. When presented with this evidence, President Roosevelt declared, "The control of American aviation has been ruthlessly taken away from the men who fly and bestowed upon bankers, promoters and politicians sitting in their inner offices, allotting among themselves the taxpayers' money."

In February of 1934, following the advice of his Postmaster General's Office, Roosevelt canceled the airmail contracts of all the aviation companies, and issued an order which directed the Army Air Corps to carry the mail. The Army Air Corps had not carried the mail since 1918, and it was a disastrous decision for the Army pilots who were not trained to fly cross-country during all types of weather, on unfamiliar air routes. By the end of the first full week of operations, five pilots died carrying the mail.

Charles Lindbergh's response to the President's decision to cancel the airline contracts was immediate. He declared Roosevelt's decision to be "contrary to American justice," and he publicly attacked him. He sent the President a letter which he simultaneously released to the press, in which he charged that the "use of the Army on commercial airlines will unnecessarily and greatly damage all American Aviation."

Lindbergh may have hated the press when he felt that it bothered him, but he lost no time in using it to his advantage when it furthered his purpose, or that of the airlines he represent-

ed. The letter to the President made front page headlines the
next morning, and President Roosevelt reacted angrily to the
personal attack. Over the next few months, and with the passing
of years, the enmity between Lindbergh and Roosevelt grew.

What had started out as an expose' on government and big
business fraud, ended up in the press as a personal contest
between two of the most famous people in America - the President and Charles Lindbergh. Ultimately, and as the United
States became inevitably drawn into the second World War, the
public sentiment turned towards the President and away from
Charles Lindbergh, who, because of his expressed admiration for
the Nazis and his anti-war activism, lost favor.

But such was not the case in early 1934. Lindbergh's prestige
had yet to peak, and his standing with the public was enormous.
The fact that Lindbergh's predictions of disaster for the Army Air
Corps materialized only added to his stature. He could do no
wrong. In truth, and with benefit of historical analysis, Lindbergh
was simply the public spokesperson for big business, in whose
interest he had a personal stake. The airline companies were only
too happy to have Colonel Lindbergh leading the charge.

President Roosevelt, realizing his predicament, carefully
extricated himself from the controversy and ordered that the
Army Air Corps cease all flights until the weather improved.
Then he proposed legislation to ensure that future contracts
would be awarded only after a carefully scrutinized competitive
bidding process. However, it would not be the last time he would
clash with Charles Lindbergh.

During the summer of 1934 Lindbergh flew the *Brazilian
Clipper*, a huge flying boat capable of carrying up to 30 passengers, on a journey across the Atlantic designed to test whether or
not regular passenger service in such planes was possible. In
eight hours he flew the ship 1,242.8 miles, averaging 158 mph.
The plane was designed by Sikorsky. Naturally, Lindbergh had
shattered the world record for a transport seaplane with this one
flight.

Shortly after, in September of 1934, Lindbergh and Anne flew
out to California to stay with her sister Elizabeth and her
husband at the ranch of Will Rogers. Rogers was a friend of the

Morrow family. During the days immediately following the "kidnapping," Rogers had been frequently quoted in the press, artfully expressing the sympathy most Americans held for the Lindbergh family. Anne's sister Elizabeth was ill at the time, and would die shortly after their visit. For Anne it was another family tragedy about to play itself out.

While they were in California in September of 1934, the Lindberghs received the phone call which would once again place them at center stage regarding the death of their son. Colonel Schwarzkopf telephoned to report that the New York Police Department had arrested a Bronx carpenter, who was a German immigrant, for the kidnap and murder of their child. Colonel Lindbergh would have to testify at the New York extradition hearing which was necessary to bring the accused back to a trial in New Jersey.

They left almost immediately for New York. There Charles Lindbergh greeted Schwarzkopf and drove to a Bronx courtroom, where he met for the first time Bruno Richard Hauptmann.

CHAPTER X

Hauptmann's arrest in September of 1934 was fully two and one-half years after the disappearance and death of the Lindbergh baby. That so much time had passed is significant. It is generally recognized that the longer an investigation continues, the colder and more stale the evidence grows. Although it is *possible* to solve a crime months, sometimes even years later, it is less likely.

What is more significant, however, is that the police shifted from a firmly held belief that a "group" of people were responsible for the abduction, to the certainty that a single individual had planned and carried out the kidnap, murder, and ransom negotiations.

After Schwarzkopf announced that "all restraints" had been lifted, he continued his probe of the Morrow's and Lindbergh's household staff members. Violet Sharpe, the maid in the Morrow home who had given contradictory accounts of where she was on the night of March 1, 1932, faced more police questioning in June, following the discovery of the baby's body. She committed suicide by drinking poison shortly after. Colonel Schwarzkopf said that the "maid had been under suspicion for a long time, as a member of the kidnap gang" and that this was a great step forward toward the solution of the crime.

Much more likely was the fact that she was emotionally disturbed, and had been involved in romantic entanglements which had accounted for her contradictory statements to police in the initial investigation. She did not want to face them again. There were rumors briefly investigated by the British Consul General in New York that Sharpe had been "cuffed around." Because she was a British citizen, the Consul General handled the arrangements for her burial.

Betty Gow, the baby's nursemaid, was for a time also widely suspected, particularly by the public. After intense scrutiny by Schwarzkopf's people, and the steadfast support of the Lindberghs, she was eliminated as a suspect. When she returned home to her native Scotland, she found that people in her own country had followed the reports of the crime closely and she found it difficult to find work.

Meanwhile, an analysis of the ladder was being conducted by a forester named Arthur Koehler who was employed by the government's Forest Products Laboratory in Madison, Wisconsin. After reading about the kidnap of March 1, 1932, he had written to Schwarzkopf and offered his services as a "wood technologist." Koehler had received his Master's of Science degree from the University of Wisconsin in 1928 and had published a book entitled *The Properties and Uses of Wood*.

After the discovery of the baby's body in May of 1932, the police sent several slivers of wood from the ladder to Koehler. They asked him if he could identify the type of wood, where it came from, and whether it could be traced to retail outlets. He filed a report which said that the wood from the slivers was from all parts of the country. Several weeks later Norman Schwarzkopf asked him to come to New Jersey.

In the latter part of February, 1933, at the New Jersey State Police training school in Trenton, Koehler examined the ladder. It had already been thoroughly checked for fingerprints - there were many, mostly from the State Police who had handled it - but as it turned out later, none were from Hauptmann. Koehler decided immediately that the carpentry work was sloppy, and noted that it had crosspieces, instead of rungs, notched unevenly into the side rails. He believed that whoever had constructed it had taken no pride in the work. He also noticed that much of the wood used in that ladder had been scarred by a dull handsaw, whose teeth had caught in the wood. The cleats had been trimmed by a plane with a dull and nicked blade.

The upright of one section of the ladder, which was called "Rail 16," and which was to become a piece of pivotal evidence against Hauptmann, had four older nail holes in it. They were square, which indicated they had been made by old, cut nails. He could not discern any traces of rust, and speculated that the rail had previously been part of something else, and that it had not been exposed to the weather. He told Colonel Schwarzkopf, "when you get a suspect, look around his premises for a place indoors where there are empty cut-nail holes, and possibly some boards to match with the ladder rail."

Koehler tried to trace the wood. He completely dismantled the ladder, and marked each piece for reassembly. Under his microscope he focused his attention on two side rails of Carolina pine, which he believed matched end to end and, he reasoned, had therefore once been part of a longer piece. He discovered a unique pattern of scarring made by two knives in the cutting heads of the machines used to mill the lumber. He concluded that the planing machine used to dress the lumber had six knives in the cutter that had trimmed the edges and eight knives in the surface cutter. By completing some elementary calculations, he also surmised that the conveyor belt fed the lumber through the planer at 232.5 feet per minute.

There were 1,598 pine mills in the Atlantic Coast states. Koehler wrote to all of them and asked if they had such a planer. Twenty-five firms responded that they did. He asked for samples of their pine stock, and decided that the mill of the Dorn Company at McCormick, South Carolina made planer marks on North Carolina pine which were the closest to those on the ladder. With the help of New Jersey State Police Detective Lewis Bornmann, Koehler traced loads of lumber from the Dorn Company to various lumber yards in the Eastern United States.

Little else was done by Koehler, until after the arrest of Hauptmann in September of 1934. Independent of his research the police formed the opinion that the people who received the ransom money were from the Bronx area. They reasoned this because of the trail of ransom money which had started to appear. It was a trail they were anxious to follow.

The Department of the Treasury had disseminated lists throughout the country which contained the ransom serial numbers. The federal agents believed that the money offered the greatest hope for resolving the case. The first of the ransom gold notes to turn up was in New Castle, Pennsylvania in June of 1932, only 60 days after the pay out to "Cemetery John." As time progressed, a few other bills surfaced elsewhere around the country, but weren't noticed until long after they had been passed.

The investigators received a boost when President Roosevelt and Congress decided to take the country off the gold standard. All gold seal certificates were to be turned in and exchanged for non-gold currency. The deadline to do this was May 1, 1933 - fourteen months after the child's disappearance. Possessing them after that date constituted an offense.

All but a small portion of the $50,000.00 ransom money had been comprised of gold certificates. People who had been holding gold certificates scrambled to exchange them at banks as the deadline approached. Bank tellers, usually quite busy, simply didn't have time to study all of the serial numbers of these notes.

Near the deadline, a man walked into the Federal Reserve Bank in New York City and exchanged $2,990 of the Lindbergh ransom money. Everyone who made such an exchange was required to fill out a deposit slip. When examined, this one indicated the exchanger was J.J. Faulkner of 537 West 149th Street, New York City.

Once notified by the Treasury, the police immediately went to that address and found an apartment house. They questioned everyone living there, but could locate no J.J. Faulkner. They asked neighbors in the area - did anyone remember any Faulkners? No one could. They compared the handwriting on the ransom notes with the deposit slip.

Although there appeared to be a resemblance, the sample was not sufficient for a conclusive opinion. They checked through old city directories, and found that a Miss Jane Faulkner had lived at that same address in 1913.

The examination of marriage license records revealed that Miss Faulkner married a man named Carl Oswin Geissler in 1921. Geissler was German. Geissler, by a previous marriage, had a grown son and daughter. The son, it turned out, had for several years prior to the kidnapping lived in the Bronx, and only a block from Jafsie. He also did business in a store where one of the ransom notes had been passed. The daughter had married a landscaper, Henry Liepold, who was also of German descent.

The police swooped down on the Geisslers and began an intensive investigation involving more than a dozen local and federal agents. They surveilled their homes. They obtained documents with Carl Geissler's handwriting, and sent these, along with the Faulkner deposit slip, to a government handwriting expert, Mr. Saunder, who worked in Washington D.C. Saunder told the police that the handwriting on all of these papers, including the deposit slip, were written by the same person. The investigative team working on the Geissler connection was convinced that they were getting close to the people responsible for this extortion.

Geissler's daughter bought a train ticket to Canada under an assumed name. She was stopped and searched at the border for the ransom money. None was found. Shortly after, her husband, Henry Liepold, sent a cable-gram to Munich to a man named Willie Krippendorf. He urged Krippendorf to take the "cheapest steamer rate possible..." To the police this meant that Krippendorf was being urged to conceal any indication of wealth. When Krippendorf arrived in the United States on May 5, 1933, he told Ellis Island officials that he was going to live with a friend, Leo Rodel in Fort Lee, New Jersey. The police discovered that Rodel was a close associate of Ralph Hacker of Palisades Park, New Jersey. Ralph Hacker was the son-in-law of *Dr. John F. Condon* and had been heavily involved in the preparations for the negotiations with Cemetery John.

Police were now convinced that they had found the "correct" group who had engaged in the extortion of money. When questioned extensively, they all denied having any knowledge of the Lindbergh case, or having anything to do with any of the ransom money. They submitted handwriting samples which were shown to several experts for comparison to the ransom notes. The experts couldn't agree on whether they were similar.

Dr. Condon viewed the three male members of the Geissler family who had by this time become quite concerned about the scrutiny they were under. Condon couldn't decide if any of them were "Cemetery John." He asked to hear them talking in the dark. When the police complied with that request, he said that Henry Liepold sounded "very much like" Cemetery John. Given this Liepold's connection to Krippendorf, and their perception that Henry Liepold might "break," the police leaned heavily on him. In October of 1933, he committed suicide.

Frustrated by their inability to develop substantial evidence against the Geisslers, the police were forced to rely on people like Dr. Condon.

Somewhat eccentric, the former school teacher was an individual who had a sense of the "drama" of life. Except for the time that the police had suspicions of his complicity in the kidnapping, Condon enjoyed being in the spotlight. He liked the public attention he had received as the Lindbergh "negotiator." When he found himself outside that public spotlight, he would make a conscious effort to draw attention to himself. One way he could do this was by "spotting" Cemetery John on the streets of New York.

On at least two occasions, the first on a bus in the Bronx in the summer of 1933, Jafsie shouted to the driver, "Stop this bus! I am Jafsie! I just spotted Cemetery John!" By the time the driver pulled over, all the passengers got off, and the police were summoned, "John" had long since disappeared. A year later, in the summer preceding Hauptmann's arrest, Condon did the same thing. Again, "John" had managed to slip away. But he was certain that he had seen Cemetary John. Each time this occurred, Dr. Condon made the front page of the paper.

Interestingly, every time that Condon was asked for a description of the man, it varied. Cemetery John was either 5 feet 8 inches tall or 6 feet tall, with either brown eyes or blue eyes, a large or small nose, a large or small chest, who had either square or pointed facial features.

Condon also visited city and county jails in several east coast cities, in a further attempt to identify the kidnapper. He viewed several thousand mug shots. Periodically, Condon would pick one out and tell police, "he's the man who gave me the money in the cemetery." When police checked, they invariably discovered that the individuals were not anywhere near New Jersey on March 1, 1932. Lieutenant Finn, of the New York City Police Department, took to calling Condon a "Screwball."

One other witness had contact with a member of the "gang" police believed they were dealing with, and that was Joseph Perrone, the New York taxi driver. On March 12th, 1932 at about 8:30 p.m., he had been hailed by a man on the corner of

Knox Place and Gun Hill Road, given one dollar, and asked to deliver an envelope to Dr. John F. Condon.

When Perrone did so, he had been briefly questioned by Condon and Colonel Breckinridge. He had said then that the man who gave him the note was wearing a brown felt hat and a brown top coat. At the time, Perrone had no idea of the significance of his encounter. Perrone, who did not get a good look at the man who had given him the note, was questioned by the police about a month later. When asked if he remembered anything unusual about the man's physical characteristics, or his appearance, he replied "no." When asked if he could identify him, or if he would know him if he saw him again, Perrone again replied "no."

Yet, during the next two years Perrone would, on several occasions, tell police that he had seen the individual who had handed him the note on March 12th. On one occasion, he identified a man named Chetel. Chetel had been nowhere near the Bronx that night. On another occasion, when investigators were working on the Geissler family, he claimed to have seen the note giver entering Geissler's florist shop. Schwarzkopf called Perrone a totally "unreliable" witness. Whether the $25,000 reward which had been posted by the New Jersey legislature, had anything to do with Perrone's sudden ability to recall the person who had hailed him, is a matter of speculation.

At about the same time the $2,990 "J.J. Faulkner" exchange was made in a Manhattan bank, two separate $500 exchanges were also made in Manhattan banks. No depositor could be identified. During the rest of 1933, only a half dozen other ransom bills showed up. The only one which resulted in a description of the person who passed the note, occurred on November 26th, 1933 at Loew's Cinema in Greenwich Village. The cashier that evening, Cecile Barr, spotted the folded $5.00 gold certificate, and felt that the man who gave it to her acted suspiciously. She called the police when she discovered that the note was on the list of the Lindbergh extortion money. The man who passed it was not found, but she described an individual about 35 years old, with flat cheeks, a pointed chin, and narrow eyes. She only saw the man briefly.

In the early part of 1934, several $5 greenbacks appeared in New York. Like the one received by Cecile Barr, many had been folded eight ways. The New York Police, along with the New Jersey Police and the FBI, were plotting the locations where they turned up on a large pin map. One or two bills surfaced as far away as Minneapolis and Chicago, but all of the rest were in New York. For the months of June, July and August, only seventeen notes were found by the Federal Bank, and those were impossible to trace. The only thing known was that they had been taken in at large department stores, or restaurants with a high volume of customers.

In September of 1934, however, a new pattern emerged. In the first part of the month, $10 and $20 gold certificates were passed at small shops. By then the $10 and $20 notes were rarely seen. When a ten spot was traced to Boccanfuso's fruit and vegetable store on Third Avenue and 89th Street, the clerk, by the name of Levantino, remembered the man who passed it. Further, he was able to give a reasonable description of him to police. A $20 bill was traced to a shoe store in the Bronx, where an assistant remembered the man who purchased ladies' slippers with it. He gave a description very similar to Levantino's.

The notes were chemically analyzed by a lab, and the report indicated that the bills contained traces of emery dust, indicating proximity to a carpenter's bench, or a machine shop. They also had a musty fragrance, which suggested that the bills had been buried or were wet, or kept where there was no air circulating. The new pattern of the emerging ransom money renewed hope among the police that they would soon be able to identify the passer.

They did not have to wait long.

CHAPTER XI

On September 15, 1934 a man driving a dark Dodge sedan drove into a gas station in Manhattan at 2115 Lexington Avenue. He paid for the gas with a $10 gold certificate. The attendant, Walter Lyle, looked at it and hesitated. He reportedly said to the customer, "You don't see many of these anymore," to which the man, speaking with an accent replied, "I've got about a hundred of them left." To be certain that he didn't get stuck for the bill, in the event the bank wouldn't accept it, Lyle wrote the plate number of the vehicle, 4U-13-41, onto the bill.

On September 17th, the bill was discovered at the Corn Exchange Bank in New York, and the manager summoned police. They quickly identified the gas station the bill came from, and spoke with Walter Lyle. Within hours they had traced the license plate to Bruno Richard Hauptmann, 1279 East 222nd St., the Bronx. They knew he was a German, and worked as a carpenter. Certain that they had at last found one of the people involved in the crime, they staked out his home. On Wednesday morning September 19th, Hauptmann stepped out of his front door, got into his Dodge, and while under surveillance, drove away. Police followed for a short distance and then signaled to make the arrest.

Forcing Hauptmann over to the curb, and with guns drawn, they quickly took him into custody. In a search of his person they found another $20 bill from the ransom money in his wallet. They asked him where he had gotten it. He told them that he had been hoarding gold certificates to guard against inflation. The police wanted to know what he knew about the Lindbergh kidnapping, and Hauptmann replied that he knew nothing about the Lindbergh kidnapping. As they were sitting in the car, one officer said to him, "You're going to fry for this."

From there Hauptmann was taken back to his home where they conducted a preliminary search of his house. His wife, Anna, was not told why her husband was being arrested, and when she asked, "Richard, what's wrong, what have you done?" he replied, "I have done nothing." When the police could find no further money in his home, they took him to the Greenwich Street Police Station for more questioning. It was here that he was shown in a "line-up" to the taxi cab driver Joseph Perrone.

When Perrone was brought to the police station he was told that they had no doubt that they "had their man" and they only needed Perrone "to verify it." Hauptmann was placed in a line-up which consisted of him and two beefy policeman of Irish descent, both of whom were over six feet tall and one of whom was still in his police uniform. Perrone identified Hauptmann as "the man."

The next day, Dr. Condon was also brought in, and according to the police, made a "partial" identification of Hauptmann. When asked what that meant, Acting Chief Inspector John J. Sullivan said that Condon hadn't "positively" identified Hauptmann as the man to whom he had given the money. Pressed further, Sullivan was asked if that meant Condon wasn't sure. "That's it," he replied. Over the course of the next several days, Hauptmann was interrogated relentlessly. He was paraded before the press, asked for innumerable handwriting samples, fingerprinted a half dozen times, denied sleep, denied access to an attorney, and finally, beaten by the police. Hauptmann staunchly maintained his innocence.

When the police went back to his house they began a more thorough, and destructive, search of the property. It was in the garage that they found an empty shellac can under some rags, containing $11,930 and another $1,830 wrapped in newspapers, altogether totalling $13,760. It was all part of the Lindbergh ransom money. It was several more days before police discovered a pistol and another $840.00 concealed in a piece of wood in the garage.

Hauptmann admitted to having used some of the money that was found in the garage, but denied that he knew it was Lindbergh money. He told the police that he had gotten the money from a man named Isador Fisch, a German Jew who was also an immigrant.

Fisch and Hauptmann had met in the summer of 1932 through a mutual friend. A diminutive man who gave the appearance of being impoverished, Fisch seemed to hit it off with Hauptmann. They developed a business relationship which Hauptmann thought was mutually beneficial.

Fisch told Hauptmann that he dealt in furs, and that with his financial assistance, they could develop a thriving furrier business. Fisch did have some experience working with hides, but only as a laborer, when he first arrived in the country. In reality he was a con man. While telling Hauptmann about his furs, he was telling other acquaintances, and their relatives, about the Knickerbocker Pie Factory.

Fisch had bought into a failing pie factory owned by two small time Italian crooks. He tried to keep it afloat, but it went bankrupt nevertheless. Long after the business was closed, however, Fisch was still convincing people to give him money as an investment in a "growing" company.

Fisch seemed to have several schemes going at once, but was careful to keep people involved in each one, separated from each other. Hauptmann did not know, for example, of the demise of the pie factory, nor of all the people Fisch had involved in it. Nor did Hauptmann know that the inventory of furs which Fisch said he was developing, was literally not worth the paper it was printed on.

Fisch had phony letterhead made up for the "Klar and Millar" firm. On one he typed a list of nonexistent furs, which he estimated to have a value far in excess of what they would have been worth had they actually existed. Hauptmann believed that the furs were worth more than $20,000, and that when sold, they would net him close to $5,000. Besides the furs, Hauptmann and Fisch invested in stocks together. Ostensibly this was the other half of their business arrangement, and for a while, they did quite well. Most of the time, it was Hauptmann who made the transactions through a stock broker.

In November of 1933, Fisch came to Hauptmann and told him that he was going back to Germany to develop an overseas connection for their fur trade. Could Hauptmann loan him $2,000 in order to make the journey? Hauptmann agreed and wrote him a check. Fisch had a brother, Pinkus, who lived in

Liepzig. It was with him, Fisch told Hauptmann, that he would arrange the European end of the import-export trade in furs.

On December 2, 1933, just before Fisch left for Germany, he arrived at Hauptmann's house and asked Hauptmann to look after a few of his things while he was away. He left two suitcases, some furs, and a package wrapped in paper tied with string. According to Hans Kloppenburg, a friend who was standing near the door, it looked like a shoe box. Hauptmann said that he would be glad to and put the wrapped package on the top shelf of their kitchen closet. He thought no more about it until August of 1934.

Fisch had told Hauptmann that he would only be in Germany for six weeks. At first he wrote Hauptmann a few cards, but by March of 1934, Hauptmann hadn't heard from him for some time. Besides the fact that Hauptmann was still unaware of Fisch's deceitfulness, Fisch had taken ill in Germany. Never a healthy man, Fisch died from tuberculosis in a Liepzig hospital on March 22, 1934. It wasn't until Isidor's brother Pinkus wrote to Hauptmann informing him of his death, that Hauptmann started looking into Fisch's affairs in earnest. He discovered the truth about the pie factory and the non-existent furs. He was angry that he had been duped by a crook.

It was against this backdrop that he discovered the money left in his care by a man who, Hauptmann figured, owed him at least $7,500. Hauptmann, himself, described what happened then:

It was about this time, in the middle of August 1934 on a rainy Sunday, when we did not go out because the weather was too bad for the child. Late in the afternoon I had transplanted some flowers, and some soil had fallen on the floor. I went to the kitchen closet to get the broom. In taking out the broom I touched the things on the top shelf with it. As I looked up to see if I had knocked anything over, I saw the little package which Mr. Fisch had given me to keep for him when he left. I had broken through the wrapping which was soaked with water, and ... I saw the yellow shine of money.

After he dried the money and counted it, he learned there was $14,600. Hauptmann knew that it was no longer legal to have large amounts of gold certificates, but also knew that they could still be passed in small amounts. Accordingly, he decided to hide the money in his garage, and began to use the $10 and $20 certificates to make small purchases in the area. He visited the fruit and vegetable store, and bought slippers for his wife in another. He readily admitted all of this when the police questioned him.

The police were persistent in their dogged interrogations of Hauptmann. They knew that the money presented them with enough evidence for an extortion indictment in New York, but they were also convinced that they could get Hauptmann to admit to his involvement in the kidnap and murder. They were very wrong. Before the Grand Jury proceedings in New York started on September 25, the police continued their efforts to connect Hauptmann to the Lindbergh home, and the actual kidnapping over two years earlier. One way to do that was to show that he had written the original ransom note "found" that night in the nursery by Colonel Lindbergh.

Late on the night of his arrest, after telling Hauptmann to copy the text of the original ransom note, Schwarzkopf presented the handwriting samples to Albert D. Osborn. He was the son of Albert S. Osborn, age 70, who was also a handwriting expert. At 4:00 a.m. the next morning Osborn Jr. told Schwarzkopf that he thought there were some "similarities, but there were also many distinctive differences" between the known and requested samples. Schwarzkopf asked whether or not more samples might help. Osborn told him that it might, and that his father would be able to look at them the next morning. Accordingly, Hauptmann was told to print some samples, and to again copy samples given to him. This included samples which were dictated to him by the police, using the misspelled words, *as they appeared in the note.*

A parade of witnesses were brought before the Bronx Grand Jury by District Attorney Samuel J. Foley, when it was convened to hear the evidence on the extortion charge. Walter Lyle was brought in to say how he had taken the fateful $10 bill. Cecile Barr, the cinema cashier who months before had only caught a fleeting glimpse of a man buying a ticket, identified Hauptmann as the one who had bought the ticket with the Lindbergh money.

Perrone testified that Hauptmann was the one who gave him the dollar to take a letter to Jafsie. A government financial analyst testified that by following Hauptmann's stock transactions, financial records, deposits, and the ransom money already found, that presto! - it totalled, plus or minus, $50,000. J. Edgar Hoover was later quoted as saying that the records, taken in total, made no sense. The New York Times carried a report that Hauptmann's stock transactions totalled more that $264,000 in the course of one year. This proved to be completely false. To this day, approximately $30,000 of the ransom money has *never* been located.

By the opening day of the grand jury, Foley asserted that he had an "ironclad case" against Hauptmann on the extortion. Asked by the *New York Times* on September 24th whether Dr. Condon had made a positive identification of Hauptmann, Foley replied, "He has not identified Hauptmann..."

But on September 25th, the police were fortunate enough to "discover" evidence which connected him to Condon. In their continuing search of the Hauptmann home, they found Dr. Condon's Bronx address and phone number written in pencil on a trim board on the inside of a closet; next to it, on the door, were the serial numbers of two dollar bills. Detective Bruckman, who found the pencil marks, was immediately brought to the grand jury by Foley, to testify about this newest evidence.

The last witness to testify at the grand jury proceeding was Colonel Charles Lindbergh. Lindbergh told how he had driven Condon to St. Raymond's cemetery to hand over the ransom money. He related how he had heard a man yell "Hey, Doc!" to Condon. He said that the words sounded as if they were spoken by a man with an accent. After he gave this information, a juror asked him if he thought he could recognize that man's voice if he was to hear it again. Lindbergh replied, "It would be very difficult for me to sit here and say that I could pick a man by that voice."

Hearing this from Colonel Lindbergh, Foley asked him to come to his office the next morning. There Lindbergh sat in a room amongst several detectives, wearing a disguise. Hauptmann was then brought into the room, and asked several times to call out "Hey Doc!" in different tones and modulations. Hauptmann did not have the benefit of legal counsel during this session, just as he didn't during any of the police questioning or the line-ups which had been conducted.

On September 26, 1934 the Bronx grand jury returned an indictment for extortion against Hauptmann for "feloniously and extorsively" obtaining from Charles A Lindbergh, father of the infant Charles A. Lindbergh Jr., the "sum of ... Fifty Thousand ($50,000) Dollars..." On the 27th of September, Foley told the *New York Times* that Hauptmann was "one of the chief perpetrators of both the abduction and the extortion, and could have possibly been the man on the ladder in Hopewell."

Foley made it clear, however, that he did not believe that Hauptmann could have successfully carried out both crimes alone. Foley stated that pending a request from the State of New Jersey for extradition on the kidnap and murder charges, he would be ready for trial in two weeks.

The New Jersey authorities were working very hard on the request. But they knew that they needed to develop evidence which would place Hauptmann at the scene of the crime in Hopewell. Osborn's conclusion that he had written the first ransom note was a start, but it was not enough.

Two things developed. First, in early October the New Jersey State Police located Millard Whited, a 37 year old farmer who, on the night of the kidnapping, had lived about a mile and a half from the Hopewell estate of the Lindberghs. Millard was very poor; by 1934 he had moved his entire family to a ramshackle "house" in Lambertville, New Jersey. He was driven to the Bronx County Jail and at a line-up positively identified Hauptmann as a man he had seen twice near the Hopewell estate. The police now had an eye witness.

After Hauptmann's arrest on September 19, 1934 the police sympathetically suggested to Mrs. Hauptmann that she move out of her rented house. They intimated that this would be to avoid the hordes of curiosity seekers who might otherwise bother her. Thinking that the police had made a helpful suggestion, Mrs. Hauptmann, with her infant son Manfred, moved in with her sister. The New Jersey State Police immediately assumed the lease and Detective Lewis Bornmann actually moved in.

A few days later Bornmann summoned to the Hauptmann house Arthur Koehler, the self-styled "wood expert." He arrived on September 28th. Bornmann brought him upstairs into the attic and showed him the attic flooring which now had a missing board. Bornmann told Koehler that he had discovered the missing floorboard by himself on September 26. This would have been one week after Hauptmann's arrest and after no less than 15 other police officers and federal agents had already searched the attic and found nothing of interest to the investigation.

Remembering Koehler's previous admonition about looking for missing wood which may have been used for the ladder, Bornmann had the ladder brought to the house so that Koehler could conduct further examinations. Bornmann theorized when he saw the "missing" plank that it had been used to make "rail 16" of the ladder.

Meanwhile, the New Jersey authorities, led by the young, aggressive Attorney General of the State, David Wilentz, moved quickly to convene a grand jury to hear the evidence against Hauptmann. Shortly before it met Lindbergh demanded, and was given, the entire police file, which he painstakingly reviewed in detail. Other writers have suggested that this convinced him that the evidence against Hauptmann was solid, and therefore removed any "doubt" about making a voice identification. However, Lindbergh also took this opportunity to closet himself with Anne and point by point go through the case the police had assembled in a determined effort to convince her of Hauptmann's guilt.

On October 8th, 1934, two days following Whited's Bronx identification of Hauptmann as the man he had seen coming out of the bushes of the Lindbergh estate, the grand jury met in Flemington, New Jersey to hear a bill of indictment on the charge of murder.

The grand jury heard testimony from the two Osborns about the handwriting samples of Hauptmann, Cecile Barr the cinema ticket agent, Millard Whited, Arthur Koehler who now testified that two of the rails from the kidnap ladder came from wood which had been delivered to a Bronx lumber yard, and once again, as the last witness, Colonel Charles Lindbergh. But in stark contrast to the statements he had made to the Bronx grand jury, Lindbergh now testified that the voice that he had heard calling out to Dr. Condon on the night the ransom money was delivered, was that of Bruno Richard Hauptmann.

This, of course, was powerful evidence against Hauptmann, and Colonel Lindbergh's effect upon the grand jury was telling. After meeting just four and one-half hours, the jury returned an indictment against Hauptmann for the murder of the Lindbergh baby. That Colonel Lindbergh had changed his testimony from the statement which he had delivered in the Bronx, did not go unnoticed by astute observers. The FBI questioned this inconsistency and expressed concern over its future effect upon the trial. The Lindbergh case was not the first, and would not be the last time, that police would generate evidence to support the conviction of a suspect who they believed was guilty. In 1989 Charles Stuart shot and killed his pregnant wife while driving home from child birth classes. He then shot himself in the stomach, and called the police from his cellular car phone. He convinced the Boston Police Department, and, through the media, most of the public that they had been robbed by a black man. Ten weeks later Stuart threw himself from the Tobin Bridge after Stuart's brother Matthew revealed their complicity in the crime.

Before Matthew Stuart's confession, the Boston Police Department announced that they had evidence from a witness who told them that Willie Bennett had confessed to the murder, and was bragging about the shooting. The Police Department even announced that Charles Stuart had "tentatively" identified Bennett. The pressure to find the black killer of the pregnant white woman was immense, and fueled daily by a media which kept the story on the front pages, and on every evening newscast. Because Charles Stuart had been believed, evidence was "found" to support the story.

In 1991, after investigating the conduct of the Boston Police Department in the Stuart investigation, the United States Attorney's office concluded that although the investigators had coerced and pressured witnesses to falsely testify against Willie

Bennett they had committed "no federal crimes," and therefore would not be prosecuted by their office. That is not to say that their conduct was proper. Certainly their conclusions were completely wrong. Convinced that they have a perpetrator, and under intense public scrutiny amplified by media coverage, police often "find" the evidence they need to support their conclusions. This is, unfortunately, as true for testimonial evidence as it is for physical evidence.

Bruno Richard Hauptmann was about to learn this lesson firsthand.

CHAPTER XII

One of the strongest objections the thesis of this book may generate is, "But the Lindbergh case is over. Bruno Richard Hauptmann was tried and convicted and his appeal was upheld, so what is all the fuss?"

That question assumes the decision-making portion of our criminal justice system to be perfect, that an acquittal before a jury means that the defendant was innocent and a conviction that the defendant was guilty. That is, unfortunately, not true.

No American jury has ever found a defendant "innocent." In those cases in which, at the conclusion of a trial, the jurors remain unconvinced of a defendant's guilt they return with a verdict of "not guilty."

This does not necessarily mean that they believed the defendant to have been innocent, or that he didn't do the crime with which he was charged, but merely that, on the evidence presented, they were not convinced of his guilt "beyond a reasonable doubt." More than one juror has approached the prosecutor or defense lawyer after such an acquittal and said, "You know, we all felt that the defendant was guilty, that he probably did it, but we weren't convinced beyond a reasonable doubt. We weren't certain, and so we found him not guilty."

The history of American jurisprudence is also filled with countless examples in which innocent men and women were convicted. This has occurred because despite the true facts the circumstantial evidence against the defendant was just too great and, on balance, tended to prove his or her guilt beyond a reasonable doubt. The United States Supreme Court has specifically recognized this possibility and has accordingly allowed defendants who maintain their innocence to still plea bargain and plead guilty, and for the court to accept the plea of guilty, even though they may actually be innocent.

This situation is not unlike the major league baseball game in which an umpire calls out a baserunner sliding into home plate to end the game. The fans in the stands might disagree. The umpire could have had a bad angle and the runner might actually have been safe. But for the outcome of the game it does not matter if he were actually safe and it does not matter how many times the instant replay showed him beating the throw or the catcher missing the tag. What matters is what the umpire called him and no matter how vociferously the runner argues, or how indignant the announcers are, or how clear the replay, the runner is out because the umpire said so.

The jury system is not perfect. The evidence is not presented by programmed machines and is not evaluated by a computer. The prosecution's case and the defense's case are presented by human beings who have chosen to be lawyers. They ask questions of and generate responses from a series of witnesses. Sometimes the lawyers ask too many questions, sometimes they don't ask enough, sometimes they ask them in the wrong order and thereby confuse the jury. No matter how well prepared a lawyer is, sometimes he or she simply forgets to ask something.

Witnesses are not much better. A witness may sit in a lawyer's office and perfectly recite their own recollection of an event. Yet at trial they may become tongue-tied, or suffer from stage fright, or not elaborate on details necessary for the jury to understand and believe their testimony. Sometimes even the most skilled examiner or cross-examiner can not elicit testimony in the way that it should be.

A witness may come from a social or ethnic background which stirs up deep-seated prejudices in a juror and makes the juror resist the testimony. So too, as is often the case in their reaction to police witnesses, a juror may want to believe and may more readily accept testimony from certain witnesses. Judges do not shed their personal background, ethnicity or social class upon entering the courtroom. With a careful judicial selection process and proper training we can hope to minimize the impact of such factors on the cases over which they preside. But judges too are human.

Individual jurors possess the same varied backgrounds and prejudices found in the general population. Courtroom education of jurors in an effort to suppress their influence is minimal, often amounting to no more than a one hour orientation session, some routine questioning prior to the start of a trial (called *voir dire*) and a few general instructions at the conclusion of the case. It is axiomatic that to qualify for service a juror should hold no preconceptions about a case. Avoiding such in a well publicized case is difficult, and often the *voir dire* process may take weeks as the court attempts to find jurors who have heard so little about the case that they are not pre-disposed one way or the other. The delay this occasions is a small price to pay to assure that the case starts with a neutral jury and the defendant is afforded a fair trial.

The Hauptmann jury was *voir dired*. At one point in the examination by defense lawyer Fischer as to whether he had made up his mind beforehand, Charles Walton, Sr. responded "Not exactly." In an effort to rehabilitate him, Mr. Hauck, assisting Mr. Wilentz for the prosecution, asked, "I understood you to answer Mr. Fischer in the beginning of his examination as to whether or not you had formed an opinion, that you said, 'Not exactly.'"

"Well ...," responded Mr. Walton, "Not more than anyone else..."

And so, Charles Walton, Sr., who had not made up his mind "more than anyone else" in America, was not only allowed to be a juror by Judge Trenchard, but also appointed its foreman.

These are the human factors, and in 1935 they were all operating against Bruno Richard Hauptmann.

In New York Hauptmann had retained Attorney James Fawcett in the extradition hearing. Although Fawcett had been unsuccessful, and New York had authorized Hauptmann's extradition to New Jersey to stand trial for the murder, Fawcett had done a credible job. It was Hauptmann's intent to keep him on as his lawyer in the New Jersey trial.

But this case had generated a circus-like atmosphere and this continued. The press, as they had throughout each stage of this case, was having a feeding frenzy. Once again they descended upon New Jersey's Hunterdon County, this time to the county seat in Flemington, to cover Hauptmann's trial. The Crime of the Century was about to become the Trial of the Century.

Each newspaper sought a competitive edge. *The New York Daily Mirror* came up with one. They hired for the defendant Attorney Edward J. Reilly of Brooklyn, a criminal defense lawyer. He was physically big; he was flamboyant; and he was sure to give a big show which would increase the dramatic effect of the trial and the public's interest in it. He also had two other attributes which proved relevant to the outcome: he was an alcoholic and he was borderline incompetent.

The Daily Mirror paid Ed Reilly a flat fee of $10,000.00 to defend Hauptmann. In return they got the big show, as did every other newspaper. But they also got something else. For the $10,000.00, Ed Reilly gave *The Daily Mirror* complete access to the defense and the defendant. *The Daily Mirror* got a pipeline.

Reilly was a member only of the New York State Bar, so he was not allowed to handle the case in New Jersey by himself. He therefore had three local New Jersey lawyers assist him: Lloyd Fischer, Frederick Pope and Egbert Rosecrans. All three were competent but their input into the defense and its direction were simply ignored by Reilly.

Lloyd Fischer arranged for Ed Reilly to stay free of charge at the home of an old college friend in Flemington. The first night there the doorbell rang, and Fischer's friend answered it. Standing in the doorway was a "lady of the night," with a steno pad in hand, who announced that she had arrived to take dictation from Ed Reilly. She was simply the first of many prostitutes who visited Ed Reilly's room on a nightly basis throughout the trial.

Reilly would also drink heavily while the trial lasted and often appeared in the courtroom the next morning extremely hung over.

The party-like atmosphere was not confined to Hauptmann's chief defense counsel. The whole town seemed to undergo an instant revitalization in the middle of the Depression. Miles of new telephone and telegraph wire were strung about town and even into the crumbling Flemington courthouse. A newsreel crew set up in the adjacent courtroom and filmed portions of the trial through a hole in the courtroom wall while an overhead microphone positioned in a broken electric fan over the witness chair recorded the sound.

Attendance at the trial became impossible. Although tickets were printed they seemed to do nothing more than spawn the growth industry of scalping.

Every hotel and motel room within fifteen miles was booked and enterprising local residents made a tidy sum renting spare bedrooms to the hordes of newspaper, newsreel and magazine people who descended on the town. Bookies moved in to take advantage of the action and one could place a bet not only on the ultimate outcome of the trial but on how long it would last, or even who the next witness would be. The action was furious.

The press corps in 1935 was heavily male dominated and prostitutes gravitated to Flemington.

Outside the courthouse an ingenious entrepreneur sold replicas of the kidnap ladder. He cleaned up.

Ed Reilly kept in the spirit of it all. He had stationary printed up for the occasion. "The Hauptmann- Lindbergh Trial" it announced at the top. "Edward J. Reilly, Chief Counsel." Down the left side of each sheet was a drawing of the alleged kidnap ladder in bright red. It is unknown if Hauptmann ever saw the stationery or, if he did, whether he truly appreciated it.

Even if he had, it was doubtful anyone would have noticed or cared. In many ways Hauptmann became the forgotten man in all this hoopla. It was as if Flemington had been awarded a sort of winter olympics with only one event, and from the beginning everyone was certain of its outcome.

But through all the money-making schemes and late night carousing, and despite the carnival-like atmosphere, Ed Reilly kept his word. For his $10,000.00 he dutifully provided the *New York Daily Mirror* with the inside story of the defense case as it progressed and *The Daily Mirror* faithfully printed it.

Those who could not buy or bribe their way into the courtroom spent their days milling about the streets and their nights carousing in the local pubs. Public opinion was unanimous. The jury in the street believed Hauptmann guilty even before the trial started and they wanted him to burn. When the jurors deliberated for eleven hours and twenty-one minutes on February 13, 1935 a crowd of over ten thousand in the street chanted, "Kill Hauptmann!" When the verdict was announced at 11:44 p.m. that night, the mob erupted in wild celebration.

It is not uncommon for the public to become enraged at certain crimes and to instinctively lash out at the first person accused of its commission. Today less than half the people in this country accept the Warren Commission's version of the assassination of John F. Kennedy. Yet do any of us doubt what the outcome would have been had Lee Harvey Oswald gone to trial for the murder in Dallas?

In 1989, when it was learned that Charles Stuart was tentatively identifying one Willie Bennett as the individual who shot and killed his pregnant wife, the public became enraged and eager for retribution. We now know that Willie Bennett was innocent. Yet had Charles Stuart continued undetected with his plan, do any of us doubt what the outcome of Willie Bennett's trial would have been?

The preconceived belief in Hauptmann's guilt which emanated from the streets of Flemington out across the nation was not the only, or most dangerous, prejudice for Hauptmann. In the courtroom itself he had to contend with Judge Thomas W. Trenchard.

It is unreliable and sometimes downright misleading to attempt to sense the true atmosphere of a trial from a neutral, dry reading of its transcript. Very often meaning and intent are conveyed as much in the tone of speech as in the language used.

Yet even a dry reading of the transcript of the Hauptmann trial reveals a clear bias on the part of the Judge. He consistently overruled any and all defense objections while sustaining any and all prosecution objections.

His treatment of Reilly, Fischer, Pope and Rosecrans was tinged with an obvious edge of contempt. On the other hand he was overly solicitous of David Wilentz, the New Jersey Attorney General who prosecuted this case.

If this prejudice is so obvious from a dry reading years after the fact, it certainly must have been obvious to the jurors. In case it was not, Trenchard went even further.

In 1935 New Jersey law allowed judges in their summations to comment upon the evidence. Trenchard took the occasion to tell the jurors who to believe and who not to believe.

With regard to each point of the defense he would paraphrase it in a mocking summary and then add a strong rhetorical, "Now, do you believe that?" Listeners at the trial have described how Trenchard emphasized the word "that" for added dramatic effect so that the question would drip with sarcasm. "Now, do you believe that?"

Trenchard summarized the defense's contention that perhaps the kidnapping was the work of a gang relying on inside help and added, "Now, do you believe that? Is there any evidence in this case whatsoever to support any such conclusion?"

Trenchard discussed Hauptmann's version of how he got the money from Fisch. After openly ridiculing it he again asked, "Do you believe that?" To ensure there was no doubt Trenchard brought it right home to them: "Was not the defendant," he asked in his charge to the jury, "the man who left the ransom note on the window sill of the nursery, and who took the child from its crib, after opening the closed window?"

But Trenchard's actions during the trial and his summary at its conclusion may have been mere icing on a cake that had long since been baked. There was a long series of factors which piled up against Hauptmann and which his alcoholic, nearly incompetent lawyer could not overcome.

There was, first of all, the fact that Hauptmann was allowed no discovery in the preparation of his defense. Discovery is a process in the legal system in which one side in a court case can learn information about the other. Hopefully, if both sides are well prepared, then all of the relevant information will come out at the trial, making the jury more likely to reach a correct verdict.

In the criminal case, discovery for an accused means, at a minimum, having available the police notes and reports, and access before the trial to the prosecution witnesses. If the prosecution has a strong case they should have no objection to revealing their evidence prior to trial. Since the defense is going to learn of it anyway, why not reveal it beforehand?

This way if a witness changes his or her story on the witness stand, or in some other way testifies differently from the way they originally reported to the police, the defense will have that to share with the jury.

For instance, imagine being a juror in a trial concerning the robbery of a liquor store. If a witness were to testify that he was in the store the day of the robbery, heard the alarm go off, and saw a six foot tall blond haired man with a droopy mustache run outside holding a bag of money in one hand and a gun in the other, and then the witness turned and pointed at the defendant seated in the courtroom and identified *him* as the man who ran out, that certainly would be an impressive piece of testimony. And if the defendant were in fact six feet tall, had blond hair and a droopy mustache, the strong temptation at that point would be to believe the witness.

But suppose that immediately after the robbery the police had interviewed all the store patrons and this witness had then told the police that at the time the alarm had gone off he had been at the rear of the store and had only caught a glance of the back of the fleeing robber's head. Although not totally certain, it had appeared to the witness at that time that the robber had short black hair.

If you were on the jury wouldn't you want to know about the witness' prior statement to the police? Doesn't that piece of information mean that perhaps the witness really did *not* get a good look at the robber, and is simply identifying the defendant as the robber to help the prosecutor who is perceived to be "the good guy?" What had seemed like a positive identification now does not seem so reliable.

But as a juror, how would you ever learn of such a prior inconsistent statement by the witness unless the defense knew about it and brought it to your attention? They could do this either by asking the witness about it or else by producing the police officer and police notes concerning the witness' original statement. Without full and complete discovery being given to the defendant, we can never be assured that the jury will hear the full story.

Hauptmann's defense team was forced to go to trial less than four months after his arrest in New York. There were over 100,000 pages of police notes, and none were given to them.

The prosecution called over 90 witnesses to testify, many more than once, yet in the less than four months of trial preparation the defense had not been allowed to take the deposition of any of these witnesses; that is, they had not been allowed to even sit with them with the prosecutor present and ask them what they knew.

On the other hand, the prosecution was allowed to know the defense case completely. Before Hauptmann was allowed a lawyer he had been thoroughly and exhaustively questioned, re-questioned and questioned again. His friends and acquaintances had been brought to the police station and interrogated. He had been forced to write copies of the ransom notes, stand in countless line-ups for various witnesses, and shout "Hey, Doc!" for a disguised Lindbergh. His home had been searched, torn apart and occupied by the police from the time of his arrest. And when they had finished with him they threw him to Ed Reilly and told his lawyers to be ready to try the case right after the holidays.

And so this, The Crime of the Century, the combination of an investigation that had lasted almost three years, had involved thousands of police officers including the combined efforts of New Jersey Police, New York Police, Federal Agents and volunteers such as Arthur Koehler, which had generated the 100,000 pages of police notes, was then tried by a broken down alcoholic and three assistants who were given no opportunity to analyze or properly prepare the case.

The lack of discovery was obvious. The trial transcript reveals countless examples where the defense team asks seemingly irrelevant questions whose answers only weakened their position. They asked Betty Gow when her brothers returned to Scotland and if they had ever been in jail. In fact they had never left Scotland and had never been in trouble with the police.

The defense was trying to follow up on wild rumors which had appeared in newspapers and on radio - often the only source of information they had about the case. As the trial progressed the defense was trying to learn about the prosecution's case. By the time they did, it was too late.

The lack of discovery was telling. Condon and Perrone had given inconsistent descriptions of the note passer, and Cemetery John, which varied markedly with Hauptmann's appearance. Yet in Flemington, both Perrone and Condon identified Hauptmann as the man they had encountered. Lindbergh had told the New York Grand Jury that Cemetery John had yelled only "Hey Doc!", and that he could not again identify that voice. Yet he changed his story and testified that Cemetery John had yelled "Hey Doctor!" and identified the voice as Hauptmann's. The Jury was never told of these prior inconsistent statements.

The police and prosecution had in their possession reports that the handwriting on the various ransom notes had been positively identified as belonging to another individual, but this was never revealed to the defense and therefore the jury never learned of it.

Millard Whited, a witness in New Jersey who identified Hauptmann as having been in the area around the time the child disappeared, had only "remembered" the incident shortly before the trial, having originally and consistently denied to the police having seen anybody. Yet the police notes detailing the fact that Whited had originally denied seeing anyone at the time, and had not come forward until shortly before the trial when newspapers began speculating who would get the reward money, was not disclosed to the defense and therefore the jury never learned of it.

The prosecution presented two important pieces of "expert witness testimony," the specifics of which are developed more fully in Chapter XIV. There were the seven handwriting witnesses who claimed Hauptmann wrote the ransom notes and Arthur Koehler, the self-described "wood expert" who claimed that a side rail of the ladder came from a floor board in Hauptmann's attic. Even if the defense team had had full and complete discovery giving them the gist of the testimony of these witnesses, it is doubtful this would have mattered, especially in light of the financial hurdles they faced.

In his opening statement to the jury, Attorney Fischer came right out and admitted that because the prosecution had seized *all* of Hauptmann's money as part of their investigation he did not have the resources necessary to retain his own experts who could explain to the jury why the rather questionable opinions offered by the prosecution's experts were incorrect.

What Fischer said was true. By the time of trial Hauptmann had no money. All of his funds, including his life savings, had been seized as evidence at the time of his arrest. The fact that Hauptmann was indigent and unable to secure the services of his own experts to help him properly present his case was considered in 1935 to be his problem. If Hauptmann went to the electric chair because he could not afford a proper defense, that was just too bad. The State of New Jersey had millions of dollars to investigate, prosecute and execute Hauptmann, but no money to help him bring out *all* the relevant facts at his trial.

When Attorney Fischer mentioned this to the jury, David Wilentz objected. He did not do so on the basis that what Fischer was saying was untrue; he objected because he thought it was unfair that the jury should know this. Judge Trenchard, of course, agreed.

The most destructive intangible concerned Hauptmann's ability to actually understand the proceedings. His native language was German and by the time of trial he had been in the country less than twelve years, most of it spent in contact with other Germans. He had married a German born woman. He spoke halting English with a thick accent.

A review of the film of the trial reveals a devastating cross-examination in which it is obvious that Hauptmann is trying to translate Wilentz' questions into German, form an answer, and translate the answer back into English. Repeatedly, before Hauptmann has a chance to complete his answer, Wilentz fires his next question at Hauptmann, who sits there struggling to comprehend.

The limited English-speaking Hauptmann should have been afforded a translator, but was not. In the absence of one the effect was overpowering. No matter how prepared his defense team had been, without a translator Hauptmann never had a full and fair chance to explain his version of the events.

Over this whole trial constantly loomed the specter of Lindbergh himself. His commitment to and involvement in the judicial presentation did not end with his review of the prosecution's case or his two days of testimony in Flemington. Each day of the trial Lindbergh arrived at the courthouse wearing a firearm in his shoulder holster which he removed only when testifying. Although neither a lawyer nor, technically, a party to the case, he sat at the prosecution table throughout the trial. He gave instructions to, and consulted with Wilentz, and no one dared object.

Anne testified briefly on the second day of the trial, was not cross-examined at all by Reilly, and hurriedly left the courthouse. But the Colonel himself stayed, strangely attracted to its unfolding drama in a way reminiscent of his morbid fascination with the police recreations of the ladder break and baby drop almost three years earlier.

Lindbergh's constant presence, more than any other single factor, served to personalize the trial, to make it not the State v. Hauptmann so much as Lindbergh v. Hauptmann and, in a larger context, American Hero v. German immigrant, good v. evil.

David Wilentz recognized this potential and exploited it. In his opening and closing he talked of Lindbergh, the hero, and pitted him against the defendant he specifically and contemptuously referred to as the immigrant non-American. Once those identities were established the trial's outcome was never in doubt.

That seemed to summarize what Bruno Richard Hauptmann faced in Flemington. Taken together, these factors do not prove his innocence. What they demonstrate is that the intangible factors in this case were running dead against Hauptmann. Each factor singularly and in combination acted to lessen the chance that the jury would review all of the evidence in a dispassionate, non-prejudicial manner to reach a correct decision. In light of the magnitude and bent of these intangibles it may have been that Bruno Richard Hauptmann's fate was sealed, regardless of the evidence.

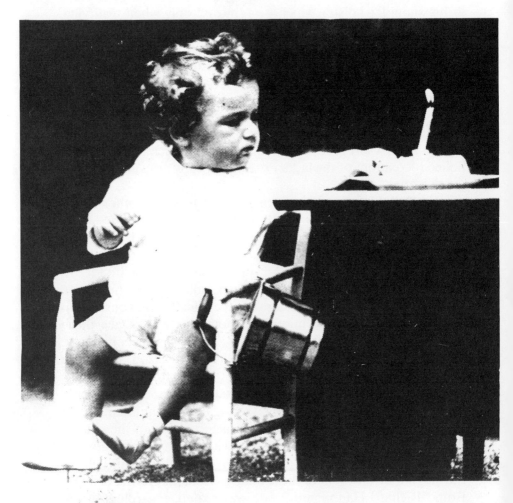

1. The Lindbergh baby on his first birthday (courtesy "New Jersey State Police Museum").

2. The ladder was found partially disassembled some 70 feet from the house. In reconstructing their theory of the crime, the police placed the fully extended ladder against the nursery window. It was never explained how an outside kidnapper would have known which window was the child's, and which one set of shutters on the whole house, could not be latched (courtesy "New Jersey State Police Museum").

3. Trooper Kelley's crime scene photo of the nursery window police concluded was used to gain entrance to the room. Lindbergh claimed to find the ransom note propped on the windowsill, after others had been in the room, and seen nothing (courtesy "New Jersey State Police Museum").

4. The nursery crib from which the child was taken. The lack of any fingerprints lead one trooper to speculate that the room had been wiped prior to police arrival (courtesy "New Jersey State Police Museum").

5. The original ransom note left the night of the child's disappearance. Note the spelling of "gut" and "anyding." Lindbergh allowed underworld figure Mickey Rossner to have access to the note, which was soon in general circulation (courtesy "New Jersey State Police Museum").

6. The child's body, found in the woods of Mt. Rose, less than three miles <u>south</u> of Colonel Lindbergh's house. Leaving the body on top of the ground, not far from the road, is consistent with an unplanned crime perpetrated by an individual pressed for time (courtesy "New Jersey State Police Museum").

Richard Hauptmann

7. Bruno Richard Hauptmann was arrested nearly two and one-half years after the baby disappeared. Executed on April 3, 1936, he adamantly maintained his innocence to the end, a fight his family continues to this day (courtesy "New Jersey State Police Museum").

Photograph of bearer

8. Hauptmann said repeatedly that the Lindbergh ransom money was given to him by Isidor Fisch, shown in this early photo (courtesy New Jersey State Police Museum").

9. Hauptmann's 1930 Dodge which he owned at the time of the child's disappearance, and which had always been registered in New York. When the authors interviewed Benjamin Lupica, he was adamant that the car with the ladder in it, which he had seen near the Lindbergh estate on March 1, 1932, bore New Jersey license plates (courtesy "New Jersey State Police Museum").

10. Notched rail 16 from the ladder as placed on Hauptmann's attic floor. The police theorized that the rail was once part of the adjacent floorboard. Governor Hoffman later asked police how rail 16 could be thicker than the adjacent board. This was never answered (courtesy "New Jersey State Police Museum").

CHAPTER XIII

If Charles Lindbergh, Jr. died at the negligent hands of his father who then fanned the ensuing investigation, a necessary pre-condition is that Hauptmann was innocent of the murder. It is not, however, necessary that Hauptmann be innocent of extortion.

Regardless of the intent of Colonel Lindbergh's March 4 invitation to intermediaries, it certainly had the effect of encouraging all sorts of fraudulent overtures which kept the police busy for two and one-half years. Without this there may never have been further ransom demands, and then where would suspicion have focused?

John Hughes Curtis approached Dean Peacock on March 6 with his "Sam" story after reading Lindbergh's invitation. He was eventually convicted of obstructing justice.

Gaston Means told Mrs. McLean of his underworld contacts after Lindbergh's invitation was widely published. He was eventually convicted of fraud.

Jafsie sent his own letter to the *Bronx Home News* on March 6 after reading Lindbergh's invitation and it certainly produced a response.

At the time of Hauptmann's trial and in the years immediately thereafter, the popular view was that Hauptmann was guilty of the kidnap, murder and extortion. There were doubters from the beginning, most notably Detective Ellis Parker and New Jersey Governor Harold Hoffman, but their voices were drowned by the roar of public approval of the verdict. There were legal scholars who were aghast at the trial, but they were considered academic eggheads.

The early journalists who wrote about the kidnapping supported the verdict. It was not until the 1950's that writers and other analysts of the crime began to be troubled by certain aspects. As more of the police notes and other pieces of the investigation were released, criticism and doubt concerning the verdict grew.

Thereafter a new line of thought developed. A series of books were written which postulated that Hauptmann could not have done the kidnapping. He was either extremely unlucky, or framed as a scapegoat by an embarrassed police force that had no real leads after two and one-half years. And, they reasoned, since he was innocent of the kidnapping his connection with the New York ransom pay-off must have been trumped up as well.

Hauptmann may actually have been innocent of any connection with the New York City ransom plot. However, that conclusion does not necessarily follow from the fact that he was innocent of the kidnap and murder. Obviously *somebody* extorted money in New York, and part of it *was* found buried in Hauptmann's garage. It is not necessary to our theory that Hauptmann was not part of an extortion. He, or someone acting in concert with him, could well have been Cemetery John in yet another fraudulent scheme. A review of the trial transcript reveals that Bruno Richard Hauptmann's conviction in Flemington for murder was based on nine pieces of evidence, or testimony, which combined to send him to the electric chair. Listed numerically they are:

1) Hauptmann was found with part of the ransom money;

2) Hauptmann was identified by Cecile Barr as having had ransom money on November 26, 1933 when he supposedly passed a Lindbergh ransom bill at her movie theater;

3) Hauptmann's closet had Dr. Condon's telephone number and address written on an inside trim board;

4) Lindbergh identified Hauptmann's voice as the one which shouted "Hey Doctor!" on April 2, 1932 in St. Raymond's Cemetery;

5) Cab driver Joseph Perrone identified Hauptmann as having given him a note to deliver to Condon on March 12, 1932;

6) Dr. John Condon identified Hauptmann as the man he met in Woodlawn Cemetery on March 12, 1932 and to whom he gave the ransom money on April 2, 1932 in St. Raymond's Cemetery;

7) Two witnesses in Hopewell and one in Princeton, New Jersey placed Hauptmann in that area on or near the day of the kidnapping;

8) Seven handwriting experts testified that Hauptmann had written the ransom notes including the original nursery note, and

9) Arthur Koehler, the "wood expert" testified that some of the wood used to make the ladder had been sold to a lumber yard close to Hauptmann's house and one ladder side rail (called rail 16) had originally been a floorboard in Hauptmann's attic.

The fact that Lindbergh ransom money was found buried in Hauptmann's garage is undisputed. Hauptmann admitted the money was his. Despite rigorous police questioning he stuck to his story that he had been given the money by Isador Fisch. At the time the prosecution ridiculed the explanation publicly by referring to it as "The Fisch Story" while more recent critics have uncovered various indicia of corroboration.

According to the prosecution's case, the address and telephone number of Dr. Condon was written in pencil on the trim board on the inside of a small closet located in the Hauptmann nursery. The closet had no overhead light and one had to remove shelves and wedge themselves backwards into the closet where they could use a flashlight to read the address and number. The prosecution argued that Hauptmann had recorded the address and number there for reference when he had to contact Jafsie.

The telephone number was a problem for Hauptmann. Its impact was compounded when the prosecution revealed that after days of intensive questioning without sleep, Hauptmann admitted having written the telephone number there. He speculated that perhaps he had done so because he had been following the case in the newspapers and had seen Dr. Condon's offer. Out of interest he might have recorded the address and number.

Defenders of Hauptmann have focused on two aspects of this statement. First, it came after six days of intensive police questioning. It has long been recognized that under coercive conditions a subject can be made to admit almost anything.

A second challenge has been that a review of the actual transcript of this "admission" discloses that Hauptmann may have been unsure in his own mind as to which closet the police were referring. This indirectly corroborates that he really had no knowledge of the writing and was just answering to stop the questioning and to be helpful - common reactions of coerced prisoners suffering severe stress.

There was other writing on the closet door which was visible when the door was swung open into the light. Hauptmann had recorded the serial number of two large bills (a five hundred dollar bill and a one thousand dollar bill) which he said he had received from Fisch. Neither bill was part of the Lindbergh ransom money although some newspaper accounts at the time erroneously reported they were. The existence of the recording of these other large bills actually tends to corroborate the "Fisch Story."

A number of critics have charged that any theory that Hauptmann wrote Condon's address and telephone number inside a closet makes no sense for a number of reasons.

First, Hauptmann did not have and never had a telephone. Even if he were Cemetery John himself, why write down Condon's telephone number in a permanent location where there was no telephone? Perhaps one might write such information on a piece of paper which he could carry with him to a pay telephone, but why write it on a fixed trim board?

Second, why write it where it was so inaccessible? Unlike with the serial numbers of the bills, to read the telephone number one had to remove shelves, wedge inside and make sure that one had a flashlight as the closet had no light. If Hauptmann were so afraid of it being discovered during a police search, wouldn't he have written it on a disposable piece of paper rather than making a permanent record? And wouldn't Hauptmann have destroyed or obliterated this piece of evidence after the ransom was paid?

Third, Dr. Condon was listed in the New York City telephone directory in the days when public telephone booths still had them attached. If Hauptmann had to call Condon from a pay telephone he could simply look up his number on each occasion. This was certainly less burdensome than checking the inside of his closet trim before he left his house.

And finally, there is some evidence that the telephone number had actually been placed there by Ed Cassidy, a newspaper reporter for the *New York Daily News* who was in the Hauptmann apartment after his arrest and needed a fresh angle for a story. Cassidy later admitted to several people that he had written Condon's address and telephone number in the closet, close to where Hauptmann had recorded the serial numbers of the Fisch bills.

At his trial Hauptmann denied having written Condon's address and phone number and indicated that he had answered contrarily in the Bronx to just provide an answer to constant questioning. If his Bronx statement was the result of lengthy and psychologically coercive grilling, this is certainly plausible.

Dr. Condon himself always doubted the authenticity of that particular piece of evidence. Interviewed immediately after Hauptmann's conviction he was quoted as saying, "To this day I cannot bring myself to accept the written telephone number and address in the kidnapper's closet ..." We will probably never know the true source of that particular piece of evidence. We only know that its reliability is questionable.

Also questionable are the identifications of Hauptmann. Cecile Barr identified him as the man who passed her a ransom bill. She testified that a man approached her movie theater ticket window where she was working as a cashier on the night of November 26, 1933 and threw a tightly folded bill on the counter. He was alone and purchased just one ticket. After completing the sale she examined the bill, fearing it might be counterfeit. It was not, but it was one of the Lindbergh ransom bills whose numbers had been circulated.

By pure coincidence November 26 was Hauptmann's birthday. He was married at the time, and his wife held a small party for his 34th birthday. Those in attendance included Hauptmann, his wife Anna, Fisch, Maria Mueller and Paul Vetterle. Mueller and Vetterle were members of the local German community and together with Hauptmann and his wife testified that they were with him at the party until 9:30 or 10:00 p.m., that he did not go to the movies that evening and that even if he had, certainly would not have gone alone on that of all nights.

Observers at the trial reported that Lindbergh's voice identification of Hauptmann, occurring as it did on the trial's third day, was very persuasive. Adela Rogers St. John, who covered the trial as a journalist for the Hearst Newspapers, immediately looked at the jury when Lindbergh pronounced this from the witness stand. "Yes," she thought to herself at the time and later wrote, "they believe." Her subsequent interviews with jurors confirmed they believed in Lindbergh's voice identification.

We would ask the readers to use their own common sense on this. Suppose you were seated inside a parked car on a New York City street on a cold night in April. From one block away a man who you do not know, have never met, and whose voice with which you are unfamiliar yells two words: "Hey Doctor!"

Then, without having seen or heard the man again, two and one-half years later you are asked to identify that voice. Do you think any such identification is possible or, if possible and made, is reliable? Regardless of how Lindbergh was involved in the child's original disappearance, isn't it likely that when seated in the Bronx and shown one man who was caught with part of the ransom money, that Lindbergh would have believed he must have been the extortionist in the cemetery? Wouldn't Lindbergh, or anyone else, have been ready to identify *any* voice he heard as Cemetery John's because he would assume that that was who he must be confronting in the District Attorney's Office?

A more accurate procedure, if one wanted to test the witness' ability to identify a voice, would have been to have Lindbergh sit in a room and have eight or ten other people behind a screen (one of whom would be Hauptmann) shout "Hey Doc!" one at a time. Lindbergh could listen to them all and even have them repeat the shout if necessary. If he could then accurately say, "Number seven was Cemetery John," then such an identification could be considered reliable. However, as the actual oral test was done with only one suspect, an individual Lindbergh knew had already been caught with ransom money, it was inherently suggestive.

This type of one person "line-up" is so inherently unfair that the United States Supreme Court has since prohibited it. If a line-up took place today like the one which took place in the Bronx on September 27, 1934, there could be no reference to it at the trial. Moreover, if the prosecution were to conduct such a "line-up", the witness would also not even be allowed to make any in-court identification of the defendant's voice unless and until it could be shown that the in-court identification was independent of any effect from the prior inherently suggestive line-up. Unfortunately for Hauptmann, this was not the law in 1935.

Cab driver Joseph Perrone identified Hauptmann at the trial as the person who had given him a note and a dollar bill on March 12, 1932. He had identified Hauptmann in a Bronx line-up. However, for all the reasons discussed with regard to Lindbergh's voice identification, this too was inherently suggestive. Perrone certainly had the opportunity to get a good long look at Hauptmann. In light of this, and his inability to describe Hauptmann, his subsequent identification of Hauptmann at the trial in Flemington is not credible.

Condon identified Hauptmann as Cemetery John. Yet his in-court identification seems to have been as much a surprise to the prosecution as it was a disappointment to the defense. At the line-up in the Bronx, Condon said Hauptmann was *not* Cemetery John and he refused to say he was. He made that statement both to New York City police officers and later to FBI Agent Leon Turrou. In fact, he told Turrou that Hauptmann was definitely *not* Cemetery John.

Between Hauptmann's arrest and trial, Condon chased around the country searching for Cemetery John, attempting to track down leads as to his identity. He did not believe that the police had the right man. Yet in Flemington he ultimately did identify Hauptmann as Cemetery John.

However, the accuracy of all of this evidence at Hauptmann's trial is really irrelevant to the issue of who killed the Lindbergh baby. Even if all of this evidence were totally true - that Hauptmann had written Condon's address and phone number in his closet, had given Perrone the money and note, had met Condon at Woodlawn and St. Raymond's Cemetery where Lindbergh had heard him shout "Hey Doc!", or "Hey Doctor!", and had passed a bill to Cecile Barr on November 26, 1933 - it does not contradict our theory. Hauptmann may very well have been an extortionist like Curtis, Means or the Cumberland Hotel Group.

There were three eyewitnesses who placed Hauptmann in New Jersey in February 1932. Millard Whited lived approximately one mile from the Lindbergh home in Hopewell. At Hauptmann's trial he claimed to have seen Hauptmann in Hopewell twice in February. One of those occasions was around February 18 when Whited claims he saw Hauptmann exit some brush by the side of the road as he drove past. Whited further testified that about one week later he again saw Hauptmann standing at a cross-road as he drove past.

Amandus Hochmuth was 87 years old at the time of the trial. A neighbor of Lindbergh's, he testified that on the day of the child's disappearance he had sat on his front porch from which he had a view of the road and lane leading to the Lindbergh estate. A car had come fast around the corner and the driver had glanced at Hochmuth as the car passed. Hochmuth testified that the car had a three section ladder inside and identified Hauptmann as its driver.

Charles B. Rossiter testified that on the Saturday before the child's disappearance he had come upon a car stalled near the Princeton Airport and stopped to offer assistance. The motorist had declined help, but Rossiter had lingered in order to get a good look at him. He identified the man as Hauptmann.

These were the only three witnesses who identified Hauptmann as being in the Hopewell area at any time near the child's disappearance.

A fourth witness, Ben Lupica, a 17 year old senior at Princeton Academy, testified that on the day of the kidnapping he had seen a car with a ladder inside drive past him as he drove home from school. Although the driver looked somewhat like Hauptmann, Lupica's description of the car did not fit either the year or color of Hauptmann's 1930 green Dodge. Lupica further testified that the car which had driven past had New Jersey license plates. Hauptmann, of course, had always had New York license plates.

The defense tried to shake these three witnesses (Ben Lupica was actually called as a defense witness) but were unsuccessful. If there were ever a justification for the allowance of extensive pre-trial discovery by the defense in a criminal case, the situation with these three witnesses provided one. Had the defense had access to the police files they would have learned, and could have shared with the jury, a number of facts of importance.

First, in June of 1932 Hochmuth had been determined to be partly blind and therefore entitled to Public Assistance. That diagnosis had been confirmed in August of 1932 when he had been diagnosed as suffering from cataracts.

After Hauptmann's execution Governor Hoffman had summoned Hochmuth to his office to determine if he was entitled to receive any of the reward money. Hoffman had his own doubts about the accuracy of the jury verdict and had heard rumors about Hochmuth. He therefore used this opportunity to test Hochmuth's eyesight by asking him to identify an 18 inch high silver cup filled with flowers which was sitting on a filing cabinet. Hochmuth identified it as a lady's hat.

The startled reaction of Hoffman and his aides apparently tipped Hochmuth that he had given the wrong answer. He then changed his answer and identified it as a bowl of fruit.

Hoffman and his aides began to question the old man closely. They had available to them what the defendant had never had: the police notes. Why, they asked Hochmuth, had you not told your story when you first learned of the baby's disappearance?

It was not until November of 1934, some two months after Hauptmann's arrest, and when the local newspapers were speculating on who would share in the reward money, that Hochmuth had suddenly come forward with his story.

And, they further asked Hochmuth, why did you change your story? When first interviewed by New Jersey State Trooper Sawyer, Hochmuth had said the car had slid into the ditch. At the trial he said it drove past. Which story was accurate?

Perhaps sensing that his chances of sharing in the reward money were slipping, Hochmuth again changed his story. He now told Hoffman that he had even more information that he had not bothered to mention earlier. Just before the baby disappeared he had met an individual on the bridge near the estate and had engaged him in a conversation. As Hochmuth was a native German he had recognized a German accent. When he queried the individual on this the stranger admitted that he was from Saxony and that his name was Hauptmann.

By that point it was now obvious to Governor Hoffman and his aides that Hochmuth was a blind, impoverished, rather pathetic individual who had not seen anything but was so desperate for money that he would tell any story to get some reward money. He eventually received $250.

Millard Whited not only identified Hauptmann as the man he had seen on two separate occasions lurking about in Hopewell, but he also testified on the witness stand that he had told police investigators this when questioned the very day after the child's disappearance.

However, a review of the actual police notes indicates that Whited had not made any such disclosure. In fact, the police notes reveal that Whited had been specifically asked on a number of occasions if he had seen any strangers lurking about in the weeks prior to the child's disappearance. On each and every occasion he specifically denied that he had.

When confronted by Governor Hoffman on this apparent contradiction, he admitted that his trial testimony was due in part to his desire to share in the reward. Whited had been promised that in return for his identification of Hauptmann he would be paid $150 up front, $35 per day for expenses, and a share of the reward money. Hoffman also learned that people who knew Whited for some time considered him an inherent liar. Again, the defense was not aware of that.

Charles J. Rossiter did not tell his story to the police until after Hauptmann was arrested and Rossiter saw his picture in the newspaper. Then Rossiter came forward and told his tale. It so happened that was shortly after he had been fired from his job for stealing company funds.

In Flemington Rossiter climbed on the witness stand and testified that Bruno Richard Hauptmann, seated at the defense table, was the motorist he had encountered by chance almost three years earlier, three days before the baby disappeared. Rossiter was positive on this and the jury believed him. Yet when he had first telephoned in his story to the New Jersey State Police they had arranged a photographic line-up for him to review, and he had not been able to select Hauptmann's picture as the motorist.

Rossiter had then been transported to the Bronx where he was shown Hauptmann. Rossiter said that he was the motorist. After seeing Hauptmann in person he was then brought into an office and asked to describe the motorist. His description fit to a tee the person he had just seen. However, his description of the motorist's automobile did not fit Hauptmann's Dodge in the least. Again, the defense was not told any of this.

As shaky as all this evidence was, as unreliable and distrustful was the testimony of these non-expert witnesses, it actually could have been worse. During the trial John Hughes Curtis had sat back and watched. The attempted swindler who had been convicted of obstruction of justice had not only received a suspended prison sentence but had been forced to pay a $1,000 fine. He still smarted from what was an expensive fine in a depression economy, and was also indignant (as he perceived it) that his reputation had been damaged.

At the time of Hauptmann's arrest, Curtis had actually been quoted in the *New York Times* as being pleased by the turn of events and hopeful that now all would come out to clarify things and, apparently, polish his tarnished image. Forever the conniver, an idea occurred to him.

Curtis telephoned Schwarzkopf and made a proposal. If Schwarzkopf would get him his $1,000 back he would come to Flemington and testify that Bruno Richard Hauptmann was the kidnapper with whom he had been dealing in Norfolk. This would seal Hauptmann's conviction.

All Curtis asked in return (besides his $1,000) was to have a picture taken of Lindbergh shaking his hand afterwards and thanking him for his help. Once that happened Curtis was confident that he would then forever be considered in the same category as Jafsie and his good name would be restored. The $1,000 and a simple handshake were certainly small prices to pay to ensure a conviction of this immigrant.

Schwarzkopf loved the idea, described it as "brilliant" and said that he would run the idea past Lindbergh for final approval.

Schwarzkopf did so. However, the Curtis offer had problems which Schwarzkopf had not originally foreseen. One, there was no evidence that Hauptmann had ever been in Norfolk or was at all familiar with the boat building crowd.

Second, Curtis had been definite in describing a group of Scandinavians with whom he was dealing, and claimed to have met. Hauptmann was German. That information could not be kept from Hauptmann's defense team since it was now a public record as the result of Curtis' trial.

Third, Curtis had been very definite in his description of having met a gang of six kidnappers. That, too, was public record. The Hauptmann prosecution was proceeding under the theory that Hauptmann was a lone wolf who wrote the original note, kidnapped and killed the baby, hid the body, sent all the follow-up notes, gave the note to Perrone, met with Jafsie twice, collected the ransom, passed the ransom money, and had the rest in his garage. If Curtis testified as proposed, the whole gang theory would have been re-opened and a jury might not be convinced that it had been Hauptmann who had actually killed the Lindbergh child.

Fourth, Curtis had been convicted at a trial at which Lindbergh had testified against him and the use of Curtis now, along with a subsequent exoneration, might call into question Lindbergh's reputation.

Fifth, the Hauptmann trial looked strong without introducing these uncertainties. There seemed to be enough evidence with Whited, Rossiter, Hochmuth, Perrone, Barr and Condon, so why take a chance? After considering it carefully, in the end Lindbergh vetoed the idea and a chagrined Schwarzkopf gave the bad news to Curtis.

What is remarkable about this anecdote lies not so much in the fact that the trial almost involved known perjured testimony, but rather what it infers about the other testimony. Writers have long criticized and questioned the veracity of Whited, Hochmuth and the others. Had Lindbergh believed that Curtis' testimony was a good idea, with little risks, would Curtis' name be added to the list of those whose testimony has been so carefully analyzed and dissected by subsequent critics of the trial?

Schwarzkopf thought that Curtis' perjured testimony was a good idea. Lindbergh, shrewder than Schwarzkopf, recognized the pitfalls. Does this imply that Schwarzkopf was willing to use other known perjured testimony by Bornmann, Rossiter and the others whose testimony was less risky than Curtis'?

The only conclusion we can be sure of is this: if Curtis had been used as a witness, whatever prior inconsistent statements he had made to the police would never have been revealed to the defense team, Judge Trenchard would have allowed the testimony in and overruled any objections to it, and the jury, as they did with every other piece of prosecution evidence in this case, would have believed.

CHAPTER XIV

The prosecution called to the witness stand seven "handwriting experts" who testified that Hauptmann had written all of the ransom notes. They also called a "wood expert" who testified that Hauptmann had made the infamous ladder in part from wood taken from a floor board in the attic of his Bronx home, and that other parts of the ladder came from wood which had been shipped to a lumber yard near Hauptmann's house where he regularly did business. These eight experts were the only ones whose testimony, if believed, directly linked Hauptmann to the disappearance of the baby as opposed to mere extortion.

Several cautionary flags are raised whenever the testimony of a so-called "expert" is offered at a trial. Both civil and criminal trials in our system of justice are predicated upon the principle that witnesses should simply relate what they know and the jury should draw any conclusions or inferences which are appropriate from that testimony.

One exception to this general rule exists with regard to expert witnesses. Some people who possess special training, knowledge, education or experience may be allowed to testify as to their opinions or conclusions on a particular matter. For instance, in homicide cases a doctor or coroner could give an expert opinion on the cause of death.

There is a concern that jurors may be overly impressed simply because a person is some sort of "expert" and may place more emphasis on that person's testimony than on others. There is also a fear that if a factual dispute exists, a juror may choose to believe "the expert" as opposed to the lay witness.

Jurors are therefore instructed that they should not give more weight to a witness simply because he is an "expert" but rather should consider all of the evidence and testimony as a whole. Because of these concerns, strict conditions are placed on expert testimony.   The expert's opinion must be based on readily accepted scientific or other recognized principles and must be based on facts known to exist in the case.   Common subjects of an expert's opinion might be the cause of death in a homicide, the medical prognosis for a person injured in an automobile accident, or the value of a piece of real estate in an eminent domain case.

An expert's "opinion" does not have to be accepted by the jury.   Often both sides in a case will produce experts who reach contradictory conclusions.   When this occurs it sometimes comes as a shock to those uninitiated in our justice system - until it is realized that an expert's opinion is just that, an opinion.

An especially troubling area of expertise is handwriting analysis.   Traditionally there have been three accepted court methods to identify who wrote a particular piece of handwriting.

The first is by asking someone familiar with the subject's handwriting to identify it.   A wife could testify, "I know my husband's handwriting and this check bears his signature."

A second method is to show the jury the handwriting in question and a specimen writing known to have been written by the defendant and then let them make the conclusion.   This is allowable even though the jurors have no specialized training.

A third method is to have a handwriting expert render an opinion.

However, the very fact that American law allows jurors to reach their own conclusions about the identification of handwriting calls into question the reliability of so-called "experts."   There is no academic training in handwriting analysis.   One does not go to college and learn to be a handwriting expert.   The allowance of jurors to make their own handwriting comparisons and reach their own conclusions is based on the recognition that there is no "science" to handwriting analysis.   One reaches the conclusion as to source because the proffered handwriting and specimen handwriting "look the same," and anyone, including jurors, can make that determination.

After Hauptmann's arrest, he was made to write as the police dictated for some 13 hours, from 9:00 p.m. on September 19 until 10:00 a.m. on September 20, 1934.   At the trial the prosecution referred to those examples as the "request writings." Also introduced into evidence by the prosecution were two other groups of handwriting: "conceded writings" composed of writing exemplars known to have been done by Hauptmann such as his driver's license application and a promissory note, and the seven ransom notes including the original nursery note.

Each of the seven handwriting experts testified that in his opinion Hauptmann wrote all of the ransom notes. The first expert, Albert S. Osborn, gave the most complete testimony with regard to the opinions.

Osborn said that he based his opinion not just on the structure or shape of the handwriting itself but also on other outside factors such as the type of words used, the misspellings, the fact that subsequent ransom notes referred to material contained in earlier notes (such as the amount of the ransom) and the use of the secret symbol.

What Osborn and the other six witnesses failed to consider, the defense neither cross-examined them on nor mentioned, was that if "Cemetery John" were just an extortionist then certainly he was *trying* to make his handwriting similar to the original nursery note (which was in general circulation thanks to Lindbergh and Rossner), was *trying* to make his words sound like those in the original nursery note, *trying* to misspell words consistently to make his notes appear to have been written by the original maker and *trying* to reproduce the secret signature to make it appear that the writer of these subsequent notes was the kidnapper who had written the original note.

Osborn and the other experts also relied on the fact that Hauptmann had misspelled words in the subsequent writings the same way that words had been misspelled in the ransom notes. The problem with that similarity, however, is three-fold.

First, the misspelling consistencies which appear in the original nursery note and in the first follow-up letter from Brooklyn are a little too pat. There are 48 words in the original nursery note, 78 in the follow-up. Two of the misspelled words in the original note ("gut" and "anyding") also appear in the follow-up letter and both are spelled exactly the same way. There was no need to use the words "good" and "anything" in the follow-up letter. Even the casual reader is left with the nagging suspicion that whoever wrote the follow-up letter went out of his way to use "gut" and "anyding" to convince a reader that the two notes were written by the same person.

Second, Hauptmann (as well as other suspects who had been required by the police to provide specimen writings) had all been dictated to and told specifically how to spell certain words in order to provide a better basis for structural comparison. However, the experts who later analyzed the writings were not told that. Hauptmann knew it, since he had been there, and told his lawyers. When his lawyers asked the experts if this were true, the experts responded that they did not know. They were giving opinions after assuming facts which they did not know to be accurate.

A third problem with the use of misspellings as a basis for the experts' opinion is the same problem which infects all of their "other factors." The misspellings, as well as the other factors and an examination of the structure, do not at all tie Hauptmann to the baby's disappearance in Hopewell.

The experts all testified that Hauptmann had written *all* of the ransom notes. Yet not once in their two days of testimony did any of the seven so-called experts discuss the original nursery note. All of their comparisons of Hauptmann's handwriting were with the *subsequent* ransom notes.

In fact, there are clear dissimilarities between some spellings in the nursery note and in subsequent notes. In the original nursery note the "sir" in the greeting "Dear Sir!" is spelled correctly. In the March 12 note to Jafsie "sir" is misspelled with an "e" at the end: "Dear Sire!" Yet no one mentioned that to the jury.

That Hauptmann could have been an extortionist trying to imitate the original note was never picked up on by Reilly and developed as a defense to the murder charge. In fact, Osborn himself hinted that this might be the case. In talking about the difference in the second ransom note he testified that, "The first two lines of the second letter are written with great deliberation and very distinctly like the writing in the first letter. The rest of the second letter is written somewhat more freely."

The opening was right there for the defense. A logical argument could have been made that whoever wrote the second note was consciously trying to imitate the first and the initial two lines of the second note reflect that. This would be consistent with that writer's intentional re-use of the words "gut" and "anyding."

The seven prosecution handwriting "experts" were not properly cross-examined in part because the information necessary to do so was unknown by the defense. And so, they testified essentially unchallenged, one by one tightening the belts strapping Bruno Richard Hauptmann into the awaiting electric chair.

The defense, although short of funds, did produce John M. Trendley, a handwriting expert of their own who testified that in his opinion Hauptmann had not written the ransom notes.

On cross-examination the prosecution attempted to ridicule Trendley by implying that he had only reviewed the documents for a mere two and one-half hours, and that this was not enough time to devote to a large quantity of writings and arrive at a credible opinion. Their effort was, to say the least, intellectually dishonest. The defense had obtained permission for Mr. Trendley to review the original ransom notes in Trenton but the prosecution had only allowed the review for a total of two and one-half hours, and at a time when a multitude of prosecution expert witnesses were also reviewing them and passing them around.

If they'd had the funds, the defense could have produced many expert witnesses to testify that Hauptmann had not written those notes. The prosecution could have produced an equal number to say that he had.

Osborn and the other six prosecution handwriting experts recognized that when they testified that they relied on the non-structural factors. Yet when considered in light of the possibility that Cemetery John may have only been an extortionist, the intangibles referred to by the seven experts lose their import as factors supporting Hauptmann's guilt.

In fact, the prosecution actually had in their possession other handwriting experts' reports, assembled before Hauptmann was arrested, which concluded that the nursery note had been written by other individuals. Shortly after the child's disappearance the police had forwarded copies of the nursery note to other police agencies to seek their assistance. On August 29, 1933 Albert Hamilton of "Chemical and Microscopical Investigators" of Auburn, New York wrote to the investigating police that he had positively identified the nursery note as having been written by one Manning Strawl, then in jail in New York. Mr. Saunder had earlier opined that Henry Liepold wrote all of the notes.

Of course this piece of exculpatory evidence was not revealed to the defense. Its importance lay not in the possibility that Manning Strawl or Henry Liepold had kidnapped the baby, but rather in the fact that it shows that handwriting analysis is not a precise science.

The prosecution's last witness was Arthur Koehler, the self-styled "wood expert." Everything which is dangerous about expert testimony was present in Koehler's testimony.

First, the field about which Arthur Koehler testified was not properly the **subject** of expert testimony. As the defense lawyers, especially **Attorney Pope**, tried to point out to the court, there is no such thing as a "wood expert." Neither author can cite or find any other examples when a "wood expert" was allowed to testify like Arthur Koehler was. Koehler was a civil servant with the federal government. His exact job description was that of a forester at the United States Forest Products Laboratory in Madison, Wisconsin. He tested trees and tree products in connection with the national forests.

He probably knew much about trees, and probably could identify different types of wood by visual inspection. However, the fact that he could tell pine from oak and birch from fir was the extent of his expertise and in no way gave him license to testify as he did, unchecked, on January 23 and 24, 1935 in Flemington, New Jersey.

But he so desperately wanted to get into the act. And in a case that had no real leads, the police in turn were desperate enough to invite him in.

Koehler had two ultimate opinions: (1) some of the wood used to make the ladder had been delivered from the sawmill to a lumberyard in the Bronx near Hauptmann's home and at which he often shopped, and (2) side rail 16 of the ladder had once been part of a floorboard in Hauptmann's attic. This testimony, if credible, would tie Hauptmann directly to the events of March 1, 1932 in Hopewell.

Koehler testified that he had examined the ladder lumber and noticed from visual observation that every eighth knife cut from the top planer and every sixth knife cut from the side planer was slightly defective. He reasoned that the top head and the side head each had one defective knife which exhibited itself once each revolution of the head. Thus the top head had eight knives and the side head six knives.

The distance between the "nicks" or defects was the distance that the lumber traveled through the planer before the head completed one revolution. Koehler referred to that distance as the "revolution spacing" and found that the distance between nicks from the top planer was ninety-three hundredths of an inch and the distance on the side was eighty-six hundredths of an inch. As the lumber passed through the planer it traveled ninety-three hundredths of an inch each time the top head revolved. Based on this rate of travel he claimed to have calculated the speed of the lumber passing through the planer at 232.5 feet per minute.

His observations up until this point are fine. The problem is that the revolution spacing was not due only to the speed of the lumber but is determined by a conjunction of two variables: the speed of the conveyor and the speed of the head.

Koehler knew this. He had arrived at the rate of 232.5 feet per minute by assuming that all top cutting heads revolved at 3,000 revolutions per minute. If they did, then a speed of 232.5 feet per minute would in fact result in a spacing of ninety-three hundredths of an inch each revolution of the top or surface cutting head.

Koehler believed that this rate of conveyor feeding was very high and therefore unique. He wrote to 1,598 sawmills or planing mills located in the Eastern part of the United States from New York to Alabama to ask if they had a planer with eight knives on top and six on the side and which could dress lumber as fast as 232.5 feet per minute. Twenty-five individuals wrote back and indicated that they did have such a planer.

One problem with Koehler's theory is that it assumed that all planing heads everywhere in the world spun at the rate of 3,000 revolutions per minute. This figure was probably a pretty good average of the speed at which a surface planer should operate.

However, when dealing with revolution spacing to the one--hundredths of an inch and making careful and supposedly precise calculations based on that, all the variables of the equation have to be exact. Three thousand revolutions per minute was not exact.

First, all planing heads are not accurate. There was no need even when the machine had been brand new for it to be calibrated to run at exactly 3,000 revolutions per minute.

Second, the speed of the head is set by adjusting a hand dial based on approximate eyeballing of the rate. Third, any machine could be worn, or out of sync, or need oiling, thereby causing it to run slower than actually set. Fourth, the gauge from which the 3,000 figure was read could be inaccurate. Fifth, sawmill heads are set at a certain speed when the feeder is dry. The resistance occasioned by lumber being fed through the planer will slow the speed of the heads, much like high grass will bog down the blade of a power lawn mower.

If the per minute revolutions of the cutting head were actually less than 3,000 (as would be likely with old, worn or not properly maintained machinery) then that would lengthen the revolution spacing on the lumber and give an artificially inflated figure for the speed of the lumber feed.

Since Koehler limited his inquiry of the 1,598 sawmills to whether they had a machine which could feed as fast as 232.5 feet per minute, he was probably eliminating many mills whose answer to that question was "no" and who therefore did not respond to his letter but could very well have dressed the ladder lumber.

But Koehler's search to find the sawmill is flawed for reasons other than the speed of the feeder. He arbitrarily limited his search to sawmills in existence when he wrote to them in 1933. We do not know when the ladder had been constructed or, more importantly for Koehler's theories, when the wood utilized in its construction had been planed.

The country was in the midst of the most serious economic depression in its history. Construction was down and businesses were folding on a daily basis. A more relevant line of inquiry for Koehler would have been, to search, if possible, for sawmills which had been in existence prior to 1932.

A third problem with Koehler's factual basis is that he arbitrarily limited his search geographically. He did not consider sawmills north of New York or west of the Appalachians. The rest of the country was ignored for no apparent reason other than it would have been much too burdensome to have written to more than 1,598. Nor was it accurate to assume that all of the wood in the ladder came from eastern trees. In fact, on the witness stand Koehler identified two cross-pieces in the ladder as having been made from Douglas fir found on the west coast.

A fourth problem concerns his assumption that only 25 sawmills in the country had the eight and six knife head combination and a fast planer. When cross-examined on this he admitted that he had no idea how many of the 1,598 had not written back. He was assuming in establishing his pool of 25 potential candidates that every sawmill owner who had such a planer would have written back and told him so.

Imagine being the operator of a rural sawmill in the Depression riddled south and receiving a letter from some guy up north telling you that he is investigating the Lindbergh baby kidnapping and trying to determine what sawmill planed the ladder lumber and do you have a certain type of planer?

Isn't the likely response to receiving this Depression era version of junk mail to just throw it away? Besides, the operator of a mill with such a planer might be fearful of the repercussions of getting involved. Will a positive response result in the impoundment of his equipment or the interruption of his operation while hundreds of agents parade through his sawmill and comb through his records? Koehler's conclusion that only 25 such sawmills existed in the country was, when considered, an absurdity. Yet no one challenged him on this.

Koehler believed in his work however. Once he had this reduced pool of 25 candidates he just assumed that the wood had been planed in one of those mills. Of the 25, two did not dress one by four pine, which left 23. He obtained samples from the suspect planer in each of these 23 and set out to find which was the culprit. What he never inquired about concerning the pair he had eliminated was whether they had *ever* dressed one by four pine. Again, his pool was arbitrarily reduced.

Of the 23 samples the one that came closest to the ninety--three hundredths of an inch revolution spacing was the M.G. and J.J. Dorn Company in McCormick, South Carolina. However, none of the Dorn samples had the unique defect marks found in the ladder lumber.

Koehler assumed that his methodology to this point had been perfect and the culprit mill had to be in the pool of 23. When none of the 23 was found to be generating wood with revolution spacing matching the ladder lumber he should have rethought his premise and re-examined his research. Instead he made another classic mistake: he began contorting the facts to fit his preconceived theory.

He testified that since the revolution spacing of Dorn lumber was closest, then the Dorn mill had to be the one. He traveled to McCormick and spoke with South Carolina State Senator Joseph J. Dorn, the owner and operator of the family mill. There he confided his mission. Dorn shut down the mill and had all of his workers thoroughly search for any scraps which would match the revolution spacing of ninety- three hundredths of an inch. Despite an exhaustive search none were found.

As Koehler droned on in Flemington, it should have become obvious to the defense team that with each assumption Koehler diminished the scientific nature of his quest. With each fact uncovered which did not fit into his theory, the likelihood of its accuracy diminished also. Another glitch was that none of the wood being produced by that sawmill had the same nicks and defects that Koehler had noticed in the ladder lumber.

This too did not deter him. Koehler simply amended his theory by now assuming that the Dorn planing heads must have been repaired after the ladder lumber had been planed. The fact that there was no evidence to support this amended theory was ignored.

What was happening to Koehler was what seemed to be affecting all those who investigated the Lindbergh baby disappearance. They all seemed to start with certain suppositions (that there was a kidnapping, that ransom demands were from actual kidnappers, that the Dorn Plant was the origin). When the facts suggested otherwise, instead of stepping back and rethinking their position, everyone seemed to simply contort the facts to fit.

Koehler inquired about the high speed planer and learned that it had been operating at its increased speed since an odd sized pulley had been installed in September of 1929. Koehler then demanded to see the books to check all of the shipments of wood from that planer since September of 1929. As the list was voluminous Koehler made another somewhat arbitrary decision which stemmed from the same cause: laziness. He copied down only those shipments made to firms north of the Potomac River.

The rationalization he presented sounds acceptable on its face: since the ladder was used in New Jersey the lumber must have come from a lumberyard in that area. Yet the hint of laziness is there and his procedure in only copying down some shipments is certainly not compatible with sound scientific investigation.

This pruning of the shipment list left a manageable forty-six railroad carloads which had been shipped to 25 firms. Eight of the carloads had gone to two firms located within 25 miles of Hopewell.

Koehler traveled to these two firms and discovered that they had both used up all of the subject lumber in their own operations and none was left. Koehler testified these two firms must not have been involved since they had used up their lumber in-house and did not sell to the public.

He apparently did not consider the possibility that an employee may have taken home a few samples of the lumber before it was expended.

Koehler and Bornmann began searching for the Dorn shipments. Eventually they arrived at a lumberyard at Ozone Park, Queens. Although the owner told them that all of the lumber from the Dorn shipment had been sold off months earlier, he remembered that he had just happened to construct some on-site bins from lumber in that shipment.

The three went out back and located the bins. One had a board protruding which Koehler cut off and examined. Although it had marks similar to those in the ladder there were two major differences. One, the blemishes were farther apart than the ninety-three one hundredths of an inch on the ladder lumber and two, the blemishes were closer to the center of the edge.

Koehler explained in Flemington that the discrepancy must have been caused by the wood having been fed at an even faster rate than the ladder lumber, which must have occurred either immediately before or immediately after the Dorn mill had changed the pulley.

At this point Koehler was clearly over-reaching. His investigation was turning up one dead end after another. But he would not back off and re-examine his process. His last conclusion was both the most damaging and the least logical. There was no reason to assume that the increased spacing had been caused by an increase in feeder speed. A decreased head speed could have been responsible. Even if there had been an increase in feeder speed it was not necessarily caused by a change in the pulley. Finally, even if the pulley were responsible, there was no reason to assume that the culprit lumber had to have been planed either immediately before or immediately after the Queens shipment. But Koehler said it did and the defense never pressed him. He testified that he tracked the two shipments of lumber planed just before and just after the Queens shipment.

The one immediately subsequent had gone to a lumberyard in Youngstown, Pennsylvania. That lumber had been trimmed at the Dorn plant one-eighth of an inch narrower than the ladder lumber. Therefore, Koehler testified, the suspect carload had to be in the one which had been shipped immediately prior to the Queens shipment and that one had gone to the National Millwork and Lumber Company in the Bronx, New York, close to where Bruno Richard Hauptmann lived and where he often shopped.

His conclusory testimony was impressive. Koehler had told the jury he was an expert on wood ("the wood expert of the United States Government" Wilentz had called him in front of the jury) and Trenchard had directly stated in court that, "I think the witness is qualified as an expert upon the subject matter" and the jury had heard that. And so, with that introduction Arthur Koehler had been allowed to ramble from the witness stand for two days. Koehler had constructed a very beautiful house for the jury, the reporters and the whole country to admire; no one seemed to notice that it lacked a logical foundation.

But Koehler did more than put the culprit lumber within Hauptmann's reach. By relating his experiences with Bornmann in the Hauptmann attic, he put rail 16 right in Hauptmann's house.

His testimony on rail 16 was not even arguably "expert" but he was allowed to give his opinion anyway. He testified that at Bornmann's request he had climbed into the attic and saw a missing floorboard. He took rail 16 with him and there was room for it to fit into the space, and the nail holes in rail 16 lined up with the nail holes he now found in the ceiling rafters.

When rail 16 was placed into the empty space there was a 14 inch gap at one end of the board and a one and one-quarter inch gap at the other. Koehler testified that by looking at the gap he could tell that the boards had once been joined.

He based this on the similarity of rings in the wood. The rings did not match up, but he speculated that could be accounted for by the existence of a knot which could have been in the one and one-quarter inch missing segment. The fact that there was no evidence of any such knot, did not alter his opinion.

Side rail 16 was two inches narrower than the remaining floorboard but he speculated that could be explained by Hauptmann having cut two inches off one edge of side rail 16 and having planed the other.

Why anyone would plane boards in a ladder which supposedly had been built to be used just once was never answered because, as was all too often in this case, that question was never asked. Psychologists would term Koehler's testimony "cognitive dissonance." In the ordinary course of events an expert would take certain uncontroverted facts, utilize an accepted theory, and apply the facts to the theory reaching a conclusion which would be presented as his opinion. Koehler took certain facts (the revolution spacing of the ladder lumber, etc.), accepted as true the conclusion or opinion (the ladder lumber was available to be bought by Hauptmann and/or came from his attic) and then developed a series of theories which allowed him to testify that the base facts led to the conclusion. He did not follow a trail to his conclusions so much as accept a conclusion and then describe from the witness stand a trail which could lead there.

Some critics have speculated that Koehler knew his testimony was worthless. An FBI memo at the time severely criticized it. Others have speculated that Koehler really believed in Hauptmann's guilt and believed that since a trail must have lead to the Bronx, there was no harm in testifying that he had actually followed it. Whichever interpretation is correct may never been known. However, after the trial Koehler tried to collect the reward money which is certainly inconsistent with his posture as having been a neutral investigator. The decision to deny him the reward by Governor Hoffman was correct.

Many critics have suggested that not only was the verdict incorrect, it was based in part on concocted evidence and perjured testimony and that Wilentz knew that.

The single most suspicious piece of evidence is the discovery of the missing floorboard. Hauptmann was arrested on September 19, 1934 and his house searched. Police had tramped over the grounds, dug up his yard, demolished his garage, searched high and low in attic and cellar, punched holes in all of his plaster walls looking for secret hiding places and other evidence, and ransacked his belongings. Police notes indicate that the attic was searched several times and nothing was found.

Meanwhile he was subjected to constant and vigorous questioning. There must certainly have come a time when the police realized that all they had against Bruno Richard Hauptmann was, at most, a case of extortion. They could not connect him to the events of March 1, 1932 and without that, all they had was another John Curtis or Gaston Means and no solution to The Crime of The Century. The police were no closer to solving this case than they had been the night they learned of the baby's disappearance.

Then, on September 26, 1934, one week after the arrest, Bornmann suddenly "discovered" the missing floorboard. He notified Koehler and together they "discovered" that side rail 16 fit into the space. Not exactly, but it fit in, and Koehler testified, the jury believed and Hauptmann was convicted.

Some have charged that Wilentz knew that the evidence was trumped. Governor Hoffman himself believed this. After Hauptmann's conviction Hoffman conducted his own investigation into the conviction. Together with Bornmann and Koehler he returned to Hauptmann's attic and placed rail 16 over the exposed floor joists. Unlike the other attic planks which had been nailed to the joists with seven nails, the plank from which rail 16 had supposedly been taken had 23 nail holes. When challenged Koehler claimed that carpenters sometimes did that with the first board to make it more structurally sound. When it was also pointed out that rail 16 was a 16th of an inch thicker than the other boards, neither Koehler nor Bornmann could offer any explanation. Witnesses report that Hoffman flatly accused them of "fabricating the evidence."

It is clear that Wilentz recognized problems with the State's theory. In his opening statement to the jury, he outlined the prosecution's theory that Hauptmann had climbed the ladder, taken the child with the idea of ransoming him, and then on his way out the window had dropped the baby, thereby crushing his skull. Reforming his plan, Hauptmann had carried away the dead child and resorted to extortion.

The defense team was generally not well prepared, although this was not totally their fault. Even when Reilly was not hung over he seemed unconcerned about the case and his questions, especially his follow-up questions, often lacked spark.

But a criminal defense lawyer, even a bad one, often has the best instincts of anyone in the criminal justice system and Reilly was experienced. Every fiber in his often inebriated body told him that this kidnapping could not possibly have been done without the aid of someone in the household.

And so Reilly spent much of his cross-examination pursuing this theory, trying to establish an inference that one of the staff had been involved. In doing so he stumbled across a point.

Charles, Jr. was a child who had always been cared for by a very small circle of people. He did not interact with strangers and had been sheltered from them. If a stranger had come into the room and removed the child he would have cried out. And despite the availability of people in that section of the house, at 9:15 p.m. no one had heard anything. Therefore, Reilly reasoned in his closing argument, the child had been taken by someone he knew.

The point may have been a small one and if left alone may have been overlooked. However, it obviously deeply troubled Wilentz as he sat there and listened to Reilly's closing argument. For when he rose and gave his closing he suddenly, in an effort to meet Reilly's challenge, changed the whole theory of the prosecution. He began by telling the jury about the disgusting person who did this heinous crime that, "[h]e wouldn't be an American..." and that he "would have to be the type of man that wouldn't think anything of forsaking his own country and disgracing his own nation; it would have to be the sort of a fellow that would leave everything behind and flee and go to another country and another land, a strange land ..." Wilentz also criticized Hauptmann, a man who claimed to be innocent, for fighting extradition to New Jersey rather than allowing himself, if he were innocent, "to come over here and prove it."

Finally Wilentz got around to Reilly's point about why the baby had not woken. "This fellow took no chance on the child awakening. He crushed that child right in that room, into insensibility. He smothered and choked that child right in that room. The child never cried, never gave any outcry, certainly not. The little voice was stilled right in that room."

This change of theory by Wilentz is absolutely amazing. If a prosecutor attempted to do that today it could be a severe tactical mistake, and might constitute grounds for a mistrial. There was no evidence of any of the "choking" to which Wilentz referred, and the fact that he suddenly changed his theory as to when the child was killed might lead a jury today, composed of more sophisticated individuals, to question whether the prosecution really had any confidence as to what actually did happen.

But in February of 1935 the question of what really did happen, like the question of whether Hauptmann really was guilty, seemed almost irrelevant in the hysteria surrounding Flemington.

Throughout Wilentz's final harangue Lindbergh sat impassively at the prosecutor's table, the American Hero overseeing the final act of the American Mystery. The American public, and more importantly this Flemington jury, believed.

On February 13, 1935, the day after Wilentz gave his summation thereby closing the lid on Hauptmann, Judge Trenchard nailed it shut with his charge to the jury. Using his prerogative under then New Jersey law to comment on the evidence, he did just that in a way which removed any chance of an acquittal. He finished at 10:22 a.m.

After some 32 days of trial, after over 90 witnesses had testified, after over one million words of testimony had been given, it took the jury only 11 hours and 21 minutes to return a verdict of guilty. When they did, the courtroom, the massing crowd outside, and all of America, erupted in jubilation. It was later revealed that the jury, upon retiring and under the careful direction of Charles Walton, Sr., who had prior to the trial not made up his mind "more than anyone else" in America, had immediately voted for guilty. They had spent the balance of the time considering a few faint pleas to recommend leniency for the defendant.

In the end they did not.

CHAPTER XV

Charles Lindbergh was at home at *Next Day Hill* with his wife Anne, and her mother, when news of the verdict came over the radio. Also present was the English writer Harold Nicolson, who had been staying at the Morrow home to complete a biography on Ambassador Morrow. The news flash emphasized that Hauptmann had been given the death sentence, and not life imprisonment.

Nicolson recounts in his diaries how the household became quiet as all conversation ceased for some minutes following the broadcast. Then, Lindbergh quietly and carefully began to recite for Nicolson the evidence against Hauptmann which Lindbergh claimed led irrevocably to the guilty verdict.

At first Nicolson couldn't understand why Lindbergh was doing that since he, Nicolson, was already familiar with the evidence. Eventually he noticed that Anne and Betty were ashen and their faces betrayed doubt. He began to sense that although the words were being directed at him, the purpose of Lindbergh's recapitulation of the evidence was for the benefit of Anne and her mother. It was, he specifically noted, a summation given in a manner to convince listeners. Interestingly enough, Lindbergh never said that Hauptmann was guilty, he merely kept reiterating that the "evidence was overwhelming."23

Hauptmann's defense team immediately filed an appeal on his behalf, and this promised to delay, at least for a short time, the first date set for his execution. It also afforded an opportunity for the new Governor of New Jersey, Harold Hoffman, to become interested in the case. Though there were few defenders of Hauptmann whose voice was heard during the hysteria surrounding this case, some newspapers editorialized on the sham nature of the proceedings. Without directly challenging his guilt, the *New York Times* said that Hauptmann was getting a rough ride to the electric chair. Privately, the FBI commented within their organization that some of the evidence, particularly the "wood" trail, was less than credible.

Governor Hoffman had his doubts. He was aware that the retired detective Ellis Parker, who was well known for his investigative skills, believed Hauptmann to be innocent. Hoffman, moreover, did not have a good relationship with Schwarzkopf, and it quickly soured as the Governor learned more about the case.

In the early summer of 1935 Hoffman secretly visited Hauptmann in his cell. They talked for well over an hour. Hauptmann implored the Governor to give him a lie detector test, or to administer truth serum. He recounted once again that he was a skilled carpenter, and would never have built a ladder like that, let alone make one from boards in his attic.

Shortly thereafter the Governor announced to the press that he had "serious doubts" about the Hauptmann case, and about the evidence which had been presented at the trial. This, of course, renewed the press fervor and brought the matter back onto the front page. A decision from the Court of Appeals was not expected until October, but the Governor's doubts provided a dramatic twist to the continuing saga. Hoffman hired an investigator to begin looking into the case which Schwarzkopf and Wilentz had put together. The more he learned, the more dismayed he became with the evidence against Hauptmann.

His efforts also struck a nerve with a narrow but growing audience. German-American groups became vocal in their flourishing belief that Hauptmann was a victim of ethnic persecution, castigated because of his immigrant status. They resented Wilentz's tactics at the trial, his frequent denigration of Hauptmann as a German, and his continued references to his non-American status. Eventually some journalists began to question the verdict. All of this fanned the continued media interest in the case, and Charles Lindbergh began to chafe at the protracted attention.

Harold Nicolson offered some acute observations of Lindbergh during this time. He recounted in his diaries that Lindbergh had a reputation amongst a wide circle of Anne's friends of sulkiness and "bad manners." He quoted one when he wrote, "She says that Lindbergh is no more than a mechanic, and that had it not been for the Lone Eagle flight, he would now be in charge of a gasoline station on the outskirts of St. Louis."24 Others shared this belief, though Nicolson appeared to have developed a fairly good relationship with Lindbergh during his stay at the Morrow home. He noted Lindbergh's disdain for the public which had made him famous, put him on a pedestal, and had allowed him to become a man of means. Once, Lindbergh told him that he "loathed" the "silly women who bring their kids up to shake my hand in railroad stations."25

The Court of Appeals rejected Hauptmann's appeal in October, 1935 and his case was immediately appealed to the United States Supreme Court. A decision was anticipated by early December, and if the appeal were denied as expected, the execution would be held in the first part of January, 1936.

By this time, Governor Hoffman had become fully engaged in Hauptmann's plight. By virtue of his own investigation, he was convinced that Hauptmann had gotten a raw deal. He attempted, without success, to remove Wilentz as Attorney General. Eventually, he succeeded in discharging Schwarzkopf as head of the New Jersey State Police. Critics of the Governor said that his motives were purely political, and pointed to the fact that Wilentz and Schwarzkopf were members of opposing political parties. They accused him of grandstanding in the press.

These criticisms are unjustified for several reasons. Although there was a growing group of doubters, their numbers remained small and the majority still supported the verdict. Lindbergh's personal popularity remained high. In part, the Governor's involvement in Hauptmann's case probably cost him his reelection. Also, long after Hoffman was out of office, and up until the time of his death, he passionately believed that Hauptmann's trial, and the evidence used against him, were a farce. He said that when he spent time with Hauptmann in his cell, he was persuaded by the young man's convincing statements, given with simple dignity. He noted how ardently Hauptmann's wife Anna argued on his behalf, firmly convinced that her husband was innocent.

Hoffman could have stayed out of the case altogether. Politically, that would have been a safer route to travel, since the majority of the public not only accepted his guilt but also sanctioned the death penalty. Instead, Hoffman went so far as to demand that Wilentz and Schwarzkopf, along with Detective Bornmann and Koehler, meet privately with him at the Hauptmann home, to prove to him that "Rail 16" was from the attic. When they couldn't, he directly accused them of fabricating the evidence.

On December 5, 1935 Hoffman publicly announced that regardless of the Supreme Court's decision, which was expected within the next few days, he would go to the New Jersey Board of Pardons to seek a commutation of the death sentence to life imprisonment. Under New Jersey law the Governor did not have the power to commute a sentence; he was merely one member of a Pardons Board.

Two days after Governor Hoffman announced to the press that regardless of the outcome of the appeal to the Supreme Court, he would go to the Board of Pardons, Charles Lindbergh told his wife Anne to pack their belongings and be ready to leave for Europe on "24 hours notice." Anne had very mixed emotions about leaving her home and leaving America, but Lindbergh was adamant.

On December 9, 1935 the Supreme Court denied Hauptmann's appeal, and his execution was set for the first week in January.

On December 19, 1935 Lindbergh called Deac Lyman, a reporter for the *New York Times*, who Lindbergh trusted, and asked him to come to *Next Day Hill*. There he told Lyman that the Lindbergh family was leaving the country, that he found the continued media attention on his family more than he could bear, and that he feared for their safety, particularly his son Jon's. In return for the exclusive story, he elicited from Lyman a promise not to publish the Lindbergh's move until 24 hours after their ship sailed. Lyman told Lindbergh that this was a huge story, and asked him if he was sure that was what he wanted to do. Lindbergh replied that he had no choice, and that perhaps they could find peace abroad. They would travel first to England, but that if that didn't work out, would look elsewhere.

Lyman agreed not to publish until after he had received confirmation that the ship had sailed, though he had to argue with his editor to do so. Knowing of Lindbergh's contempt for the press, Lyman's editor was not certain that Lindbergh hadn't given the story to other papers and he dreaded being scooped.

On December 22, 1935, only two weeks before the scheduled execution, Charles Lindbergh and his family boarded the U.S. passenger freighter, the *American Importer*, and left America. It would be over three years before Lindbergh would return to the United States. The four column headline in the *New York Times*, which ran the morning after their departure, exclaimed, "LIND-BERGH FAMILY SAILS FOR ENGLAND TO SEEK A SAFE, SECLUDED RESIDENCE; THREATS ON SON'S LIFE FORCE DECISION."

In fact, Charles Lindbergh fled the country. It is no coincidence that his escape from the United States occurred just before Hauptmann's scheduled execution, and at a time when Governor Hoffman's investigation into the evidence was bringing greater public scrutiny. Charles Lindbergh did not want to be around during that scrutiny. Lindbergh had once again, when it was to his advantage, artfully manipulated and used the press for his own purposes. The *New York Times* gave the story the angle Lindbergh had wanted them to, that the family was leaving since it was no longer safe for them in the United States. Deac Lyman's "scoop of the century", as his peers called it, earned him the Pulitzer. The *Times* editorialized that it was a sad commentary on the American society that its greatest hero could not live in his own country.

But not everyone saw it that way. Several major papers called Lindbergh a "quitter" and argued that had he simply behaved like heros were supposed to behave with an adoring and sympathetic public, he would have been left alone. Several of Lindbergh's closest advisors had made similar arguments.

As it turned out, Hauptmann's execution was delayed further when Governor Hoffman granted a stay, attempting to get enough votes from the Board of Pardons to commute the death sentence. He was unable to do so. Hauptmann died in the electric chair at 8:47 p.m. on April 3, 1936, at the State Prison in Trenton, New Jersey. The legions of reporters who had expected a last minute confession of guilt from Hauptmann, were disappointed.

In fact the prosecuting authorities offered Hauptmann a deal. If he would make a complete confession about his involvement in the kidnapping they themselves would go to the Board of Pardons and seek a commutation of the death sentence. They too were disappointed. Hauptmann again, and for the final time, proclaimed his innocence.

Having fled the country, Lindbergh installed his family in a remote section of Kent, England where he rented *Long Barn*, an estate belonging to Harold Nicolson. There he was safe from the prying eyes of the American press, and uninvolved in any further developments in the Hauptmann matter. The Lindberghs lived there for two years. He used this time to pursue his "aeronautical" interests, while Anne continued to write. Generally, Lindbergh was left alone by the English.

Charles and Anne made several flights to Europe, and one to Russia to inspect aviation plants and facilities. These were reported in the press, and prompted an invitation in May of 1936 for Lindbergh to travel to Germany for an inspection. The invitation was from Major Truman Smith, G.S., the Military Attache' to the American Embassy in Berlin. Smith wanted Lindbergh to give him an estimation of German air strength so that he could report on Hitler's growing military machine.

Lindbergh accepted Smith's invitation and flew to Berlin on July 22, 1936, landing at the Staaken Military Field. On his first visit he toured the German fighter wing, and spent some time at the Air Research Institute. The Germans were very pleased to have Lindbergh in their country, and he was well received and extremely well courted by the Nazis. He was allowed to speak with the pilots and engineers, and given full access to the employees. Lindbergh noted that they were very open with him, with the exception of the employees at the Air Research Institute where he tried to discuss rocket technology.

Although Major Smith tried to keep Lindbergh away from the political echelon this proved difficult. Smith was especially concerned about Hitler, who Lindbergh had expressed a desire to meet. While the Major was successful in keeping Lindbergh from Hitler, he was not so with Hermann Goering, Hitler's number two man, and Chief of the German Air Wing. Goering gave a formal luncheon for Lindbergh at his official residence. From this first meeting a special relationship developed between Lindbergh and Goering.   It was a relationship which Goering successfully developed for his own, and the Third Reich's, purposes.

Goering was part Swedish and greatly admired the country. He knew that Lindbergh's grandfather emigrated from Sweden, and made much of having this in common with him. Goering was disappointed when he learned that Lindbergh didn't speak any Swedish. The Germans went out of their way to impress Lindbergh, and saw to it that his comments and his travels around Germany received international attention. Lindbergh was impressed. He became more so with each trip.

Following his first visit, he wrote a report for Smith which stated that the German air strength was growing rapidly, was superior to that of the French or the Russians, and was on an escalating curve which would rapidly overtake that of Great Britain and the United States. In September of 1936, he told Harold Nicolson that Germany had the most powerful air force in the world.

Following his second visit to Germany one year later, Lindbergh told Nicolson that the German Luftwaffe was "ten times superior to that of Russia, France, and Great Britain." By this time France and England were alarmed at Hitler's growing military machine, and his clear statements of expansion. Lindbergh, however, maintained that Britain should make an alliance with Germany.

Again, Goering exploited Lindbergh's prominence during his visit. Lindbergh expressed admiration for the German people, praising their "sense of order," their "efficiency, virility, and technological skill."[26] Even as the crackdown on Jews began, Lindbergh was unconcerned with their plight, and thoroughly impressed with the nation being built by the Nazis. All of

Lindbergh's action and statements were being reported in his own homeland. There was a growing sentiment in the United States that Lindbergh was "overly" impressed with the Germans. Many Americans were uncomfortable with his pro-Nazi statements.

In late 1938, Lindbergh moved his family from England to Channel Island of Iliec, off the coast of France. His neighbor was Dr. Carrell, the scientist with whom he had maintained a relationship since their work at the Rockefeller Institute in New York. He continued to be an admirer of both Dr. Carrell and his theories on racial origin, and they spent much time together.

In his book, published in 1935, Dr. Carrell argued for the preservation only of the strong. "Only the elite makes the progress of the masses possible," he wrote. There should be no interest in "encouraging the survival of the unfit and the defective..." These, he concluded, should be gassed.

Lindbergh visited Germany a third time between October 11th and October 29th, 1938. It proved to be his most fateful one. At a stag dinner at the American embassy in Berlin, Marshall Goering awarded Lindbergh, on behalf of the Fuehrer, the "Service Cross of the German Eagle," the Nazi's highest civilian award. Lindbergh accepted it. Anne immediately sensed that his acceptance would not be well received in America. She called it his "albatross." Lindbergh seemed unperturbed. But even Anne's instincts couldn't guess at the scope of negative reaction in America to this Nazi symbol.

Only two weeks after the presentation, the Nazis began their government sponsored anti-Semitic riots of early November, 1938. Hundreds of Jews were killed, thousands had their homes, possessions, and businesses destroyed, and the most vicious and repressive measures ever systematically employed against a people began in earnest.

Lindbergh was openly castigated in the American press. Editorials demanded that he return his "Nazi decoration." He refused to return it or to comment on it. As to Germany's policies against the Jews, Lindbergh wrote, "I do not understand these riots on the part of the Germans. It seems so contrary to their sense of order and intelligence. They have undoubtedly had a difficult 'Jewish problem,' but why is it necessary to handle it so unreasonably?". Legions of Americans were outraged at his comments about the "Jewish problem." It would not be the last time Lindbergh made anti-Semitic remarks.

Instead, Lindbergh actually considered moving his family to Berlin. He made two other visits to Germany between late October, 1938 and January of 1939. Ostensibly this was to negotiate a purchase and exchange of aviation parts between Germany and France. Lindbergh was supposedly a go-between to facilitate an agreement, and met again with Goering to persuade him to approve it. However, there is ample evidence that Goering was simply once again manipulating Lindbergh. He even joked about it with his staff, since the Germans had no intention of selling parts to France.

The campaign to convince Lindbergh, and through his reports the French, British and Americans, of the invincibility of the German Air Force, was complete. Lindbergh was certain that because of her air power Germany could not be defeated. He alarmed Joseph Kennedy, then Ambassador to England, and frightened William Bullit, the Ambassador to France. He fervently believed that in a European war, victory would go to the Germans. Sensing correctly that one was imminent, he finally abandoned plans to move to Germany, and returned with his family to America during April of 1939.

He was immediately contacted by Major General Arnold, who asked Lindbergh to brief him on the status of the air forces of the European nations. Lindbergh restated his conviction that the Luftwaffe was unbeatable. General Arnold asked Lindbergh to return to active duty so that he could advise the United States Air Corps in matters of advanced aviation. Lindbergh refused.

In September of 1939, Hitler's war machine rolled into Poland, bringing England and France to immediately declare war on Hitler's Germany. Almost at once, Lindbergh began speaking out against any involvement in the war by the United States. He argued that it was strictly a European matter, and that it need not involve the United States.

While President Roosevelt generally agreed that war should be avoided, he instinctively recognized the threat that would be posed by a Nazi dominated Europe. When France fell and Great

Britain became the only power resisting Hitler on his western borders, Roosevelt knew that the United States could not let England fall. Lindbergh, on the other hand, felt that it did not matter, that helping England could only prolong the war, and that the United States must not intervene under any circumstances.

This once again put Lindbergh directly at odds with the President. Lindbergh began speaking around the country against American involvement in the war, in any manner. When President Roosevelt proposed the Lend Lease Act to help a crippled and ailing England, Lindbergh spoke out directly against Roosevelt. At first Lindbergh was quietly reminded by the administration that as an officer in the reserve armed forces, it was his duty not to speak out against his Commander in Chief. This didn't work. Not only did Lindbergh continue to speak out, the Nazis continued to quote his speeches in their own propaganda efforts. They even dropped leaflets on their enemies with his statements printed on them.

Lindbergh joined the America First Committee, a group which supported isolationism, and opposed American involvement in the War. While the group only existed between September of 1940 and December of 1941, it received significant press attention. The Committee developed a reputation for virulent speech making and agitation. Two agents from the Axis powers managed to penetrate the Committee during its existence.

The President was so disgusted with Lindbergh, that he called Lindbergh a "Copperhead" at his news conference on April 25, 1941. The Copperhead reference was an unambiguous message that Lindbergh's patriotism was in question. Three days later, Lindbergh sent a telegram directly to the President, which he released to the press beforehand, in which he resigned his commission as a reserve officer in the Air Corps.

Once Lindbergh could clash with the President and still hold popular support, but this was quite another story. Lindbergh was rapidly losing favor with the public. As his fervor grew, his statements became more inflammatory. In a Readers Digest article, he wrote, "Only a Western wall of race and arms can hold back the infiltration of inferior blood and permit the white race to live at all in a pressing sea of yellow, black, and brown." The real threat, he argued, came not from Germany, but from Asia, Africa, and Russia.

Anne's mother publicly opposed him, as did Anne's sister Constance. But the full wrath of the public and the press did not occur until after a speech Lindbergh delivered in Des Moines, Iowa on September 11, 1941, for the America First Committee. He stated that there were three groups "pressing" the country to war, the British, the Roosevelt administration, and the Jews. "Instead of agitating for war, Jews in this country should be opposing it in every way, for they will be the first to feel its consequences. Tolerance is a virtue that depends upon peace and strength." Continuing on, he added, reflectively, that, "Large Jewish ownership and influence in our motion pictures, our press, our radio and our government, constitutes a great danger to our society."

The reaction throughout the country was immediate. A major newspaper said, "The voice is Lindbergh's, but the words are the words of Hitler."27 Others suggested that Lindbergh should take his anti-Semitic beliefs, and his Nazi medal, and move permanently to Germany. Even the America First Committee disavowed Lindbergh's speech, and issued an apology on the Committee's behalf. Trans World Airlines stopped billing itself as "The Lindbergh Line," and in his home town of Little Falls, Minnesota, they quietly painted over the water tower which had so prominently proclaimed the community as his birthplace.

When the Japanese bombed Pearl Harbor on December 7, 1941, and Germany declared war on the United States, Lindbergh tried, through the Secretary of War's office, to regain his commission. President Roosevelt flatly refused to allow him to return to the service. No one came to his defense, and Charles Lindbergh, the Army Air Corps trained aviator, remained a civilian the entire time the world was at war. Lindbergh never wavered, even following the great conflict, in his conviction that he had been right. He never repudiated any of his statements. He never returned the "Service Cross of the German Eagle."

The public wondered for a time what had happened to their hero; that he had so changed, that he had become a bigot and an anti-Semite, that he seemed to lack compassion for the plight of individuals suffering under the terror of oppression. After a time, these questions waned, and the Lindbergh of old, the Lindbergh who had crossed the Atlantic, alone and brave, reemerged in the public's consciousness. What they did not recognize, and did not know, was that the Lindbergh to whom they had been briefly exposed during the pre-war years was the real Lindbergh. These attributes were as much at play during that time as they were during the death of his son in 1932. To admit error was simply not in his character.

CHAPTER XVI

So much has been written about Charles Lindbergh and the baby Lindbergh case, so much has appeared on television and in the movies, that it is sometimes difficult to remember that the case was real. It was not a novel, a Hollywood movie or a television show. For purposes of ascertaining what really happened this is regrettable, because novels, movies and television shows always have a clear cut, unambiguous conclusion that informs us with moral certainty "who did it." In the television series *Perry Mason*, with ten minutes remaining in each episode we could always count upon a witness chair confession from the real killer. In other television mysteries, during the final explanation, the audience is shown via flashback the true course of events. We hear it or we see it, and there can be no doubt.

It is unfortunate that the Lindbergh baby disappearance is not such a work of fiction, for if it were we too would know with moral certainty, with proof absolute, who did it. But this is a real case, like thousands of others, and like so many cases the truth can only be reached by examining the evidence piece by piece to ascertain what theory is best constructed from them.

There is no smoking gun here. In presenting and writing this book we have generated no death bed statement by a witness who now admits to having seen Lindbergh climb the ladder that night; we have uncovered no long lost confessional letter in the Colonel's own handwriting; we have found no Zapruder-like videotape of him disposing of the body in Mount Rose.

But that does not mean that the case against Colonel Charles Augustus Lindbergh is weak. It is not a weak case. It is a circumstantial case.

To those not directly involved in the criminal justice system the term "circumstantial evidence" is often synonymous with "weak evidence" or "no evidence." This is not accurate.

If we are sitting at home on a snowy winter evening and look out our living room window to see a stranger walking across our front yard, then we have direct, first hand evidence of that trespass. We saw it. If we had had a video camera handy we could have filmed it.

If we do not glance out our window, but instead upon arising the next morning go out into the new fallen snow and discover fresh footprints across the front yard, we have circumstantial evidence that someone walked across that area. We did not see it, we have no statement from anyone who saw it, we have no videotape of it happening, yet there is no doubt that it did happen. This evidence that someone did walk is different from direct observation, yet no less reliable.

So too is the case of the Lindbergh baby disappearance. When jurors are assembled to decide a person's fate in a criminal case they first listen to the evidence produced during the trial. After this they are then "charged" with the law; that is, the Judge reads to them the law they are to apply in the case. And they are told that as jurors they are to use their common sense and their life long experiences when evaluating the evidence.

There was no smoking gun in the case against Bruno Richard Hauptmann. No one saw *him* coming down the ladder on March 1, 1932, or disposing of the body in Mount Rose. There was no film of his action. Despite rather rough treatment by the police he never "confessed" to the crime or otherwise admitted his complicity in it. Even at the end, when he was offered the chance to save himself from the electric chair if he would just "tell the truth," he maintained his innocence. He could have saved himself with even a fabricated story but did not choose to do so. The case against Bruno Richard Hauptmann was "only circumstantial" yet it was enough to send him to the electric chair.

The case against Colonel Charles A. Lindbergh, although never considered by the police and therefore not pursued, is much stronger. When each piece of evidence is independently examined, analyzed, considered and interpreted in light of the known facts and our own common sense, it supports the theory that Charles A. Lindbergh, and not anyone else, was responsible for the death of his child.

Any solution to a crime whose perpetrator is not "caught in the act" begins with an examination of the crime itself. When this is done here, the pieces fit to form a theory which points directly at Colonel Lindbergh.

When the police arrived at the home on March 1, 1932 they were immediately troubled by the same facts which have troubled students of the crime since. For all the criticism which Colonel Schwarzkopf has had to endure over the decades, his original instincts were correct. They just did not, or could not, point him in the right direction.

There was, first of all, the problem of the knowledge of the "kidnappers" that their target was available. The early reaction of the police and the media was that this was a brilliant crime, well thought out, planned and executed. That belief stemmed in part from the fact that since the Lindberghs were never there during the week the kidnappers must have had fantastic intelligence to know that an exception had been created for that evening.

Yet that makes no sense. If the kidnappers did have excellent intelligence and the plan was brilliantly mapped out, they would have learned that the Lindberghs were only there during the weekends and never during the week. They would have had no reason to be in the Hopewell area on a weekday night, let alone plan a weekday kidnapping. If they were set on executing the crime in Hopewell they would have planned a weekend kidnapping.

This problem, immediately recognized by the police, gave rise to their original theory that perhaps the kidnapping was an "inside job," that the kidnappers not only had good intelligence about the Lindberghs' general habits but also had inside information that contrary to habit they would be home that particular night. Many writers who have subsequently looked at this case, even those who disbelieve the Hauptmann as kidnapper theory, have speculated on an unknown kidnapper or gang who learned that the Lindberghs would be there that night, recognized the opportunity that afforded them, and took advantage of that opportunity.

The problem is, what opportunity? None of these chroniclers has ever bothered to address this question: what was so special about March 1, 1932? Let us assume that this theory is correct, that a gang of knowledgeable kidnappers stalked the family and studied their habits. They learned that every weekend the

Lindberghs are in Hopewell, during the week Englewood. Then, through incidental information or pure chance, they discover on March 1 that contrary to pattern the family will be in Hopewell this very weekday evening. They could not have learned this earlier since Colonel Lindbergh had only made the decision that morning. If this is so, why was there any need to rush out to Hopewell to kidnap the child that evening?

So many journalists have talked of this moment in terms of the kidnappers seeing their opportunity and seizing it. But what opportunity? Even assuming the kidnappers preferred to make their move in Hopewell, the Lindberghs were there every Friday, Saturday and Sunday night. Certainly a well planned kidnapping would have a higher chance of success than a last minute decision.

The fact that the child was taken on a Tuesday evening when he was not supposed to be there is not consistent with a well planned kidnapping plot. Although the "well planned crime" theory has found some favor with later analysts, including those who believe Hauptmann innocent, it is not a logical conclusion.

If this were a real kidnapping there is always the possibility that the child was taken by a kidnapper who had no intelligence at all concerning the family. Someone may have just blindly driven to Hopewell, found the house on a day when the Lindberghs just happened to be there, and successfully abducted the child. Pure dumb luck. This should not be too quickly discounted either and if true, might actually be consistent with the Hauptmann as criminal theory.

But any proponent of such a theory would still have to explain how the "lucky" kidnapper then knew which room was the child's, and, more disturbingly, which shutters did not latch. Again, blind luck could be cited, but as the improbabilities mount the possibility of this as a viable explanation decreases in direct proportion.

There is another possibility that was never explored by the police and yet is consistent with the facts. The child was there that evening because Colonel Lindbergh had ordered the child to be there. He told the police and others that he ordered this because the child had a cold and therefore he did not want the child to make the trip from Hopewell to Englewood.

What he never explained (because no one ever asked him) was why not? The child had had the cold for a while and in fact was improving. Colonel Lindbergh had not prevented the child from travelling in the rain on the previous Friday from Englewood to Hopewell when the cold was much worse, so why prevent a return trip now that the child was better?

Second, what risk was there in the trip? The Lindberghs had a heated car, and servants to bundle and cover the baby to and from the car. Besides, anyone who has ever had a child knows that children have many, many colds and some seem to have one continuous cold from November to April of each year. Even in 1932 this should not have prevented an automobile trip.

Third, Colonel Lindbergh was not the type of person who ever really expressed over concern for his children or their health. He himself engaged in many extremely risky pursuits. His attitude towards his children had always seemed to be to not pamper them, to make them tough. He had thought nothing the previous July of forcing Anne to leave their then thirteenth month old while they embarked on a planned six month flying tour of the Orient. His biographies are also filled with accounts of his treatment of his other sons in which he forced them, as toddlers, to climb hills even though they were exhausted. Prior to Charles, Jr.'s disappearance his father had tossed pillows at him while the baby was toddling in an effort to knock him down.

Lindbergh wanted to make his children "tough," perhaps as his father had made him, when he refused to pull Charles from the swirling waters of the Mississippi. Colonel Lindbergh's actions on March 1 in showing such concern over a mild and fading cold is atypical behavior for him.

Fourth, even more disturbingly for the Colonel's later explanation, is that Anne herself, in a letter written March 2, 1932 to her mother-in-law which discusses the kidnapping, indicates that the child's cold had been completely cured and the temperature gone by Monday, February 29, the day before the Colonel's order to remain.

Under all of these circumstances, does Colonel Lindbergh's explanation for his actions ring true? Or, is it more likely that Colonel Lindbergh wanted the child there in Hopewell that evening for some other purpose, to do something that he could not do in Englewood?

We know that Colonel Lindbergh enjoyed playing very sick and cruel pranks on people. The term "practical jokes," although invariably used by his biographers, does not accurately describe the treatment he inflicted on others. There is no humor in putting kerosene in a man's water pitcher, causing the victim to be hospitalized after gulping it. The victim could have died from that "prank" and then what would we think of the Lone Eagle? There is no humor in putting a venomous snake in the bed clothes of a fellow military officer known to be deathly afraid of snakes. That victim could have died, if not from the snake bite then certainly from a heart attack. Ask any person deathly afraid of snakes what their reaction would be if they came home and after undressing pulled down the blankets only to find a venomous snake. Bed time would never again have the same meaning.

But these actions of Colonel Lindbergh, whether intended by the Colonel as "practical jokes" or whether indicative of something more sinister, were not confined to victims outside of his family.

There was no humor when the Colonel, during a dinner engagement with Amelia Earhart, suddenly, and without provocation, dumped a glass of water over Anne's head, spoiling her new silk dress. As George Putman noted in his description of the incident, silk stains when wet.

The incident was not funny. It was unprovoked and cruel. The Lindberghs had just recently met Amelia Earhart and the incident accomplished nothing other than embarrassing and humiliating Anne.

In Putnam's account he described how Anne got up and moved to the end of the room where she stood with her back to the other occupants. Amelia Earhart feared that Anne was crying. Suddenly Anne turned and dumped her glass of buttermilk all over the Colonel. Putnam concluded (perhaps hoped) that what Amelia had witnessed was a practical joke by the Colonel and an equally clever response by Anne.

But was it? What is humorous or clever about the Colonel's actions? What is funny about humiliating one's spouse in public?

As bad as that incident was, it did not mark the nadir of the Colonel's "jokes" towards his family. A few months prior to the baby's disappearance Colonel Charles A. Lindbergh, the Lone Eagle, had taken the baby from its crib and hidden him in a closet. The house had been thrown into an uproar as the family panicked that the baby had been kidnapped. Lindbergh let the ruse last for twenty minutes before the infant was discovered.

Is that funny? We can speculate about the reactions of the man finding a poisonous snake in his bed, or Bud Gurney as he lay in a hospital. Those are bad enough. But what was Anne's reaction when she actually thought that her baby had been kidnapped? What would any parent's reaction be?

As sick as that was, it actually may not have been the first time Lindbergh used a kidnapping scenario as a vehicle for one of his cruel performances. The coincidence of the April 1929 kidnapping threat to Constance Morrow is troubling.

Occurring just one month before Charles' and Anne's marriage, most of the Morrow family was out of the country. Dwight Morrow was on post in Mexico City as the American Ambassador. With him were his wife, oldest daughter Elizabeth, and Anne. Newspaper accounts of the day reported that the three Morrow women would be leaving Mexico City by train to begin their return to New York. The engagement had been announced and although no date had been publicized, newspapers were speculating on a June wedding. Ambassador Morrow was expected to remain in Mexico until shortly before the event.

Newspaper accounts place Charles Lindbergh on the east coast flying out of and into Roosevelt Field on Long Island.

The only Morrow family member in the country was fifteen year old Constance who was a student at Milton Academy, an exclusive girls' boarding school in Milton, Massachusetts. She embodied every aspect of the victim towards whom Colonel Lindbergh like to direct his "practical jokes." Like her older sister three years later, she was alone, cut-off from her family.

On April 24, 1929 she received an envelope. In it was a ransom demand. She would be kidnapped and killed unless her family paid a ransom. She was to tell no one else and get the money from her father. Once she had the money she was to await further instructions. The amount of the ransom was an even fifty thousand dollars.

In two weeks a second letter arrived. It instructed her to put the money into a box and place it in the wall behind an estate in nearby Westwood, Massachusetts.

By this time the police had been alerted and Lindbergh knew of their involvement. An actress placed an empty box in the wall and police detectives staked it out. No one picked up the box and the matter was soon forgotten.

But the parallels between that incident and the March 1, 1932 incident are striking. In both cases a note was used as the communication. In both cases the ransom amount was the same to the exact penny. Perplexingly, both notes do not give instructions for how the ransom is to be paid, but both indicate that further notes will instruct the victim.

That is suspicious. It is atypical for a blackmailer or other extortionist not to give all the demands and instructions in the first communication. Compare that with the practice of current international terrorists who make an extensive list of demands in their first communication and negotiate down from there. A second note only increases the chance of the perpetrator being detected while sending it, and also gives the victim and authorities time to prepare. Subsequent notes only make sense if there are ongoing negotiations, which there were not in either case. Both were simply demand cases.

Both subsequent notes, in 1929 and 1932, mandate that the money be placed in a box. Would a kidnapper care if the money were placed in a satchel, envelope, paper bag or even just loose with a rubber band around it? A subsequent note in the 1932 incident goes so far as to describe the exact dimensions of the box.

Was the Constance Morrow kidnap threat a product of Charles Lindbergh's sick mind? The case is too old, the clues too muddied, and the information too sketchy to answer that question definitely. But it has all the earmarks of a Lindbergh "practical joke."

And, three years later, so too did the March 1 incident. Only this "practical joke" went wrong, terribly wrong for Charles Lindbergh. The evidence suggests that the whole aftermath was an effort by him to intentionally cover up his blunder by making it look as though the child had been kidnapped by a third party.

Although this book is the first to suggest Charles Lindbergh himself was the kidnapper, the authors were not the first to suspect him. In the minutes after the child was discovered missing, two people immediately believed that the Colonel had taken the child as a sick joke. These people were Betty Gow and Anne Lindbergh. In a letter to her mother-in-law the day after the child's disappearance, Anne recreated the events of the evening before. She asked her mother-in-law to destroy the letter after reading it. The elder Mrs. Lindbergh did not. In the letter Anne wrote, "At ten Betty went into the baby, shut the window first, then lit the electric stove, then turned to the bed. It was empty and the sides still up. No blankets taken. She thought C. had taken him for a joke. I did, until I saw his face."

And these initial suspicions by Anne and Betty were not, as Anne implies, quickly dismissed in the minutes following the discovery of the empty crib. For in the months and years that followed, a review of the observations of others indicates that Anne retained her doubts even after Bruno Richard Hauptmann was arrested, tried, and convicted.

CHAPTER XVII

Much of the post-trial analysis of the Lindbergh kidnapping case has been directed towards ascertaining whether Bruno Richard Hauptmann, as opposed to some other individual or gang, did it. Our inquiry is more basic. Was there even a kidnapping?

As discussed in the previous chapter, any potential kidnapper could not have known that the Lindberghs would be in Hopewell on March 1. But that point is not conclusive in ruling out a kidnapping because the kidnappers could have been stupidly lucky and discovered the Lindberghs at home by pure chance. That is possible. However, there are other aspects of the incident which combine to make this extremely unlikely.

The first is the question of how a kidnapper would know which room was the baby's. Although later critics of the Hauptmann as perpetrator theory have used this to buttress their belief that Hauptmann could not have done it alone, they still concede that that factor points to a well ordered gang of kidnappers. Why no evidence of such a gang has ever surfaced has never been explained.

But there is a deeper problem. They inevitably assume that the information concerning the location of the child's bedroom was learned through surveillance. As recently as 1986, Ludovic Kennedy in *The Airman And The Carpenter* speculated that a lonesome watcher in the woods surveyed the house hour after hour, night after night until a knowledge of the interior structure and the movements and habits of its inhabitants was learned.

Although this makes good fodder for novels, movies and television, the reality is quite different. Any law enforcement officer can attest that visual surveillance of a house, even by a well trained officer, is of limited value. It may reveal, and not always with certainty, who goes in or out, but it is virtually useless for ascertaining what transpires inside or how the interior is set up. The family house was a rambling mansion filled not only with the Lindberghs but with their servants. This compounds the problem.

To prove this point the authors invite the reader to try it. Choose a house in a section of the city with which you are unfamiliar and stake it out. How long do you think you will sit in your car staring at a dark house (if no one is home) or at the same lit window which shows no movement, before you realize what a waste of time it is? A few weeks? A few nights? A few hours?

Police use "stake-outs" for limited purposes and usually only to ascertain if a particular person went in or out of a particular door.

The Lindbergh's house was even more difficult. Where would such an observer stand? The house was set back in the woods, eliminating surveillance by someone sitting in a parked car. The house was huge, with a large wing on each side which served to block all except one side at a time from observation.

The weather would have made surveillance even more difficult. Any observations would have been during weekend nights in January and February of 1932 when it would have been frigid, standing in the surrounding woods while studying a house through binoculars. How long would anyone have done this before quitting?

Access would have been a problem. Some analysts have speculated that the house's remoteness would have aided a spy in the woods. But that remoteness also mitigates against there having been any such observer. The structure was located in a small community off a dead end dirt road. A potential spy would have had to park his car where any household member or neighbor would have noticed it and probably stopped to investigate or offer assistance. The risk would be too great.

It is not logical that the house was under surveillance, or if it were, that anything of much value was learned. The question remains as to how a potential kidnapper would have learned which bedroom was occupied by Charles, Jr. And if a kidnapper would not have known, who would have? The answer, of course, is any member of the household. The staff were fully investigated and cleared. Charles Lindbergh was never investigated, and he knew the location of the child's bedroom.

But even aside from the knowledge of the bedroom's location there is the nagging question of access. Only one set of ladder rail holes was uncovered. Access was attempted only through one window, and it was the only window in the house with shutters which could not latch. Even assuming that the house was under constant surveillance during the winter of 1932, the most observant, experienced and intelligent spy could not have learned which set of shutters could not be latched from inside.

Recognizing this problem, Kennedy went so far as to speculate that the spy must have fixed that one pair of shutters so that it would not latch. The improbability of this action aside, the problem with the theory is that the shutters would not latch because they were warped. It is beyond rational belief that a kidnapper stood on a ladder day after day pouring water on a second floor shutter so that it would warp a certain way.

Again, to the extent that these facts tend to support one theory or another, these tend to support the theory that there was no kidnapping through the window.

There is also the problem of the dog never barking. The dog was a high strung Boston Terrier, and during the ensuing investigation everyone noticed that the dog would bark at the slightest provocation or arrival of a new police officer. Yet the dog had not barked that night, a fact duly noted by the police and one that caused Colonel Schwarzkopf concern.

Perhaps the dog would not have barked at merely a noise in the yard, but can anyone reasonably argue that the dog would not have been relegated to paroxysms of barking had an intruder been sensed in the house? However, *Wahgoosh* would not have barked had Colonel Lindbergh simply entered the nursery. Again, to the extent that this factor supports one theory or the other it tends to support the theory that a household member, as opposed to a stranger, entered the nursery.

There is also the problem of the location of the ransom note. It is logical to suppose that had there been a kidnapper he would have prepared the note beforehand, placed it in a sealed envelope, and left it when he picked up the child.

We would ask the reader to imagine him or herself as the kidnapper. You climb into a child's nursery with a kidnap note in your pocket, you approach the crib and lift out the child. Where do *you* leave the note? Picture the scene, and before reading on, answer where you leave the note. Don't you leave it in the crib? Isn't that the most logical place to leave it, to ensure that it will be seen by the parents?

Yet the note was not discovered there, but on the radiator beneath the window with the non-latching shutters and with the ladder rail holes below. A real kidnapper who came in through that window would have no interest in leaving a trail to show the police how he entered. He would want to leave the note in the place where it would most likely be found.

However, if the note were placed after the crib had been searched, then it could not be credibly placed in the crib and had to be left elsewhere. Its placement on the radiator drew attention to *that* window as the point of ingress and egress. The location of the note was not consistent with a *kidnapper* having come through the window, but was consistent with a person trying to convincingly show that a kidnapper had come through the window.

Similar concerns exist with regard to the location of the ladder found 70 feet from the house. The police theorized that the kidnapper had begun to remove the ladder, but then had, for whatever reason, changed his mind and abandoned it. After the discovery of the body and the arrest of Hauptmann, the prosecution theorized that he had brought the ladder with him and intended to leave with that potentially damaging piece of evidence. However, after the child was killed, Hauptmann abandoned the ladder and fled with only the body.

What the prosecution never addressed was why any kidnapper would change his plan and leave the ladder. Certainly any kidnapper would have planned to carry off both the ladder as evidence and the child as booty. The unexpected death of the child should not have altered that part of the plan. The death occurred when the ladder split. Even after that event the perpetrator had risked the additional noise of removing the ladder from up against the side of the house and had begun to carry it off. Toting the ladder and a dead child was no more difficult than the anticipated burden of the ladder and a live one.

Neither was the ladder abandoned because the perpetrator was interrupted. If Colonel Lindbergh were correct about the 9:15 p.m. cracking sound, we know that this elicited no further investigation. No alarm was sounded until the child was discovered missing some 45 minutes later.

Why then did someone remove the ladder from the side of the house and begin to carry it off some 70 feet only to change his mind and abandon it? What is plausible is that whoever took the child out the window had not planned on carrying away both the ladder and the baby, if it was never their intention to depart the grounds with the child. If Lindbergh planned to merely walk around to the front door and announce, "Look who I met in New York," he would not have planned to remove the ladder. It was only when the ladder broke and the child died that he would have felt compelled to remove both to carry through on a kidnap story. Only after attempting to carry them both would he have realized that he could not, and had to abandon one.

Furthermore, the scenario of a kidnapper dropping the child and killing him, and then immediately and coolly reformulating his plan into an extortion bluff, does not at all fit with abandoning the body above the ground less than three miles from the house. Once the kidnapper got safely away from the scene with the body and formulated a new plan, he would want to hide the body absolutely to best effectuate the new plan.

The combination of the body's placement and the ladder's location is not consistent with the later ransom demands. The ladder's placement served the same purpose as the note on the windowsill. It was an arrow which pointed to a third party having used the ladder to gain entrance through that particular nursery window. Without the ladder being left no one might ever suspect an outside perpetrator.

There is also the problem of the lack of fingerprints. No prints of Bruno Richard Hauptmann (or any other potential kidnapper) were ever found on the ladder, the chisel, the windowsill, the note or elsewhere in the nursery. By itself this might not be surprising. The prosecution speculated that

Hauptmann had worn gloves at all times and moreover, had worn some type of masking material over his shoes to prevent any shoe print identification.

Such a conclusion, when examined in a vacuum, seems plausible. If a potential criminal were aware of fingerprint analysis he or she would avoid leaving prints. Rather than carrying around a cloth and dutifully wiping every surface after touching it, the logical course of conduct by such a person would be to wear gloves.

However, there is more here than that. If a kidnapper came through the window he not only wore gloves but apparently went around the nursery and carefully wiped all surfaces clean of *any* fingerprints as no prints of anyone were discovered.

Why would a kidnapper do this? What difference would it make to a kidnapper if fingerprints of Betty Gow, Anne Lindbergh, Ollie Whately, or the baby himself were discovered in the nursery?

However, if Colonel Lindbergh had planned to take the child through the window, he certainly did not plan for the joke to last so long that the police would be called in and begin fingerprint analysis. Therefore, Lindbergh would not have bothered to wear gloves and his prints would have been on the ladder, outside the window casing, inside the windowsill, on the crib and other places that ordinarily one might not expect them to be.

Once he dropped the baby and decided on following through with the kidnap story, he would have realized the problem his fingerprints caused. When discovered by the police in these locations they would point suspicion towards the Colonel. At that point he had to engage in a frenzied wipedown of all surfaces in and outside of the nursery to remove any prints linking him with the disappearance. He would have thereby caused the rather odd results discovered by the police: the lack of *any* fingerprints. As one trooper said at the time, "I'm damned if I don't think somebody washed everything in that nursery before the printmen got there." At the time no one thought much about that statement.

There is also the problem of the time of the "kidnapping." If there were a kidnapping, either by Hauptmann or by a gang, why would they have removed the child at 9:15 p.m.?

There were five adults living in the house, two males and three females, all relatively young and in good physical condition. There were firearms in the house. There was a telephone which connected the outside world. Evidence of its existence was manifest as the wires were strung above ground to the road. No one in the house went to bed early. The house was on a dead end road.

Let us assume hypothetically that you, the reader, are planning to kidnap the Lindbergh baby. You locate the house, you ascertain which room is the nursery and which shutters do not latch. You are sitting in the woods with your homemade ladder. People are up in the house and the lights are on. You notice some people moving about the house.

The baby is put to bed at 7:30 p.m. He is checked again at 7:50 p.m. If you know anything at all about babies, or if the nursery note is accurate when it says "we have been planning this a very long time," you know babies wake up, fuss, and are changed again before the household retires.

You have $50,000.00 at stake. If caught you will be vilified and prosecuted to the fullest extent of the law. You want to get in, take the baby, and get away with as long a head start as possible.

Do you enter the house when everyone is still up and about and when, even if you escape detection, you run the risk of someone checking on the baby shortly after you depart (maybe even while you are still on the ladder) and telephoning in the alarm? You might not even make it to the nearest cross-road.

Or, do you wait until the middle of the night when everyone is asleep, when even if they awake their reaction time is slowest? If the baby is not discovered missing until the morning, a four or five hour head start is assured.

Are we to believe that a kidnapper walked up to a well lit house in the early evening, placed a heavy ladder against the side, climbed up, forced up a window, tumbled in the room and removed the baby rather than waiting a few hours until conditions for success would have been immeasurably greater?

Yet that was the only time for Lindbergh. He wanted to secure the disappearance of the baby before anyone realized he was home. He could then witness their reaction when it was discovered and, perhaps, he could himself dramatically present the baby and thereby triumph in his own success.

But the last factor may be the most significant, although it has largely gone unnoticed. The initial investigation by the police led them to conclude that the kidnapper must have parked an automobile by the side of the road several hundred yards from the entrance to the driveway. He then cut through the woods to the edge of the clearing where he studied the nursery. At approximately 9:05 p.m. he cut across the short clearing to the house with his ladder and climbed to the window. After the ladder break he carried the body back through the woods to his car and drove off.

Although the testimony at Hauptmann's trial was unequivocal that no footprints were found, this theory was logical and had been well publicized. Newspaper articles in the days immediately following the kidnapping had gone so far as to include detailed diagrams of the kidnapper's probable route through the woods to and from his get-away car.

Obviously no kidnapper would have pulled into the Lindbergh driveway to commit The Crime of the Century. The driveway was a narrow one-lane gravel affair that wound back one-half mile from the road to a turn-around near the garages. If a kidnapper were foolish enough to park in the driveway he risked detection should a household member attempt to leave the house via automobile. Worse for the kidnapper was the possibility that while he remained parked, a late night visitor or returning household member might drive in behind him, thereby not only discovering the crime in progress but also cutting off his escape. Since no kidnapper would be that stupid the published maps were logical.

Yet around the end of March Betty Gow and Elsie Whately found one of the child's thumbguards at the edge of the driveway approximately 100 yards from the road.

The prosecution devoted no attention to this discovery in their arguments at the trial, and Betty Gow and Elsie Whately made only passing references to it in their testimony. The prosecution recognized that the discovery did not link Hauptmann to the kidnapping. On cross-examination of Gow and Whately, Ed Reilly only insinuated that their discovery had been trumped up. No explanation was offered by him as to what purpose this would have served.

In fact Reilly's challenge may have just been instinctual. Like everyone else he knew that no kidnapper would have used the driveway that evening and therefore he just didn't believe that the thumbguard could have been found there. However, since he recognized that it was not probative as to whether Hauptmann, as opposed to someone else, was the kidnapper, he too did not spend much time on the point.

Reilly was wrong in asserting that the discovery was fabricated. What he failed to realize is that the discovery of the thumbguard was an important piece of evidence supporting Hauptmann's innocence. The lawyer had fallen victim to the assumption which everyone else in this case had: that there was a kidnapping.

The thumbguard had been discovered in the driveway because the child had been in the driveway that evening. We now know that at that time the child was either dead or in extremis. The child did not voluntarily throw off the thumbguard; it fell off when his body was jostled, as may have occurred when it was placed in the back of an automobile.

Everyone was correct. A kidnapper would not have used the driveway. However, Charles Lindbergh had no reason not to. He knew no one else would be arriving after him. Besides, there was no risk if he were discovered in the midst of playing his joke. Its success did not hinge on his having to park by the side of the road and tramp through the damp woods. He could park in the driveway 100 yards from the road but still out of sight of the house and complete his mission. When fate forced him to alter his plan, and he decided to carry away the body, he had to put it in his car. It was there that the thumbguard fell off, to be discovered one month later.

Each of these factors have troubled other observers of this crime, including the original investigating police authorities. But they have all tried to fit these factors into a theory that alternatively either Hauptmann was, or was not, the perpetrator of a kidnapping. An objective analysis of these factors indicates that each is consistent with a theory that there was no kidnapping.

CHAPTER XVIII

The factors discussed in the preceding chapter all suggest that there was no stranger and no abduction through the nursery window. However, neither those factors by themselves, nor in conjunction with each other, compel one to the inescapable conclusion that the child's disappearance was therefore caused by Colonel Lindbergh. For that one has to examine his actions on that night.

Lindbergh had left instructions that once put to bed Charles, Jr. should not be disturbed until Ms. Gow went to bring him to the bathroom for the final time at 10:00 p.m. His proffered reason was that he did not want the child "spoiled," but there was no evidence that the child was being spoiled, or that any corrective action was necessary.

Yet Lindbergh gave that order. That command served another purpose. It ensured that once the child was put to bed no one in the household would dare venture into the room to surprise a visitor. It ensured the sanctity and security of the room, if the child cried out. It presented to Lindbergh his very own window of opportunity.

A second puzzling action of Lindbergh's on the night of the "kidnapping" was his having "missed" the New York dinner. The event was big. His attendance at it had been well publicized. He was a man who, despite his assertions to the contrary, seemed to thrive on the accolades he received from an adoring public and never missed an opportunity to revel in them. He was a man who demanded punctuality and exactitude and was intolerant of its absence in others.

Yet he did not attend. His later explanation, that he simply forgot, although never questioned or doubted by the police, his biographers or even by later students of this crime, simply does not ring true. Charles Lindbergh was many things, but forgetful was not one of them.

Instead, Colonel Lindbergh telephoned his wife that evening to tell her that he would be a little late. Not very late as would be expected if he were attending a dinner party, but a little late. His 8:25 p.m. honking horn arrival was in fact later than usual, as Anne stated in her March 2 letter to her mother-in-law and testified to under oath at Hauptmann's trial.

No one ever asked the Colonel why he was late or where he had been for that period of time, or who could corroborate a later than usual departure from New York. The Colonel never volunteered any explanation. The police never asked him, they never checked his story and he was never asked about it at the trial either by the prosecutor or by the defense during cross-examination.

He could very well have actually left New York at his usual hour, driven back to Hopewell, parked in the driveway, taken the child, and all the while not be missed. After all, he was not expected until later. If Lindbergh left work at his usual time and arrived at his house at the usual time he would have had sufficient time to go in the correct window via ladder, take the baby out the window, accidentally drop the baby onto the granite ledge below, realize that the baby was dead from the massive head injury, think quickly, drive three miles south to a wooded area with which he was familiar, leave the body in the woods and drive back home.

And when Lindbergh drove up the second time at 8:25 p.m. he honked his horn in the driveway. Why would a man honk his horn upon arrival home? He did it for the same reason anyone honks their horn, to draw attention to himself, to say "I am here, notice me." Lindbergh wanted it noticed that he was arriving home then.

Charles Lindbergh went upstairs to wash up for dinner. The bathroom was located next to the nursery. Yet despite the fact that he ostensibly had not been home in two days and therefore had not seen his first (and at the time only) child in that time he did not peek in on him.

Isn't it logical for any parent who comes home after his or her only baby is in bed to peek in on them? If the reader has never been the parent of a 20 month old then ask someone who has. It is normal; it is customary.

Yet Charles Lindbergh did not do it. He did not because he knew there was no child in there and he did not want to be the one who raised the alarm. Let someone else discover it. He was not going to draw attention to himself.

After dinner he and Anne went into the library for just five minutes. At approximately 9:15 p.m. he claims to have spoken to Anne about a snapping sound he had just heard coming from outside.

There are two interesting aspects about this "event." First, if Lindbergh had heard a cracking sound, one of such a note that it caused him to comment about it to his wife, why didn't he investigate? They did live in a secluded area; there were no neighbors within a half mile; no one was expected to visit. Why didn't he pick up his rifle and charge outside then? This certainly would have been consistent with his character.

Yet he did nothing, because he did not want to charge outside and find the broken ladder and no one in the yard, the woods or on the road. He instead wanted to record for Anne that when the snapping sound occurred he was inside with her, and the "kidnapper" therefore had time to get away.

If the snapping sound was of such magnitude that Lindbergh not only heard it but commented upon it, why didn't anyone else hear it? Betty Gow didn't hear it. The Whatelys didn't hear it. Anne, who was seated in the same room as Charles, didn't hear it. Apparently the dog never heard it because he barked at even the slightest noise. Only Charles Lindbergh "heard" it. The reason? Because there was no snapping sound at 9:15 p.m.

The evidence on this is overwhelming. Only Lindbergh ever claims to have heard that noise. In her statement to the police Anne never mentions the noise. In her March 2, 1932 letter to her mother-in-law not only does she not mention any noise, but she specifically states twice that "we heard nothing," and later, "[n]o noise heard."28

At the trial she was never asked by the prosecutor if she had heard any noise and, in fact, was never even asked if she remembered Charles commenting on a noise. If we assume that the prosecutor had reviewed her testimony with her prior to the trial then we can safely assume that not only did she not hear any noise, but she could not recall her husband commenting on one. This raises an even more intriguing possibility: that not only was there no noise but perhaps there was no such comment by the Colonel.

This is the type of glaring absence of testimony that a competent defense lawyer should have picked up on and asked Anne about during cross-examination. Even if the theory of his defense was that there was a kidnapper but it just was not Hauptmann, Attorney Reilly still should have asked Anne about the noise to at least cast doubt on the accuracy of the 9:15 p.m. estimation. If he could have hinted that the kidnapping occurred earlier it would have strengthened Hauptmann's alibi defense. But Reilly asked no questions at all of Anne.

An interesting aside to the non-barking dog concerns the various participants' explanations. At Hauptmann's trial Reilly pursued the issue. His intent was to try to raise the inference that the dog didn't bark because a household member, as opposed to his client, had removed the child. He was hoping to convince the jury that the child had been removed by Oliver Whately (who had died before the trial began) or by Betty Gow.

The witnesses all knew what Reilly was attempting, yet they all, with only one exception, admitted that *Wahgoosh* was a good watchdog who would have barked at any stranger.

Betty Gow admitted that he had not barked that night. When Reilly asked if the dog generally barked when strangers were around she responded, "Yes, as I remember it, he did."

When Attorney General Wilentz asked Elsie Whately if *Wahgoosh* were a "barking dog or a quiet dog" she replied, "Well I always thought he was sharp; if he heard a noise he would bark..."

Anne Lindbergh was not asked any questions on cross-examination. However, in her letter to her mother-in-law of

March 3 she mentions the oddity of the dog's not having barked and adds, "[h]e has been barking ever since."29

These are honest responses by three household members. Only one gave a contrary response, and that was Colonel Lindbergh himself. When asked by Reilly if *Wahgoosh* were "[a] good watchdog?" Lindbergh replied, "I would not say that he was particularly a good watchdog." Later the Colonel admitted that the dog did sometimes "bark but that was not a regular thing." After conceding that the dog had not barked that night the Colonel hastily added, "[b]ut I would not expect any from that dog."

Why was Colonel Charles Lindbergh so obviously troubled by Reilly's efforts to focus on the dog not having barked? Reilly was going after Gow and Whately and yet their answers to his questions were consistent with the facts. What caused Lindbergh to be so defensive on this issue?

When Betty Gow came downstairs into the Colonel's library at approximately 10:00 p.m. and asked if he either had the baby or knew where he was, Lindbergh replied "no" to both and bounded upstairs. Apparently he and Betty arrived at the nursery at approximately the same time that Anne entered from her passageway. It was the Colonel who spoke first.

Consider the scenario logically. Let the reader assume that he or she has a 20 month old male toddler. The child is put to bed in a crib in a room on the second floor of a large, rambling mansion. The windows are shut and are still shut when the toddler is discovered missing from the crib.

What is the first thing that a parent would logically do or say? What is the first thing that you, the reader, as a parent, would think? Is your first thought that someone must have driven out to your remote home, put a ladder against the outside wall, removed the child and closed the window afterwards?

No, of course not. Your first thought is that the child got out of the crib and crawled or toddled off somewhere, either in pursuit of a favorite toy or stuffed animal or else to find another place to sleep. Children forever want to sleep in "mommy's bed" or "on the couch." Your first instinct upon discovering your child out of his crib is to look for him.

But not Charles Lindbergh. He apparently was clairvoyant. While Anne and Betty Gow were still innocently wondering where Charles, Jr. was, Colonel Lindbergh, without looking for the child or suggesting any other alternative, simply announced, "Anne, they have stolen our baby."

There was no hesitation. Colonel Lindbergh immediately drew attention away from any other alternative and planted the seed that the child had been kidnapped. He needed to draw attention away from the truth. He knew that if he did not convince Anne and Betty immediately of a real kidnapping there was a chance that they would suspect the truth, that this was one of his sick practical jokes.

In fact, he was correct. In the March 2 letter Anne stated that both she and Betty had originally harbored the same suspicion when they discovered the baby missing: that Colonel Lindbergh had taken the baby as one of his cruel jokes. It was only Lindbergh's statement, "Anne, they have stolen our baby," coupled with his expression at the time, that diverted Anne's suspicion away from the Colonel onto a possible unknown third party.

Had Lindbergh led, or even allowed, a search of the mansion for the child, the whole kidnapping theory might not have been accepted by the household and Lindbergh knew it. Two months earlier Lindbergh had hidden the child in a closet, creating a household panic that the child had been kidnapped. A frantic mother had searched the house for the child to no avail. Lindbergh howled in glee at his wife's anguish. If he suggested or organized yet another house search everyone would recall the previous one and no one would believe there had been a kidnapping. Suspicion would immediately focus on him, suspicion which might never dissipate.

Thus he had to immediately plant the idea of the outside kidnapping. He did two things. He did not search the house which he knew would be to no avail. And he immediately stated that the child had been kidnapped.

He did not search because it was futile. He said the baby was stolen because he knew the baby was not to be found nearby.

These two actions, taken together, come as close to constituting a confession as exists anywhere in this case.

There is one other incriminating aspect to his statement. In the excitement attendant to the discovery of the empty crib, Lindbergh made a slight slip. His statement was, "Anne, they have stolen our baby." Those exact words were reported in the police notes, and testified to by Betty Gow at the trial. Every writer since then who has researched the case has reported those as the exact six words Lindbergh uttered. "Anne, *they* have stolen our baby."

At that point there was no other evidence of a kidnapping. The ransom note had not even been found, let alone opened and read. Yet, Lindbergh used the plural word *"they."* It was not until the note was opened that it was learned that it claimed, *"we* have your baby."

Since Lindbergh had not opened the note at that time and supposedly did not know what was in it, how did he know to use the plural "they?"

Consider this rationally. If you discover your child's crib empty and suspect foul play, wouldn't you instinctively say, "our baby has been stolen!" Why would you use "they?"

Who does "they" refer to? Lindbergh's use of "they" was a slip. He knew the note claimed kidnapping by a group. He knew what was in the unopened note because he had recently written it.

Lindbergh proceeded into his own room and loaded his rifle while instructing Whately to call the local Hopewell Police.

Although it is somewhat suspicious that under those circumstances a parent would delegate that important task to someone else, it's possible if he or she believed the abductor to be still close by and that someone else could call while he set off to recover the child. Under those circumstances delegation of the responsibility of securing police help is plausible.

But what is neither plausible nor likely is Lindbergh's subsequent choice of telephone usage. He himself made two telephone calls. The second one was to the New Jersey State Police to inform them of his son's kidnapping. The first was to his New York lawyer, Colonel Henry Breckinridge.

Again, we would ask the reader to imagine himself in the position of the father who fears that his child has been kidnapped. Who do you call first? Wouldn't it be logical to call the police to enlist their assistance? Why did Lindbergh call his lawyer? What need did Lindbergh have, or think he had, at that time, of a lawyer? A lawyer protects a client's legal interest. What legal interest did Lindbergh fear might be in so much jeopardy that he would call him before calling the state police to inform them his child was missing?

Of course Lindbergh and Breckinridge are both dead and these questions cannot be put to them. And even if we could, Lindbergh might invoke the attorney/client privilege to avoid an answer. But even without an answer the question remains, and Lindbergh's preference in who he called first is disturbing. Did Lindbergh fully confide in Breckinridge? Did he tell him that he had made a colossal goof, had inadvertently killed his child in a moment of foolhardiness, and now, to cover up such a blunder from media and public ridicule, had concocted a kidnapping hoax? Did he enlist Colonel Breckinridge's help in this scheme as personal advisor and lawyer?

We do not know and probably never will. However, we do know that Colonel Breckinridge immediately dropped whatever he was doing in New York and rushed to Lindbergh's side where he remained throughout the kidnapping ordeal, the ransom demands from, and negotiations with, various alternative parties, and the pay-off of a ransom and discovery of the child's body in May. Colonel Breckinridge advised Lindbergh, counseled him, supported him in his power tussle with the police and participated in virtually all of the various steps in the investigation and ransom pay-off. Keeping in mind the function of a lawyer, even a high powered one like Breckinridge, would a lawyer devote so much attention if Lindbergh were merely a victim? Breckinridge was there to protect his client, but only Breckinridge and Lindbergh knew why Lindbergh needed protection.

After the calls, Lindbergh dashed outside, ostensibly to look around for the kidnappers. During his absence, Anne, Betty and the Whatelys did what had apparently not occurred to the Colonel to do: they logically began to search for Charles, Jr.

They found nothing, and presently Ollie Whately joined Lindbergh outside where the Colonel instructed him to proceed into town to obtain flashlights. When the Colonel returned to the house he went back up to the nursery. It was here, he later claimed, that for the first time he spotted the sealed ransom note.

The discovery of the note at that time is troubling. If the note had been left by a kidnapper why wasn't it seen earlier? The Colonel had immediately suggested kidnapping upon seeing the empty crib. Why hadn't a note been spotted, or at least looked for?

Even more troubling is the fact that after Colonel Lindbergh had dashed outside Betty, Anne and Elsie Whately had searched for the child. Wouldn't it have been logical for them to start by thoroughly searching the child's room? In closets, behind radiators, under bureaus and in commodes - all must have been searched. Yet they had not seen any note propped on the radiator by the fateful window.

Perhaps they hadn't seen it because it wasn't there. It wasn't there because no kidnapper had left it.

And what about the Colonel's actions upon "finding" the note? These are also suspicious. He called Betty Gow upstairs to show her the location of the note. Ostensibly, the purpose of her being summoned was so that she could go back downstairs to the kitchen to get a knife, which she did. But what purpose would that have served? If he decided to open the note and damn the fingerprints, he wouldn't have needed a letter opener. And if he did need a knife it would have been quicker for him to dash downstairs and back up with one than calling Betty to make three trips. The only logical purpose for her being summoned was so she could corroborate his having found the note.

Once he had the knife he did not use it. The instinctive reaction of any parent who believes his child has been taken and who then discovers the existence of a probable note from the kidnapper is to rip it open.

Yet Lindbergh did not touch the note. Further, he ordered all in the household to refrain from touching it. He explained that this was to save any fingerprints or other evidence which might remain. It certainly is true that not tampering with or handling

230 Ahlgren -- Monier

any piece of evidence in a criminal investigation makes it more likely that the police can secure relevant evidence.

The restraint claimed here is admirable. But is it believable? Are we to believe that Lindbergh not only resisted ripping open the note to learn its contents but also had the cold presence of mind to order others not to touch it? He didn't need to open that letter because he knew its contents. Opening that letter was not going to lead to his son's safe return, because he knew his son was already dead.

CHAPTER XIX

If it were only Lindbergh's behavior immediately before and on the night of the kidnapping which was atypical, it would be tempting to ascribe this to a coincidental series of statistical aberrations. His prank of hiding the baby two months earlier might be a coincidence.

Perhaps he just happened to order that the baby not be disturbed.

He might have just "forgotten" his speaking engagement on the same night that another unrelated and unrevealed errand caused him to arrive home late.

Perhaps a sudden whimsy led to honking his horn as he drove up the driveway.

It is possible he was just too tired that night to look in on his son in the one and one-half hours between his arrival and the discovery of the empty crib.

Maybe he had exceptionally sharp hearing and so was the only one who heard a snapping sound.

Perhaps upon seeing the empty crib he had had some sort of extra-sensory hunch that the child was stolen and that a search of the home would be fruitless, and further that a gang ("they") was involved.

Perhaps Lindbergh was a person of extraordinary restraint and self-control and so did not open the note.

Perhaps Lindbergh had other pressing business to discuss with his lawyer that was more important than notifying the police about the kidnapping.

We know he was a calm individual. In fact when the local Hopewell Police arrived they found Anne, Betty Gow and the Whatelys in an agitated state, as could well be expected under the circumstances. However, Deputy Chief Williamson remarked that although the other household members were agitated he found

Colonel Lindbergh very calm and collected throughout that evening. And Anne, writing to her mother-in- law on March 2 remarked that following the kidnapping she noticed her husband to be "*marvelous* -calm, clear, alert and observing."30

If the above were the only factors we could say, although perhaps not convincingly, that by themselves they are not persuasive.

However, Lindbergh's behavior in the days following the kidnapping remained more consistent with the actions of a participant attempting to hide his involvement, than with a victim's behavior.

First of all, there was his insistence on heading up the investigation. The traditional explanation has been laudable: he was so concerned with the return of his child that he wanted to be personally involved to ensure the project's success. And the image the press created was noble: Lindbergh conferring with his advisors, Lindbergh keeping abreast of developments and reviewing options, and later Lindbergh traipsing off to New York to personally deliver ransom money.

It was, without a doubt, ultimate macho. Charles took charge while Anne, the distraught and pregnant mother, stayed home and wrung her hands in anguish.

The problem with the image is that Colonel Lindbergh did not just participate in the investigation, he headed it. He insisted not only on being informed of all developments, but also on making all decisions. He actually threatened to shoot any policemen who made a move without him.

Was it because he was concerned for his son and wanted to help? This traditional explanation was, and has been, readily accepted. But Colonel Lindbergh was not stupid. He knew that he was not a policeman or otherwise trained in criminal investigations. He knew that the personal advisors he brought in on the case, Colonels Breckinridge and Donovan, were also not trained criminal investigators. He had supposedly been so cool and logical in not touching the nursery note and ordering all others to similarly refrain. If he knew enough to defer in that circumstance to experts, why then did he insist that he be in charge of the criminal investigation?

The answer is that it was the only way to ensure that he knew what the police were discovering, who they were suspecting, and to ensure that they did not come after him. What criminal would not want to head the investigation of his own crime?

Neither can Lindbergh's insistence on being in charge be ascribed to any unease he had with the abilities of the New Jersey State Police. If that were the case then why, when J. Edgar Hoover sent an FBI agent to assist in the investigation, did Lindbergh coldly rebuff the offer?

To the FBI he was openly hostile and would provide no information. Special Agent J.M. Keith in a report to Hoover on April 9, 1932, summarized that it was obvious that Colonel Lindbergh was keeping things from him.

Why would the supposed victim/parent, concerned about the return of his son, refuse help from the one agency in the United States whose experience and training made it the best candidate to solve the crime? After all, he accepted help from an untold number of cranks, kooks, tipsters, clairvoyants and assorted underworld hustlers who paraded through the case. Did he oppose help from the FBI precisely because it was in fact the one agency in the United States with the experience and training to solve the crime? Did the thought of FBI involvement frighten Lindbergh?

Instead, from his Hopewell headquarters he directed two simultaneous courses of action. On the one hand he systematically blocked every logical police procedure which might have led to the discovery of helpful information. At the same time he replaced good solid police procedure with his own methods, which had no other purpose than to obscure the trail and create as many false leads as possible which led away from Hopewell.

In line with blocking accepted police practices is Lindbergh's reaction to New York Police Commissioner Mulrooney's plan to stake out the mailboxes in the area from which the ransom notes were being mailed. The first follow-up ransom note by mail had arrived at Hopewell on March 5, 1932 having been postmarked in Brooklyn on March 4, 1932 at 9:00 p.m. Mulrooney suggested the logical possibility that the kidnapper lived in Brooklyn and the next note might be mailed from that area. A team of detectives could be assigned to watch every mailbox which would in turn be fitted with a device to hold each letter. After every letter was mailed the detectives could retrieve it, check the address and, if the letter were addressed to Lindbergh, follow the mailer.

Yet this suggestion, which was sound, logical and which epitomized good solid police work and could have led to the uncovering of the kidnapper (if there were one), and the rescue of the child, was vetoed by the child's father. This man, who prided himself on his cool, his logic, his almost emotionless calculating mind, vetoed it.

In fact, he did more than just veto it. When Lindbergh learned what Mulrooney was about to do he hysterically forbade it and threatened to have Mulrooney broken if he crossed him on this. With Donovan and Breckinridge by his side, and given Lindbergh's general social standing, he probably could have done it.

Mulrooney backed down. It was just one example of how good police procedure in this case was countermanded by a direct Lindbergh order.

Subsequent Lindbergh apologists have argued that this position was motivated by his concern for the welfare of his child and the desire for his safe return. The fact that another ransom note was mailed from one of the mailboxes which would have been staked out has been characterized as unfortunate. Lindbergh just happened to be wrong on that point.

If this were an isolated incident where Lindbergh just "made a mistake" in his handling of his son's disappearance that explanation might be more persuasive. The problem is that the Mulrooney incident was one of a whole series which were more than just "unfortunate."

If the subsequent ransom notes were in fact false and were being mailed by someone who, whatever his motivation, was not a kidnapper, and if Lindbergh knew this, then Lindbergh would not want that person caught. The discovery that no kidnapper was making ransom demands might cause the authorities to rethink their investigation. There is too much in his reaction to, and his control of, police actions to attribute them all to "mistakes in judgement." Is it believable that he just happened to be wrong about the Mulrooney plan, that he just made a mistake with regard to assuming command of the investigation, that he was just too grief stricken to make the right decision about including the FBI and sharing information with them, that later on in the investigation he just happened to show poor judgement in attempting to prevent the recording of the serial numbers of the ransom money, and that he just made a mistake in forbidding any stakeout or surveillance of the ransom pay-off area?

Are these just "errors in judgement" by the man who was so composed that when he spotted the nursery note he knew enough to protect its evidentiary value? Not likely. These "mistakes" appear to fit a pattern of behavior in which Lindbergh deliberately sabotaged the investigation.

Lindbergh's actions in the days immediately following the child's disappearance also seemed designed to invite fraudulent claims, create misleading clues and provide a rich, albeit false, breeding ground for police investigative ventures.

Lindbergh immediately decreed two things about the kidnappers for which there was no factual basis. First, he announced that the kidnappers were connected with the underworld or organized crime and second, that they were from New York. He then steered police efforts in both of those directions despite the fact that there was nothing in the note, or in the circumstances of the disappearance, to suggest that either underworld characters or New Yorkers were involved.

Pursuing this line, he brought into the case Rossner, Spitale and Bitz. One has to again ask why an intelligent, coldly rational man would involve randomly picked small time New York con men and divulge to them the most secret, intimate details of the kidnapping and the ransom notes, including the important "secret signatures" used to identify the kidnappers.

Lindbergh had to know the outcome of such a course of action. His March 4, 1932 invitation to the kidnappers to have their representative contact his representative, is nothing more than an open invitation to fraud, an inducement to attract a virtual cavalcade of flim-flam artists and fraudulent negotiators.

Rossner saw the nursery note and may have even had a copy of it. He could have been the source for whoever mailed the first follow-up letter on the evening of March 4 from Brooklyn. When it arrived, he went off to New York with it. Thereafter followed a flood of further ransom demands, notes, tips and people claiming either to have special knowledge of, or be in contact with the kidnappers.

While on the one hand Lindbergh firmly excluded Mulrooney and the FBI, on the other he actively solicited thugs like Rossner, Bitz and Spitale, adventurists like John Curtis, known swindlers like Gaston Means, dizzy socialites like Evalyn McLean and blowhards like Dr. Condon. Only his efforts to involve incarcerated gangsters like Al Capone, were stymied. As Alan Hynd originally titled his essay on the case, "Everyone Wanted To Get In On The Act."

Whenever the police investigate a major crime they try to keep its details secret. One reason is so that they will be able to later assess the reliability of subsequent confessions and leads.

Lindbergh knew that. Yet, through the involvement of these other parties, and the release of his public statement, he purposely revealed details of the kidnapping, thereby making it easier for fraudulent overtures. Why would he do this? Was it to improve the likelihood of the child's safe return? It is hard to see how that pattern of behavior would lead to anything except chaos.

Or, was it for a more sinister purpose? Did Lindbergh know that without his public appeal there would be no real leads, no real kidnappers with whom to negotiate, and that no real demands would be made by anyone knowing the signature code? His actions in the days immediately following the child's disappearance are inconsistent with those of a grieving father anxious for his child's return. They are, however, consistent with a perpetrator anxious to spread suspicion as far and wide as possible and to create countless clues for the police to chase.

When the police did develop a sound avenue of inquiry that could have led to the solving of the crime, or at least the uncovering of relevant clues, Lindbergh vehemently and consistently obstructed that path. When the time came to pay the ransom to Cemetery John, the money was to be loaded in a box. The police, quite understandably, began to record the serial numbers of the bills before they were put in the box. Yet

Lindbergh again objected and tried to prevent the recording of the bills. Again we have to ask why.

His stated rationale, and the one most advanced since then, was his desire not to interfere with the return of his child. However, this was not logical. The plan was that the money was to be handed over and the child returned simultaneously.

Once the child was returned Lindbergh had no interest, or should have had no interest, in the protection of the kidnappers. If the serial numbers were recorded then the money might be tracked weeks, months or even years later and the crime thereby solved. In fact, when the serial numbers were recorded it was their trail which led to Hauptmann's arrest.

Why then oppose that? Once the child was returned, Lindbergh should *want* the crime solved and the kidnappers caught.

Although the evidence on this point is sketchy, some speculation is possible. One possibility is to relate this incident to the 1929 attempted extortion on Constance Morrow. In both cases the amount of the ransom was exactly the same, $50,000.00. In both cases the money was to be put in a box. In both cases the source of the funds was not the Lindbergh family but the Morrow family, whom Lindbergh disliked and who felt the same about him. But, the Morrows were wealthy and it was their family which ultimately paid the $50,000.00 ransom for the Lindbergh baby.

Suppose, for whatever reason, that Charles Lindbergh was behind both of these incidents. The letter to Constance Morrow in 1929 may have been a cruel joke, or, it may have been a way for Lindbergh, a person not born to independent wealth but who was about to marry a woman from wealth, to get money from his future in-laws whom he detested. If so, the Constance Morrow incident may have been in part an extortion attempt gone awry.

Suppose that the March 1, 1932 incident was a practical joke gone bad. The "kidnapping" was an effort to cover Lindbergh's stupidity. As he developed the cover and invited negotiations he began getting ransom demands which he, and only he, knew were fraudulent. He knew that Cemetery John had to be a con man.

He then found himself in a position where he had to deliver $50,000.00 of his in-laws' money to a person he knew was not the kidnapper, and could not lead to the return of the child. Wouldn't that money be better spent towards the purchase of a new airplane or some other similar expenditure?

Accordingly, Lindbergh might very well have developed a plan to pocket a portion of the ransom money. If he got $50,000.00 and only turned over $18,000.00 or $19,000.00 to the kidnappers, who was going to complain? The extortionist obviously didn't have the child so he would not be heard from again.

Doesn't this scenario make more sense as to why Lindbergh opposed the recording of the serial numbers? Keep in mind also that the balance of the ransom money, with the exception of that found in Hauptmann's garage or passed by Hauptmann or someone else earlier, never turned up.

There is another clue which seems to have been overlooked.

The "kidnappers" had said that the $50,000.00 was to be placed in a box of a certain size. When Lindbergh and his associates had tried to do that in New Jersey they discovered that the money would not quite fit. Ultimately, the money was stuffed in and Lindbergh had to kneel on the box to close it.

Yet when Jafsie got the box from Lindbergh at St. Raymond's Cemetery and handed it to Cemetery John the latter insisted on counting the money. Jafsie's testimony was that John opened the box and flipped through the loose bills. Realizing that he did not have time to count it he said, "It's okay I guess," and simply closed it. He had no trouble closing the box and certainly did not have to kneel on it. Is this because the box now contained less money than it had in New Jersey? Did Lindbergh get cold feet and later destroy the money he knew to be marked and, if so, is that why the bulk of the ransom money has never been recovered?

Lindbergh also opposed the staking out of the site for the delivery of the ransom money and the following of the "kidnapper." Was it to protect his child, whom he claimed to expect to be safely returned, or was it to prevent the discovery that there had been no kidnapping?

Lindbergh's actions throughout this period, consistent with a theory of him as perpetrator, were not limited to his involvement in the police aspect of the case, or to his negotiations with the claimants. His personal decisions also were directed towards leading the trail elsewhere while covering up any real clues.

In addition to negotiating with anyone and everyone, Lindbergh was constantly on the move. He flew over the Buzzards Bay area to look for the boat, *Nelly*. When the child's body was discovered, Colonel Lindbergh was at sea, searching for yet another boat. Again, Lindbergh was leading police investigators away from Hopewell, this time to boats in the Atlantic.

Lindbergh's reaction to the whole Jafsie intervention is consistent with his knowledge that Jafsie could not lead to either the return of his child or the discovery of the kidnappers.

When Jafsie first approached Lindbergh the Colonel did not believe him. He instead believed Jafsie to be part of an extortion plot. This was despite the fact that the ransom notes which Jafsie received had the secret signature code. Why was Lindbergh so certain Jafsie was only an extortionist and not dealing with the real kidnappers? In fact, in order to watch Jafsie, Lindbergh had Colonel Breckinridge move into Jafsie's apartment.

And finally, when the child's body was found on May 12, 1932 it was certainly clear then that the child would not be coming home alive. The case was elevated from a kidnapping to a murder. When the body was found the only remaining issue was "who did this?" And the most important piece of evidence in any murder case is invariably the body itself. An extensive autopsy with toxicology tests and a pathological examination is the accepted method to detect the exact cause of death and glean possible clues.

Again, Lindbergh, the supposedly logical, intelligent man made a decision which could not possibly be attributed to a desire on his part to catch the kidnappers. Lindbergh identified the body in the morgue after a 90 second examination. He then ordered the body cremated. He did this before any toxicology tests, pathological exam, or a full autopsy could be undertaken. He was Lindbergh, and his orders were carried out to the letter.

Within the hour, the remains, and any further evidence or clues they may have provided, were destroyed.

CHAPTER XX

When the child's body was found, Lindbergh's efforts came to a grinding halt, and so did the influx of tips, leads, ransom demands and offers of help. Once Lindbergh stopped, the case stopped.

All that remained for the investigation of the case was diligent, laborious police work. With Lindbergh's direct involvement at an end, so too was the craziness of the preceding two months. As Colonel Schwarzkopf said, "everything is different now," and thereafter strict police investigative techniques were the rule.

The course of the police investigation and ultimately the arrest, trial, conviction and execution of Bruno Richard Hauptmann are discussed elsewhere in this book. However, Lindbergh's actions subsequent to the discovery of the body, although not always directly related to the investigation, are still illustrative and supportive of the proposition that he, and not some third party, was responsible for his son's death. Factors concerning the discovery of the body itself also support that position.

There were the issues of why the child was killed; how the child died; why and how the body was left where it was.

At Hauptmann's trial the prosecution attempted to answer these questions by fitting the known facts into their "Hauptmann as Lone Wolf" theory. They argued, without supporting evidence, that Hauptmann's original intent had been to kidnap the child and hold him for ransom. Towards that end the original nursery note had been left.

However, on the way out the window the ladder had broken, and Hauptmann had slipped and dropped the child, crushing his skull. In a panic Hauptmann had dumped the baby's body in the woods close to the road and fled back to the Bronx. Once there Hauptmann had recovered his wits, assumed that the body had not been found, and continued with his plan to collect the ransom.

In addition to the fact that there was no evidence for this scenario, there were also several problems with it which were never explained during the course of the trial.

For instance, if Hauptmann had taken the child to hold for ransom, what was his plan? Hauptmann lived in a two-family home in the Bronx. At the time he had no children. The prosecution was satisfied that Hauptmann's wife Anna had no knowledge of the kidnapping and was not part of any plot.

So what was Hauptmann going to do with the baby? Would he tell Anna he found it and they ought to keep this 20 month old toddler for a few days? What was he going to tell his neighbors, that his curly haired "nephew" from Germany had arrived unexpectedly, and just happened to look exactly like the baby whose picture was suddenly appearing on the front page of every newspaper in America? What was his plan?

There was no evidence that he had rented any other apartment or room in which to keep the baby, and how could he without a neighbor, or his wife, finding out about it? The prosecution further maintained that Hauptmann acted alone, without accomplices, agents, co-conspirators or helpers. So, if he were going to hold the baby for ransom, what was he going to do with it in the meantime? The prosecution never answered this and the question was never asked.

The second problem never addressed is why Hauptmann, discovering that he had killed the child, would dump the body at all, and if so, why so close to the Hopewell home?

If a kidnapper dropped the baby and killed him, why take the body with him? Wouldn't the kidnapper have been better off to have left the body and fled through the woods to his car? Lugging the dead child certainly would not prevent detection of the crime, because the crime would be obvious as soon as the child's absence was noticed. These actions would not be logical. The facts as they are known do not support the prosecution's theory.

However, a clever prosecutor might argue that neither do the facts disprove the original theory. In fact, in his opening statement to the jury, Wilentz argued that when Hauptmann had accidentally killed the child, he instantly and coolly reformulated his plan and took the body in order to maintain a modified version of his ransom scheme.

But if so, why would any kidnapper then have dumped the body so close to the Lindbergh home where the likelihood of its discovery was increased? Once he got the child into the car wouldn't he have been better able to hide it the farther away he drove from the Lindberghs? Wouldn't it be logical that the closer an area was to the house the more intensely it would be searched?

There is also the problem of the location of the body. The Bronx is north of Hopewell, New Jersey. The body was found in Mt. Rose, three miles south of the Lindbergh home. If Hauptmann kidnapped the child, dropped him, and in a panic decided to dump the body, why would he drive south, away from his destination? His route back to the Bronx would not have taken him to Mt. Rose, and driving north would have afforded him many secluded areas to dump a body. Driving south, dumping the body, and then doubling back, only prolonged his time in the area, thereby increasing his chances of apprehension. The body was dumped south of Hopewell because it was not dumped by a person heading back to the Bronx, but by a person merely looking for any place to dump a body.

One could theorize that Hauptmann was still guilty but that the prosecution was wrong: namely that Hauptmann's intent all along had been to kill the child and then hide the body as part of a comprehensive plan in which he would not have to care for the child but could still collect a ransom. Wilentz changed his theory and adopted this one in his closing argument.

There are four problems with this. First, the body was lying on top of the ground, which is consistent with the child having been dumped there in a panic by a person who had not planned to murder the child. If Hauptmann had planned to murder the child, wouldn't he have brought a shovel and buried the evidence?

Second, the body was found close to the road - William Allen had only gone into the woods far enough to go to the bathroom when he found the baby. This too, is consistent with a person having hurriedly dumped it.

Third, the body was close to the Lindbergh house, which again is consistent with the child having been killed unexpectedly and then quickly dumped there by a person who did not have time to travel far.

Fourth, even if the child were intentionally killed by Hauptmann, there remains the problem of why he would first proceed south, thereby forcing himself to double back.

These factors are inconsistent with any theory except the theory that Lindbergh did it. If Lindbergh inadvertently killed the child and decided to hide the body, he would have had a limited time before he would have to return and make an appearance.

In his moment of panic shortly before 8:00 p.m. on March 1, he would have realized he had to dispose of the body. Since he had told Anne that he would be only a little late he could not travel too far. When the Lindberghs were building their house they had lived in nearby Mount Rose. The Colonel had traveled in the area while supervising the construction. He was familiar with the terrain and knew the woods there.

The spot where the body was left was less than three miles from the Hopewell home. Traveling the country roads at even the reduced speed of thirty miles per hour would result in a total round trip travel time of twelve minutes.

Once in the woods he would have left the body quickly. There was no time to go too far into the woods. There was no time to dig a grave, nor did he have an implement to do so. Any delay in the woods would increase the chances of being caught. He would leave the body on top of the ground, hurriedly covered with some brush and leaves. The total time needed for this would be between two and three minutes.

Assuming he had been poised to begin his "prank" upon Betty Gow's 7:50 departure from the nursery, the total time in the nursery at Hopewell and on the ground below would be less than seven minutes.

The total time necessary, at the outside, would be twenty-two minutes. Assuming that the 7:50 and 8:25 times are accurate, the Colonel would have had an extra thirteen minutes to wait in the woods to assure that Betty had left the nursery, to sit on the ground outside the window afterwards and reformulate his plan, drive a little more cautiously to Mount Rose and carefully exit his car before entering the woods, and still return by 8:25 p.m. to be only slightly late. The facts concerning the location of the child's body support not the case against Hauptmann, but rather the case against Lindbergh.

Although his actions after the discovery of his son's body were not directed towards controlling the investigation, they still support the proposition that it was Lindbergh who caused his own son's death. Moreover, the doubt originally experienced by Anne Lindbergh endured, persisting even after Hauptmann's conviction.

Upon Hauptmann's arrest, the evidence against him was presented to Lindbergh. The Colonel carefully reviewed it, organized it and then took it to Anne where he spent some time convincing her of the strength of the police case. No one knows exactly what went on at that meeting or what was said; but it is clear that Lindbergh felt compelled to convince his wife of Hauptmann's guilt.

The traditional explanation by his biographers has been that Lindbergh was a cautious man who wanted to carefully review the evidence to ensure that Hauptmann was the guilty party and not the victim of a witch hunt. His own careful review of the evidence might in fact be explained by such an eccentricity in his character. However, this does not explain why he then felt compelled to take the evidence to Anne to convince her. She certainly did not share that eccentricity. Did he feel compelled to convince her because she doubted?

There is a common pattern of behavior in criminal cases where the victim or victims believe in the guilt of the accused right from the start. They participate in the investigation and trial with zest, determined that the accused be convicted.

There is another pattern of behavior, although not as common, which sometimes occurs in violent crimes - the victim, or in murder cases, the victim's family - participates in the investigation and sits through the trial because of a need to know what happened. Even if they know "who did it," they want to know about the last moments of their loved one.

But both authors of this book are unaware of other cases in which a husband and wife, or other joint victims who (supposedly) had the same degree of knowledge of the crime, differed so much in either their involvement in the investigation or in their expressed certainty of the guilt of the accused.

Lindbergh, for whatever reason, felt compelled to convince Anne of Hauptmann's guilt. The obvious deduction is that she doubted and his efforts were designed to erase that doubt.

Why did she doubt? When we view her uncertainty in light of her letter to her mother-in-law on March 2, 1932 in which she stated she originally suspected her husband, the urgency of the Colonel's efforts to convince her is subject to a darker, more unsettling interpretation. She doubted because she suspected her husband. Since he was trying to erase her doubts even after Hauptmann's arrest, can we infer that she still suspected him?

Lindbergh's actions also become more understandable during this period. One of the most dangerous times for the culprit who believes he has committed "the perfect crime" occurs not immediately after the initial cover-up, but later, when suspicion focuses on another. The actual perpetrator finds himself in a quandary. Although most people might believe that the perpetrator would jump on the prosecution bandwagon and point a finger at the falsely accused, this rarely happens. It is too risky.

On the one hand he may be tempted to state and later to testify that "that is the man I saw lurking outside my house the night my wife was killed," since if someone else is convicted the actual perpetrator will probably be safe forever.

However, what happens if he states that the accused is "the one," only to have it turn out conclusively, when additional information is uncovered, that the person he has identified could not have possibly done the crime? Everyone will remember the accusation, and the inquiry may shift to why there was a positive identification of an innocent person. Of course the perpetrator can claim that he just happened to be wrong, but the questions will linger.

The solution for one confronted with this dilemma is to tell the police that he is unsure and then keep his eyes open. If while maintaining his uncertainty, the proof of the innocence of the wrongfully accused surfaces the real perpetrator is safe. In fact, at that point his professed uncertainty may serve to heighten his credibility. Only when the actual perpetrator learns that the evidence against the wrongfully accused is overwhelming is it safe for him to throw in with the prosecution.

This was the situation with Charles Stuart. When Stuart gave a description of the black man who killed his wife, police focused on one William Bennett. Yet despite police prompting, Stuart would only initially say that the picture of Bennett "looked like" that of the gunman. Had Stuart's plan not ultimately unraveled, he no doubt would have testified against Bennett at the latter's trial, identifying him positively as the gunman and thereby assuring Bennett's conviction.

Lindbergh found himself in the same quandary. To jump on Hauptmann too early, to positively identify his voice as the one at the cemetery was risky if Hauptmann ultimately proved his alibi. Lindbergh's actions following Hauptmann's arrest, his original reluctance to identify Hauptmann's voice, his demand to personally review the police file to ascertain the prosecutorial merit, and then after seeing what other evidence the police had, only then publicly identifying his voice at the trial, and his willingness to lie at that trial, are all actions consistent with Lindbergh as perpetrator. Although these actions have previously puzzled Lindbergh biographers and other students of this crime, they are readily understandable when viewed in the context of Lindbergh as killer.

Once Lindbergh ascertained that the case against Hauptmann was strong and a public commitment to that position was not risky, he then had to convince Anne. Yet it is still unclear just how successful he was. Even after the jury returned the guilty verdict against Hauptmann on February 26, 1935, there is Harold Nicolson's observations of the Lindberghs when they learned of the verdict over the radio.

Anne was white and very still and even at that point Nicolson read doubt on her face. The Colonel then went on at length with Nicolson, outlining the strengths of the prosecution's case. At first Nicolson was perplexed as to why Lindbergh would do this, since he was intimately familiar with the case. Then he realized that although Lindbergh was talking to him he was actually speaking for the benefit of Anne, whose face still bore traces of doubt.

The import of this should not be minimized. Anne Lindbergh and Betty Gow had both, back on March 1, 1932, suspected Colonel Lindbergh. Now, almost three years later and after a jury had convicted Bruno Richard Hauptmann, Anne's face still betrayed doubt and Colonel Lindbergh was still attempting to convince her. One can only wonder how long her doubt remained and if in fact it ever disappeared - Anne told the writer Ludovic Kennedy that if a miscarriage of justice had taken place, she did not want it glossed over.

Once Lindbergh became convinced of the strength of the case against Hauptmann he would have found it safe not only to convince Anne, and to throw in his lot with the prosecution, but also to lie under oath at Hauptmann's trial.

He lied that he could identify Hauptmann's voice as that of Cemetery John's "Hey Doctor!"; he lied that he had never doubted or questioned his ability to recognize the voice; and he lied that he had never suspected Jafsie. He also lied that *Wahgoosh* would not have barked. By then the case against Hauptmann was like a rushing waterfall and there was no risk to Lindbergh of throwing in another bucketful.

Even after the trial, conviction and execution of Bruno Richard Hauptmann, the subsequent actions and deeds of Colonel Lindbergh call into question not only the guilt of Hauptmann, but Lindbergh's belief in it.

Hauptmann was a German. At the time of his arrest he was still a German citizen. He spoke with a heavy German accent. In World War I he had fought in the German army.

His prosecutor, David Wilentz, was Jewish. When interviewed much later about the case, Wilentz admitted to having anguished over this fact and had considered not personally prosecuting the case because of the troublesome appearance which might be presented by his prosecuting a German. South Jersey was full of German immigrants and he did not want to lose a conviction due to some public perception of impropriety. After wrestling with the issue, he eschewed such concerns and took the case.

It is hard, if not impossible, to ascertain the exact cause of a person's prejudice, racism, or other bigotry. Certainly a bad experience with a member of a particular ethnicity can be a contributing factor. If the police version of this case is correct and if Colonel Lindbergh believed this version, then a German killed his son in 1932 and was brought to justice by a Jew in 1935. Yet before that decade had ended Lindbergh had become extremely pro-German and pro-Nazi and at the same time an anti-Semite. In isolation those developments might not be noteworthy. But when viewed in conjunction with what Lindbergh claimed to believe as the facts in his son's death, his later racism is more than ironic, it is troublesome.

We do not wish to argue that if there had been a kidnapping that experience coupled with the subsequent trial should have made Lindbergh either pro-Jewish or an anti- German bigot. If it had not, he could have been commended for resisting such low forces.

Yet isn't it more than ironic that he went full speed in the opposite direction? Ironic, that is, unless in fact he never believed that a German had killed his son and a Jew had rightfully prosecuted. Perhaps his subsequent staunch support of Germany on the eve of World War II was motivated in part by a subliminal guilt that a German had died after being falsely accused and prosecuted by a Jew. Ultimate rationalization could easily come into play here as Lindbergh could come to believe that he was not responsible for Hauptmann's death, Wilentz was.

If so, the rationalization did not stop there. Neither did his efforts to convince others that Hauptmann was guilty, even after the latter had been executed. Lindbergh's *Autobiography Of Values* was published in 1976, a project begun and mostly completed before his death in 1974. In the book he devotes portions of just thirteen paragraphs to the kidnapping and murder of his son, the ransom negotiations, the subsequent two and one-half year investigation, the trial and the impact of all of this on his family.

The details he does present are clearly filtered. Although he does not mention the snapping sound, he emphasized that he was in the parlor with his wife. Yet in the one and one-half hours from his return until the child was discovered missing only about five minutes were spent by Lindbergh in the parlor. Was this a further effort, forty years after the incident, to reinforce his alibi?

He also talks of having worked "with Federal, State and City police" yet the reality is that he refused to work with the federals or help them in any way. His relationship with the State and City police was not so much a working relationship as one of master and servant. He also discusses obtaining the ransom money from J.P. Morgan and how "[t]heir bank clerks selected gold notes and listed the number of each one as a step towards the eventual apprehension of the kidnapper." He does not mention that he opposed this step.

And lastly, he admits to stealing away from the United States on December 22, 1935 while Bruno Richard Hauptmann languished on death row in Trenton but attributes this to a desire to protect his family. He does not admit his love affair with Nazism or the Third Reich.

Lindbergh's later actions, consistent with a theory of him as perpetrator, do not stop with the overt actions of his relationship with Germany, Germans and Nazism or the revisionist history of the case advanced in his *Autobiography Of Values*.

The biggest admissions of all, the unalterable behaviors of Lindbergh which speak volumes across the decades since that fateful night in March of 1932, and which serve to point straight at the Colonel as the party responsible for his son's death, are actually three non-actions.

The existence of a mere thirteen paragraphs in his autobiography devoted to the kidnapping, its aftermath and the misleading presentation contained therein, indicate an effort to hide the facts from the public. But the effort did not stop with the public. For with just one exception when a stranger came to the door claiming to be Charles, Jr., Lindbergh never discussed the kidnaping with his other children. This effort to hide, to cover-- up, to prevent discussion, extended to the end of his life.

Prior to his death he left specific instructions for the handling of his remains on his passing. Pursuant to those instructions, he was dressed in a khaki work shirt and pants, wrapped in an old Hudson's Bay blanket, and placed in a plain wooden coffin in which he was buried. Yet no one bothered to ask, or perhaps no one thought to consider, why this man, who apparently was not an advocate of cremation, had ordered his twenty month old son cremated forty-two years earlier.

Instead, the press recapped his life and extolled his virtues. They discussed all that he accomplished, the places he traveled, the causes he championed and all the people he met. Yet in this review lies the greatest admission by non-action of all. For in those last four decades of his life after his son died, not once after March 1, 1932 did Colonel Charles A. Lindbergh ever again play or attempt to play one of his so-called "practical jokes" on anyone.

The only conclusion that can be reached is that Colonel Lindbergh had learned his lesson from the one that had gone awry.

EPILOGUE

As the authors of this book, neither one of us claim to have definitely and ultimately "solved" the Lindbergh kidnapping case. However, looking at the various theories which have been popularly advanced: Hauptmann as Lone Wolf, Hauptmann as merely an extortionist, Hauptmann as innocent victim, and, our theory, Lindbergh as killer, both authors agree that the scenario in which Colonel Lindbergh killed his son by accident, and used a kidnapping story to cover his idiocy and protect his public reputation, is by far the most probable. Whether there is now sufficient evidence by which Colonel Lindbergh, were he still alive, could be convicted of negligent homicide beyond a reasonable doubt, will have to remain an academic question.

If we do not believe in the certainty of his guilt we clearly can not hope to persuade the reader, and that has not been our intention. Rather, from the outset it has been to put the events of March 1, 1932, and the aftermath, into a logical and plausible framework, and to suggest a theory which has never before been considered. We believe that the framework which we have offered is the most likely and is most consistent with the facts now known to be true.

This book does not totally break new ground and we owe a debt of gratitude to those who have researched and written about the Lindbergh case before us. As we researched and reviewed previous independent investigations, we realized that many came so close yet never made the next sequential step in logic to Lindbergh as killer; perhaps because such a step was seen as too terrible, more likely because it was not seen.

Alan Hynd in a 1949 article for *True Magazine*, "Everyone Wanted To Get Into The Act," was one of the first to understand that the case against Bruno Richard Hauptmann was shaky. He perceived the inconsistencies of the prosecution's case, the illogic, the impossibilities and the endless unanswered questions. He concluded that whether innocent or guilty Hauptmann certainly got a rough ride to the death house.

Alan Hynd did a good job, and his article helped put us on the track. He also researched and had available facts not known at the time of the trial. But Mr. Hynd was laboring under some extraordinary disadvantages that may have prevented him from uncovering the full story. Because he wrote the article before the Freedom of Information Act, the prosecution and police file and notes were not available. The real fatal flaws in the 1935 conviction remained hidden.

Anthony Scaduto in his 1976 book *Scapegoat* came one step closer. An excellent crime reporter, Mr. Scaduto was able to cleverly obtain, review and include in his book many previously unknown details of the police investigation and prosecution's case. He also, for the first time, learned and related that Colonel Lindbergh had lied on at least three occasions at Hauptmann's trial. He concluded that Hauptmann was improperly convicted on mistaken, erroneous and/or trumped up evidence. Yet he wondered in the book why Colonel Lindbergh, a person of otherwise impeccable character, had lied. Not seeing the obvious and being yet another person enamored with Lindbergh's personality, he theorized that it was to spare Anne any additional trauma an unsolved case might spawn. The noblest of purposes was ascribed to this less than noble man.

Ludovic Kennedy in *The Airman And The Carpenter* concluded categorically that Lindbergh had lied and Hauptmann was innocent. The analysis stopped there.

Yet we do not mean to criticize these earlier works. It should be kept in mind that it was the intention of Hynd to show the problems of the Lindbergh case, the intention of Scaduto to show the problems with Hauptmann's conviction and the intention of Kennedy to show that Hauptmann was innocent. None of these earlier works can be criticized for not "solving" the Lindbergh case because it was not their intention to do so.

Besides, we had two major advantages over the previous journalistic investigations. First, we had available their works as a basis and reference frame. We can no more criticize them for not solving the Lindbergh case than Daniel Boone could criticize Christopher Columbus or Lief Erickson for not discovering the Cumberland Gap. Like Columbus and Erickson, the writers who have gone before us, although not going as far, have in many ways made a greater contribution to the topic.

But our second advantage is more telling. All the prior post-conviction investigations were done by journalists. They were good journalists, and in fact Hynd and Scaduto were excellent crime reporters. But they were still journalists, with a journalistic orientation of being outside the criminal justice system looking in. A good crime reporter has his nose up against the glass, but he or she is still outside looking in.

The two authors are both players within the criminal justice system. We have assembled, dissected, analyzed and tried criminal cases ranging from simple theft rings to first degree murder. We have sat with criminal defendants in the glare of the detectives' interrogation room and the quiet sanctity of a lawyer's office and have listened to them talk about their plans, their motives, their actions and their reactions. At times we both have to think like a criminal, to put ourselves inside the crime as it unfolds and options are weighed, choices are made. We base that on our experience. We have relied heavily on that experience in this book.

Writing this book has been difficult. We all learned about Colonel Charles Augustus Lindbergh in elementary school and we have all thrilled to the movie *The Spirit of St. Louis*. For all Americans Charles Lindbergh remains one of the icons of our youth. To suggest that he would have been better portrayed in the movie by Anthony Perkins than Jimmy Stewart has not been easy. To suggest that Charles Lindbergh was a murderer (for even if he only negligently killed his child his lies strapped Bruno Richard Hauptmann in the electric chair) is in many ways like suggesting George Gipp died of AIDS.

We do not want to be reckless and we do not think we have been. We are both sensitive to the fact that Colonel Lindbergh is dead and can not defend himself. It was never our intention to take a cheap shot at the man and what we have done in this book should not be construed as an attack upon his contributions to aviation.

But another side has to be told. Traditionally Colonel Charles A. Lindbergh has been treated like a god. There is not an unflattering biography of him. True, most of the biographical work on him was done pre-Watergate when criticism of our heroes and leaders was minimal. Yet one of the best biographies of him is called *Charles Lindbergh: The Last Hero*, and one can only wonder even before reading it how accurate and objective such a work can be.

In every biography, every major character flaw of Lindbergh is twisted into an admirable trait. The cruel behavior he directed at those he disliked or who otherwise crossed him is everywhere written off as examples of his practical jokes. When he made Anne, then seven and one-half months pregnant, fly across the country in an open cockpit airplane and at one point flew so high that when they landed she was so sick from oxygen deprivation that she had to be hospitalized for several days, and when he later lied to the press to cover his blunder, the biographers cited the episode to show what a trooper Anne was. When he flew his airplane in highly risky configurations jeopardizing the lives of himself, his passengers and innocents on the ground, they talked reverently of his courage. When Charles, Jr. was learning to toddle and the Colonel tossed pillows at him to knock him down, they applauded his skill in making his son "tough." When he supported the Nazis in the 1930's they spoke admiringly of his desire to keep American boys from being killed in a European war. And when he lied at Hauptmann's trial, lies which contributed to Hauptmann's conviction and execution, they whispered of his sensitive compassion in trying to end this terrible ordeal for Anne.

It is true that after researching Lindbergh neither one of us like him very much. Was he a killer? Definitely? Possibly? Probably. We may never know for certain. But just because the answer may never be known does not mean that the question should never be asked.

The unfortunate thing is that it was not asked in 1932. If we are right, then not only did a very serious misdeed go unpunished but the perpetrator duped others into creating more victims: an innocent man's life was cut short by the electric chair, a young wife and new mother was deprived of her husband's love, and a young toddler was deprived of his right to a father. The unnecessary police investigation alone caused two suicides, the incarceration and deportation of Red Johnson, and the wholesale arrest and harassment of countless innocent Americans. All because the right questions, all the questions, were not asked.

There is enough blame to go around here and no single scapegoat should be chosen. There are several factors which led, either singularly or in combination, to the injustice of Hauptmann's execution and Lindbergh's evasion of justice.

When the *Titanic* sank in 1912, cavalier optimists ascribed it to a statistical aberration due to an errant iceberg. This made everyone feel better, and safer. But to do so was a disservice to those who had perished. By learning from the *Titanic* the world could be safer, for the disaster could not be blamed on just an errant iceberg without attention being given to the failure to heed the iceberg warnings, the failure to proceed cautiously at night, the failure of the pilot to turn the ship in response to the lookout's warning of an iceberg dead ahead and the failure to have enough life boats. No tragedy has just one cause and the Lindbergh case is no exception. We learned from the *Titanic* and we should learn from Lindbergh.

Some of the factors which led to the tragedy in Hopewell, the Bronx, Flemington and the death house in Trenton were products of the times, and as long as we guard against history repeating we should avoid similar tragedies in the future. Other factors are still with us, and a study of the Lindbergh case teaches us to become and remain vigilant to prevent these factors from recurring.

The first easy target is the police, and much criticism has been directed at Colonel Schwarzkopf's handling of this case. Yet it is too easy to dismiss this tragedy as Colonel Schwarzkopf's blunder. It is true that he made two mistakes: he did not consider the Lindberghs as suspects and he allowed the person who should have been his chief suspect to head the investigation.

Colonel Schwarzkopf has been roundly criticized for this second mistake. However, we should bear in mind that he was not the only one to make it. Commissioner Mulrooney in New York was also faced down by Lindbergh and it is doubtful if any police official in 1932 would have reacted differently and not abdicated his authority to Colonel Lindbergh. We do not put our heros on pedestals as we once did and, hopefully, never will again.

Similarly, police techniques in child abuse prevention and detection have improved tremendously since 1932. If the Lindbergh case scenario repeated itself today, certainly Colonel Lindbergh would be at the top of the list of suspects. In the sixty years since this case we have learned that child abuse, spousal abuse, alcohol abuse, sexual abuse and incest are not confined to a particular financial class or ethnic group. Because of the recognition of the value of police training and education in the last twenty years, police are no longer mere para-military foot soldiers. They are trained to know that familial abuses are truly egalitarian American crimes: they infest families without regard to race, color, creed, national origin, financial position or social status. That was not accepted as true in 1932; it is today.

The prosecution has also been nominated as a scapegoat by many critics of the Lindbergh case. Certainly they too are good candidates. David Wilentz had available to him information which tended to show that Hauptmann was innocent. There is strong circumstantial evidence that Wilentz had possession of Hauptmann's ledger book which would have bolstered his alibi defense but did not disclose it to the defense. Certainly Wilentz must have known that several key witnesses such as Condon, the New Jersey witnesses, the cab driver Perrone, the movie theater ticket clerk Barr, and Lindbergh himself were all testifying in a way inconsistent with earlier statements they had made, and that such prior inconsistent statements were not available to the defense.

If the jury had been apprised of such facts they may have voted to acquit. Wilentz either knew or should have known that other handwriting experts had attributed the nursery note to other third parties. If that had been disclosed to the defense and the jury, it would have at least demonstrated that no handwriting expert was credible. The jury might then have been persuaded to discount all of the expert testimony linking Hauptmann's handwriting with the nursery note. Without that, they may have voted to acquit.

Some critics have charged more. Scaduto insinuates and Kennedy directly states that Wilentz knew that much of his case was fabricated, that Bornmann had manufactured the attic/rail board connection and that Condon's telephone number in Hauptmann's closet had been put there by an over- eager newspaper journalist. Wilentz said nothing about this evidence, the jury was not told the whole story, and Hauptmann was electrocuted.

If true, this is certainly reprehensible. An innocent man died because of a prosecutor's zealousness. Yet a blanket condemnation of Wilentz is also somewhat unfair. The condemnation stems from our view of the case in hindsight. To correctly analyze what David Wilentz did we have to ask why he did it.

First and foremost, David Wilentz probably believed that Bruno Richard Hauptmann *was* guilty. If so, then it would be an injustice if he were acquitted. Thus all efforts must be directed at convicting him and if the existing evidence is not enough then the addition of tainted or manufactured evidence only helps achieve the correct result. If the road to hell is paved with good intentions then interposed in that tar is rail 16 of the ladder.

But more than "good intentions," the source of the problem with the prosecution of this case can be traced to the roles that lawyers, and in particular prosecutors, were perceived to have. A lawyer was, and even is today, supposed to represent his or her client zealously. The prosecutor's client is "The State" or "The People." His interest is perceived to be the conviction of the criminal. If both the prosecutor and the defense lawyer swing with everything they have then the jury can sift it all out and reach a correct verdict.

The problem with that scenario is two-fold. One, it assumes that both sides are hitting fairly and that both are producing all the real facts for the jury. When one side starts manufacturing evidence then the accuracy of the system is thrown off. If David Wilentz justified what he did on the basis that the correct result (conviction) would therefore be reached, he was in effect substituting himself for the jury. He would be changing the system in favor of his own: prosecutor as judge and jury.

Second, under contemporary theories of the role of the prosecutor, it is no longer considered that the interest of the State is always to secure a conviction. What if the accused happens to be innocent? More recent analysts would say that although in all cases the interest of the accused may remain acquittal, the interest of the State is for a *correct verdict*. In the case where an innocent defendant stands accused the interest of the State would be in an acquittal.

Under this philosophy the prosecutor has an obligation to provide to the defense all exculpatory material or evidence in their possession; that is, material or evidence which tends to show that the defendant is in fact innocent. Although this may not seem radical, it only stems from the United States Supreme Court's declaration of such in the case entitled *Brady v. Maryland* decided in 1963. Prior to that, prosecutors often acted the way critics have accused Wilentz of acting in this case.

The judiciary and criminal justice system itself also deserve some blame. In 1932 many of the constitutional protections which we have today did not exist. They did not because judges and courts would not enforce them. Random arrests, searches and seizures were commonplace. Henry Johnson spent 18 days in jail without being charged with anything before being deported into obscurity. Henry Johnson was only the best known of these "other" victims of the Lindbergh investigation. Hundreds of persons were stopped, arrested, searched, detained and their rights violated with no factual or legal basis.

That is how police solved crimes then. Unfortunately, it is too often how they solve them today. If you round up enough of the "usual suspects" you will eventually catch the guilty one. That the technique works only makes it a more difficult practice to eradicate. The anguish of the Henry Johnsons is not enough to do so.

The judiciary of 1932 turned a blind eye. Not until Earl Warren did the United States Supreme Court begin to change these practices. Bruno Richard Hauptmann was beaten by the police in the Bronx, and when the issue was raised in the trial in Flemington the Judge dismissed the allegation as irrelevant, ruling that a New Jersey court had no jurisdiction to concern itself with a New York police beating. After a discussion at the bench the trial proceeded, the beating forgotten.

Judge Trenchard, like David Wilentz, was result oriented. For whatever reason, whether it was his belief in Hauptmann's guilt, deference to the Lindbergh name and power, or recognition of the popular position, Trenchard's handling of the trial was a farce. By his rulings during the trial and his summation to the jury at its close, he basically instructed them to convict Hauptmann, and they did just that. A result oriented judiciary is, unfortunately, not a characteristic of our criminal justice system which we shed with the great depression. The popular perception of judges in this country is as a type of law enforcement officer: the perceived chain of law enforcement hierarchy is policeman, prosecutor, judge. When a criminal defendant is released from the system the public reaction is often "how could the Judge let him go?" The very question reflects the prevailing attitude that the Judge is the top cop whose interest should be conviction.

That attitude is too often shared by members of the judiciary themselves. Judges are, by their very selection process, political players. One becomes a State Court Judge either by getting appointed by the governor or by standing direct election. Often governors will accompany a judicial appointment with the caveat "a person who has always been tough on crime and who will continue to be so from the bench." A governor wants to make popular appointments. When a civil libertarian surfaces on the bench it is usually because their orientation was not known prior to their appointment.

In those states where judges are directly elected the campaign can be abysmal. Judges often advertise their record of toughness on crime and television commercials have aired showing incumbent judges standing in front of slamming jail doors. These are the people who too often, even today, become judges and worse, once judges, engage in result oriented judicial decisions. We saw the repercussions of this in 1935.

But the last scapegoat is perhaps the biggest. Hauptmann faced a brutal line-up in Flemington, New Jersey: a police force which did not fully investigate, which abdicated its control and which may have tinkered with the evidence; a prosecutor who at the least was negligent about preventing this and at the worst was its architect who did nothing to ensure a fair or correct verdict; and a judicial system which both condoned and elaborated on the police and prosecutor's misdeeds. In the face of this Hauptmann had the right to expect his lawyer to fight. Maybe the deck was too stacked, the odds too insurmountable. Perhaps given the prevailing climate and the state of the evidence, his conviction was lawyer-proof. Regardless, he had the right to expect that his lawyer would meet with him before and throughout the trial, be well prepared and prepare him well for the trial and his testimony in it.

It never happened. Reilly had his money up front and was not going to get any more. He had his fee and whether he did a good job or a lousy one would not effect his financial situation. All he cared about was getting the case over as quickly as possible. The outcome was irrelevant.

Ed Reilly's defense of Bruno Richard Hauptmann was perhaps the most shameful aspect of this whole tragedy. We can expect the police, the prosecutor and the Judge to act as they did, and we can even forgive it if we believe that in their misguided zeal they were trying to direct what they perceived to be the correct verdict. But Ed Reilly's role is indefensible.

There is a strong temptation in writing about an event like this to reach some sort of philosophical conclusion, to find in the deaths of Charles Lindbergh, Jr., Bruno Richard Hauptmann, Violet Sharpe and Henry Leipold, in the incarceration and deportation of Henry Johnson, and in the wholesale invasion into the rights of countless others some meaning, some wisdom learned that made it all worth while, to assuage our fear that all did not suffer in vain. However, history is not a zero sum game in which a lesson of equal value springs forth from every tragedy. Rather, it is a continuum along which we progress, strengthening with the experiences we gather. Armed with that strength we can look back and again learn to question, to challenge, to doubt, to ask why, to not blindly accept at face value. This was not done in 1932 with Colonel Charles Augustus Lindbergh. It was not done in 1989 with Charles Stuart or in 1990 with Christine Lane. We must learn.

AUTHORS' NOTES

This project began early in 1990 when Attorney Greg Ahlgren inadvertently came across the reprint of the Alan Hynd article on the crime. Even though he knew little about the case initially, certain aspects troubled him as he read on. These, and his own experiences in defending people charged with crimes, raised his suspicions.

After mulling it over for a few days he photocopied the article and sent it off to Chief Stephen Monier without annotation or indication of suspicion. The Chief called back and shared the same concerns. It quickly became a book project.

There was no shortage of research material available. A number of books and articles have been written about the crime. There is much biographical work on the Lindberghs themselves. In addition, we obtained original police notes, original diaries of the principles, and the transcript of the Hauptmann trial.

As we delved into the material we noticed that the other writers had all looked at the case retrospectively - there was a kidnapping in 1932; did Hauptmann do it? We used our own experience and training as a criminal investigator and trial lawyer to look at the case prospectively from the time of the initial police report of the child's disappearance - these are the clues; what probably happened?

The advantages that we bring to this case are discussed elsewhere. What is important is that we tried to investigate this case as it would be investigated today, and should have been in 1932. We also tried to investigate it without regard to the identity of the victim's father. That clearly was not done in 1932. Doing so we quickly concluded that the investigation may have been built around a fundamentally false assumption. There may not have been a kidnapping.

In presenting our thesis we have stated certain "facts" of the case. Where we have encountered conflicting evidence, we have not necessarily presented those factual patterns most consistent with our theory, but rather those which we feel are most likely to be accurate.

One example in hundreds concerns the time of Lindbergh's honking horn arrival on March 1, 1932. We have said that it was 8:25 p.m., thereby giving him a 35 minute window to accomplish his deed. This is some ten minutes more than he needed.

Yet the 8:25 p.m. figure is in dispute. In her often cited letter to her mother-in-law of March 2, Anne placed the time at 8:20 p.m. Although this makes his opportunity narrower, our thesis is still possible. Betty Gow testified to an 8:30 p.m. arrival. Some researchers have pegged the time at 8:35 p.m.

Although the latter estimates (of 8:30 p.m. and 8:35 p.m.) make Lindbergh's window of opportunity larger, and our theory easier, we have rejected them in favor of the 8:25 p.m. arrival. We took that from the testimony under oath of both Anne Lindbergh and Colonel Lindbergh during the Hauptmann trial.

We did not lightly reject the other estimates. However, in considering them and the circumstances under which they were given, we found the sworn statements by Anne and the Colonel to be the most credible. Betty Gow's estimate has to be taken in conjunction with her estimate of a slightly later time as to when she had left the nursery. In any event, Lindbergh's window of opportunity as defined by her (30 minutes) was still sufficient.

The 8:20 p.m. estimate in Anne's letter was produced by a distraught mother writing furtively under the stress of the moment. The 8:35 p.m. figure which exists in other writings seems to have no factual basis.

As we continued our research there were four major aspects of this case which deeply troubled us and seemed to have never been fully investigated.

The first concerned the 1929 extortion note to Constance Morrow. Newspaper articles in the *New York Times* at the time of Hauptmann's arrest tipped us to its existence. The similarities between the two were extraordinary. Yet in the trial, no reference was made by either side to the earlier extortion attempt. Most writers have not even mentioned it. When it has been noted, it has only been to show an unfortunate chain of circumstances that haunted the Morrow family, or to suggest that

Colonel Lindbergh therefore had "kidnapping experience" which he could rely on in this case. We determined to try to find that note.

The second aspect which deeply troubled us is Charles Lindbergh's own failure to recall what he did on the afternoon of the kidnapping. All of the accounts of his whereabouts are vague. We know that he did not attend a scheduled speaking engagement that evening, but he himself could not describe in detail what time he purportedly left the office, where he went, whether or not he had a dentist appointment, and so on.

His testimony at the trial gives the clearest indication of this conspicuous memory failure. On direct examination he said only that he "had spent the day in New York." On cross- examination, Reilly had asked him to outline his movement that day. He again tried a curt answer, but Reilly pressed him:

Q. Now, will you give us an outline of your movement on Tuesday?
A. Tuesday I was in New York during the day.
Q. Where?
A. I don't recall in vivid detail where I went. I think I went to the Pan-American Airways office, probably to the Trans-Continental Air Transport offices. I was at the Rockefeller Institute during a part of the day and I believe that I stopped at my dentist's that afternoon late, to the best of my recollection.

Does it seem probable that generations of Americans can remember in detail their whereabouts and activities during momentous occasions, such as the day of the Kennedy assassination, but that Charles Lindbergh would be unable to account for his time following his departure from work, and his arrival at home - on the very night his first born son disappears? Since the police never considered Colonel Lindbergh a suspect, the ability to accurately, precisely, and corroboratively reconstruct where he was during that entire day and afternoon, has been lost forever.

The last two aspects which troubled us concerned two witness/participants. The first was Robert Thayer, the young lawyer in Colonel Breckinridge's law office. Immediately following the child's disappearance, he was as involved as Breckinridge in advising Lindbergh.

Thayer was a young, ambitious, aspiring lawyer, and married to a Standard Oil heiress. In March of 1932 he was 30 years old, with a promising legal and social career.

He liked to rub shoulders with "underworld types" and was responsible for bringing Mickey Rossner into the case. He was the one who answered the telephone the night Dr. Condon called. At the outset, he participated at the highest level and attended virtually every strategy session.

Then suddenly, without warning, and without explanation, he disappeared from the case. He was not part of the later investigation, played no role in the arrest of Hauptmann, and, most strangely, was never called as a witness in the 1935 trial.

While other authors have noted this, it especially disturbed us. A few writers theorized that perhaps it was because he would have contradicted some of the minor points about which Dr. Condon testified.

To us his absence was more sinister. Attorney Thayer would have been the perfect set-up witness used by a prosecutor to present an overview of the events in Hopewell during the Condon/Cemetery John negotiations. He could have testified as to how he became involved in the case, how he brought in Rossner, what happened the night Condon telephoned and traveled to Hopewell, and what the strategy was with regard to the New York City pay-off. Knowing that Condon's credibility would be in issue, the prosecutor would have wanted an ingenuous Thayer to help establish that credibility.

Yet Thayer was not called as a witness. Lack of money or desire to be expeditious could not explain it. A host of minor witnesses were brought to the trial every day, sat through it for weeks, and then gave brief testimony on obscure points.

Could Thayer's absence possibly be because he had been told something by Lindbergh or Breckinridge, or had inadvertently discovered something, which made him, for reasons of conscience, disassociate himself from the case? If as a lawyer he had learned that Lindbergh had killed his own child, he would have had an ethical obligation to not further participate in the perpetration of a fraud, to not further aid and abet Lindbergh's deception.

However, those same ethical obligations would have mandated that he not tell anyone what his client had told him or Breckinridge. His only alternative would have been to withdraw from further participation in the hoax. We did not believe his disappearance from the case to be a voluntary one. From what we have learned, Thayer loved both the criminal law and his personal involvement in criminal cases. He certainly relished his role in this, "The Crime of the Century." We determined early on that if Thayer were still alive we had to find him.

The last loose end concerned Sebastian Benjamin Lupica, the Princeton Preparatory senior who claimed to have seen a car with two sections of a handmade ladder in it at about 6:00 p.m. on March 1, 1932, near the Lindbergh estate. Lupica had been subpoenaed by the prosecution to the trial but had not been called by them as a witness. Instead, he was called by the defense and examined by Attorney Fischer.

His testimony was that he had been standing by the series of mailboxes at the driveway leading to the Lindbergh estate. He was interested in a piece of mail addressed to him and had stopped to read it. Around the corner came an automobile which had stopped up the dirt road and pulled off to its left as if waiting for him to pass. When Lupica proceeded towards the car he noted it to be a dark blue or black 1929 Dodge sedan with New Jersey license plates. The driver of the car was alone, between 35 and 40 years old, and had thin features. He said that he could not identify Hauptmann as the driver and had never told anyone that he could.

On cross-examination David Wilentz came close to adopting Lupica as his own witness. He elicited from him that there was only one man - not a gang - in the car. This specifically rebutted a defense theory that only a "gang", (and therefore not Hauptmann) could have carried out the crime.

Wilentz also asked Lupica about a prior identification attempt and whether:

Q. The man you saw on the night of March the first resembled Mr. Hauptmann?
A. That Mr. Hauptmann had a resemblance to him.

Wilentz also showed Lupica a newspaper clipping which contained a purported quote by Lupica identifying Hauptmann as the driver. Lupica denied ever having identified Hauptmann as the driver. Later Wilentz asked Lupica whether:

Q. You told everybody in the world that the man you saw on March first in an automobile with a ladder in it looked liked Hauptmann, isn't that right?
A. He has a resemblance, yes.

In his summation Wilentz referred to Lupica's identification. The clear impression any observer of the trial was left with was that Lupica had seen a man driving the car who closely resembled Hauptmann, but that Lupica just could not bring himself to actually identify the kidnapper from the witness stand. Newspaper articles at the time actually referred to Lupica "having wavered on the witness stand" in his identification of Hauptmann.

Every other researcher has passed over the exchange between Lupica and Wilentz. However, as we read and reread his testimony, there were two things which stood out. First, it is obvious that Lupica was not agreeing with Wilentz' contention on cross-examination that Hauptmann looked like the driver. He twice corrected Wilentz, a man much his senior and legally trained, by asserting that the man he saw only "had a resemblance" to Hauptmann. Wilentz argued that this constituted a *de facto* identification.

Second, the fact that Lupica was called as a defense witness and not as a prosecution witness, stood out immediately.

After all, Hauptmann also owned a Dodge, and although it was a green 1930 model, the description was sufficiently close to raise the inference that Lupica was simply mistaken about the year and shade of color. Moreover, Lupica could confirm the existence of one man - and not a gang - as the kidnapper and thereby rebut, as of the date of the kidnapping itself, a defense theory.

Why hadn't Wilentz called Ben Lupica to the witness stand? Lupica was present in the courtroom and available every day. Since Wilentz presented a comprehensive case, calling an array of even minor witnesses to cover obscure points, why didn't he call the one man who may have actually seen the kidnapper near the Lindbergh estate on the day of the crime?

In all the books and articles written since the event, no other writer had focused on this, and we could find no reference that anyone had ever gone back to ask Ben Lupica what he had seen in that car on March 1, 1932. Could it be that what he had seen had caused Wilentz not to risk using him as a witness? We made a note early on that if Ben Lupica were alive, he too, had to be located and interviewed.

We did this with the knowledge that Ben Lupica might also be the one witness who could summarily disprove our theory. Surely he knew Lindbergh, his neighbor, and one of the most famous men in America at the time, by sight. Wouldn't he have recognized him had Lindbergh been behind the wheel?

Having cataloged these issues, we began by looking for the note. Milton, Massachusetts police Chief Richard G. Wells was very helpful and courteous, and granted us complete access to his records. In fact, the records from that period had been kept.

When crime reports were made to the desk sergeant they were entered on his daily desk blotter. That desk blotter existed and the text of that contact appears elsewhere. Other officers working on a case also kept day books with their notes. The day book which would have contained the notes on this case has disappeared. No receipt or note indicates why it is missing. A check with Milton Academy was similarly unfruitful.

Neither of the two witnesses were easy to track. There were no Robert Thayers practicing law in New York State. The historical records of the state bar showed that Robert H. Thayer had been admitted to practice in 1928, but no further information about him, even whether he was still alive, was available.

The American Bar Association also had no record of him. Had he disappeared, we wondered?

A random telephone check of all Robert Thayers gave us our first clue. One Robert Thayer informed us that he was not the one we were looking for, nor was he a relative. When asked, we shared the purpose of our search. He indicated that although he had never heard of Attorney Thayer, about six months before our call, he had received a similar inquiry from the British Broadcasting Corporation. They revealed to him that they had traced our Robert Thayer into intelligence work for the United States government, but had lost him there.

Armed with this new information, we renewed our efforts. Relying on other contacts and sources, we eventually learned that he had passed away on January 26, 1984. His wife was also deceased but we were able to locate and speak with his son.

What we learned from him did nothing to dispel our theory. Thayer had indeed been involved in the inner working of the Lindbergh case in its early stages, but had suddenly, and for reasons he never revealed to his family, disengaged himself from the case and even from the employment of Colonel Henry Breckinridge.

He worked briefly as an assistant District Attorney in New York, and then took a job overseas with the U.S. State Department. Although classified as a diplomat (he was later appointed an ambassador by President Eisenhower) everyone in his family knew that he was actually engaged in covert intelligence work and used his diplomatic postings as a cover. By the time of Hauptmann's arrest and trial, Thayer had long been assigned out of the country.

Who had so assigned him? We were aware that Breckinridge had been an assistant Secretary of War in the Wilson Administration and retained influence in foreign service circles. Had Breckinridge gotten Thayer out of the country, and if so, why?

The trail however, seemed to end there. Robert Thayer's oldest son told us that he was only two years old when this all happened, and he had no recollection of it. As he grew up he was generally aware that his father had been involved with the "Lindbergh case" but his father pointedly never talked about it. If Attorney Robert Thayer had felt an ethical obligation to get out of the case, and for that matter to leave Breckinridge's employ, he may have also made an ethical decision to never violate any confidences.

Finding Sebastian Benjamin Lupica was even more difficult. Ultimately, however, we learned that he was still alive. When we contacted him, he agreed to meet with us.

We spoke with him on June 12, 1992. He was retired after 37 years as a research chemist. Although mentally alert, personable, and engaging, he was suffering from Parkinson's Disease. To our astonishment, he revealed that despite all the books that had been written about this crime, not once had anyone ever made an effort to speak with him about his observations.

We spoke with him in his apartment, in the presence of his wife and daughter. At the end of the two and one-half hour session, we both realized that those who had tried to clear Hauptmann's name in the New Jersey courts, without ever having taken Ben Lupica's deposition, had missed out on a tremendous opportunity.

In some way Mr. Lupica seemed relieved to speak with us. He had never read any of the books written about the crime, and his wife related how just the week before, he had refused when she had suggested that they watch a PBS documentary on it. He was upset at the way the crime had been treated by journalists in 1935, and therefore distrustful of how they may have treated the facts since. The fact that we were not professional journalists, had contributed to his decision to speak with us after 60 years. As he put it, "I want the truth to come out."

Ben Lupica's parents (and his wife's parents) were Italian immigrants who had originally settled in New York City. When Ben was still young his parents had purchased a tract of land in the Sourland Mountains to attempt farming. His family was poor, but they worked hard at the family farm in the Depression.

In 1931 Ben graduated from high school. However, he knew he had to improve his academics to get into a good college and so in 1931-1932 he lived at home while attending Princeton Preparatory School in nearby Princeton, New Jersey. Every morning he would drive to school and return in the afternoon.

Ben was only vaguely aware of Lindbergh. As a boy struggling through the Depression, with a goal of obtaining college, he did not pay much attention to current events. In the days before television, he had no idea what Lindbergh looked like.

Moreover, although he was aware that Lindbergh had purchased the land in Hopewell, and that construction was under way, he did not know that Lindbergh was living there.

On March 1, 1932 Lupica had stopped his car at the row of mailboxes to retrieve his family's mail. As he stood there reading a letter, he saw the other car come around the corner and pull over to its left about 100 yards away. As the dirt road was narrow and two cars could only pass with difficulty, he assumed that the other driver had pulled over to make room.

Ben got back in his car and proceeded towards the other car. He had no reason to pay attention to the other car or its driver. He thought the other car might be a Dodge, but was absolutely certain that it had New Jersey license plates, which he saw clearly.

As he squeezed past, he paid no attention to its driver and had only an impression of a man "between 30 and 40" wearing a Fedora. There were two sections of a homemade ladder stretched from the rear left of the passenger compartment across the seat back to the front right near the windshield.

He stated unequivocally, after 60 years, that he could not identify Hauptmann as that driver. That driver, he said to us, "could have been anyone, anyone in the whole world." When asked what the resemblance was that he had told the police that the driver had to Hauptmann he responded, "they were both white." That was the resemblance that Wilentz and the press had referred to as an "identification" of Hauptmann.

Mr. Lupica also told us that he had never identified Hauptmann as the driver. At the time of Hauptmann's arrest, newspaper reporters were not above manufacturing interviews and one New York paper wrote an article claiming that they had interviewed Benjamin Lupica, and that he had identified Hauptmann as the driver. Ben was so irate, he had written a letter to the paper protesting its publication. It was this article Wilentz had shown him on the stand in an effort to impeach his lack of identification at trial.

Ben Lupica also told us that the morning after the crime, before he had heard about it, he was driving to school when he stopped to give a ride to a neighbor. The passenger asked Ben if had seen any strangers the night before and Ben described his encounter.

At this point they arrived at the Lindbergh driveway and the neighbor excitedly exited. Ben noticed swarms of police standing around with a dazed or shocked look on their face as hordes of newspapermen and photographers paraded over the grounds. Not knowing what was going on, and not at that point even aware that Lindbergh was residing there, Ben drove on to school, where he learned of the crime.

That afternoon, upon his return home, the police visited him. They took him to the Lindbergh estate for questioning. There he met Charles Lindbergh. Never having seen either the Colonel or a picture of him, it was a big moment. However, when Ben was introduced to Lindbergh as a person who had seen a car with a ladder in it the evening before, Lindbergh became agitated and distraught, and mumbled something about concern for his wife.

That was the only reference we ever found of Lindbergh not being cool and calm throughout all of this. As we listened to Ben Lupica the same thought crossed both of our minds.

We also asked Ben where he thought the kidnapper would have put his car, were he to approach the house. He immediately said "right in the driveway leading up to the house." He explained that he thought it would have been virtually impossible to traverse the woods, fields and terrain if someone had parked on any of the lanes surrounding the Lindbergh acreage.

Ben also described the trial. He knew both Amandus Hochmuth and Millard Whited. He described Hochmuth as a blind, senile old man who testified as he did for the money; money which Ben himself was offered, but for which he refused to change his testimony.

During the trial Ben Lupica sat next to Whited and during breaks he and Whited conversed. Whited constantly pumped Ben for details of his encounter with the car, and when Whited finally testified, it became clear to Ben that Whited had taken the threads of Ben's details and wove them into the fabric of his own manufactured story. Ben knew that Whited, too, had done it for the money, and it sickened him.

We asked him if he believed Hauptmann was guilty. He responded that he did not know. Sitting through the trial 57 years earlier, he had thought then that the proceedings were a sham, and even as a young student, he had been offended that Lindbergh himself had sat at the prosecution table throughout the entire trial.

He had heard Hauptmann testify and we asked him if he had believed him. He paused a long while before answering, "yes, I did believe him. But the money, the money was found in his garage. That is what sunk him, and that's what makes me think, I just don't know."

Both of us were very impressed with Benjamin Lupica. Despite his physical failings, his honesty and integrity shown through. As we listened, both of us, wished that more of our cases could be blessed with witnesses like Ben Lupica.

Despite the effects of Parkinson's, at the conclusion of the interview, Ben Lupica rose out of his chair to shake our hands. He looked us in the eyes and asked, "Am I the only one still alive?" Other than Anne Lindbergh and Anna Hauptmann, both aged, Benjamin Lupica is the only major figure in this case still alive.

The following players, in the Crime of the Century, are now deceased:

Colonel H. Norman Schwarzkopf, head of the New Jersey State Police, and the architect of the most famous kidnapping investigation in the history of the United States. Heavily criticized for what many have termed a "fatally flawed" investigation, Colonel Schwarzkopf was steadfast in his firm support for Charles Lindbergh, and in carrying out his wishes when conducting the investigation. His son, General H. Norman Schwarzkopf, was the commander of Operation Desert Storm.

Oliver and Elsie Whately were the Lindbergh household staff members who served as butler and cook for Charles and Anne Lindbergh. Oliver Whately actually died before the trial.

Betty Gow was the Scottish nursemaid to baby Charles, the "little eaglet," and who was widely suspected at one point, of having been involved from the inside in the kidnapping. Charles Lindbergh was resolute in his defense of her.

Violet Sharpe, the household staff member of Mrs. Morrow, Anne's mother, was subjected to intense police scrutiny, and ultimately committed suicide.

David Wilentz, the young, aggressive attorney general of the State of New Jersey. He parlayed his fame from the successful prosecution of Hauptmann into a long and distinguished legal career. He became active in the Democratic Party and his son, Robert Wilentz, is the presiding chief of the New Jersey Supreme Court.

Still alive, Anna Hauptmann has steadfastly maintained that her husband was innocent of the crime, and has refused to accept the verdict rendered by the jury in Flemington. Anna never remarried, and along with her son Manfred, merely an infant at the time of his father's execution, has never given up the fight to clear Bruno Richard Hauptmann's name.

Represented by Attorney Robert Bryan of San Francisco, Anna unsuccessfully sued the State of New Jersey for that purpose. Although the New Jersey courts dismissed her suit, she has reviews, and a request for a post humus pardon, pending with the New Jersey governor's office, and a judicial board of review.

In her last televised interview at the age of 92, Anna Hauptmann made an unusual appeal to Anne Lindbergh, asking Anne to help her reveal "the truth about this matter." Anna Hauptmann has also said publicly that, "I am waiting for the truth to come out. When it does, I die next day. And I die in peace."[31]

Ben Lupica also wanted the truth to come out. The authors believe that it is time it did.

FOOTNOTES

1. Charles Lindbergh, *The Spirit of St. Louis* (NY, 1953)
2. Alan Hynd, "Everyone wanted to Get Into the Act"
3. Charles Lindbergh, *Autobiography of Values* (NY, 1977)
4. Lindbergh, *Autobiography of Values.*
5. Lindbergh, *Autobiography of Values.*
6. Lindbergh, *Autobiography of Values.*
7. Kenneth Davis, *The Hero* (London, 1960)
8. Lindbergh, *Autobiography of Values.*
9. Lindbergh, *Autobiography of Values.*
10. "Dear Abbey", *Manchester Union Leader*, December 23, 1990.
11. Anne Lindbergh, *Bring Me A Unicorn.*
12. Sergeant's Book, Milton, Massachusetts Police.
13. Lindbergh, *Autobiography of Values.*
14. Anne Lindbergh, *North to the Orient* (NY, 1935).
15. Anne Lindbergh, *Bring Me A Unicorn.*
16. Anne Lindbergh, *Hour of Gold, Hour of Lead.*
17. Ibid.
18. Ibid.
19. Ibid.
20. Trooper Bornmann's reports.
21. John F. Condon, *Jafsie Tells All* (NY, 1936).
22. Anne Lindbergh, *Hour of Gold, Hour of Lead.*
23. Charles Lindbergh, *Autobiography of Values.*
24. Harold Nicolson, *Diaries and Letters* (NY, 1966).
25. Nicolson, *Diaries and Letters.*
26. *The American Experience*, "Lindbergh."
27. *San Francisco Chronicle.*
28. Anne Lindbergh, *Hour of Gold, Hour of Lead.*
29. Ibid.
30. Ibid.
31. Ludovic Kennedy, *The Airman and the Carpenter.*

BIBLIOGRAPHY & SOURCES

The authors found the following books to be helpful sources of information on the Lindbergh case:

Brant, John and Renaud, Edith. *True Story of the Lindbergh Kidnapping*, Kroy Wren, NY, 1932.

Canning, John, Editor. *Unsolved Murders & Mysteries*, Treasure Press, London, 1990.

Condon, John F. *Jafsie Tells All*, Jonathan Lee Publishing Corporation, NY, 1936.

Demaris, Ovid. *The Lindbergh Kidnapping Case: The True Story of the Crime that Shocked the World*, Monarch Books, Conn, 1961.

Haring, J. Vreeland. *The Hand of Hauptmann*, Hamer Publishing Co, Plainfield, NJ, 1937.

Kennedy, Ludovic. *The Airman and the Carpenter: The Lindbergh Kidnapping and the Framing of Richard Hauptmann.* Viking, NY, 1985.

Osborn, Albert D. *Questioned Document Problems*, Boyd Printing Co., Albany, NY, 1944.

Scaduto, Anthony. *Scapegoat*, Secker and Warburg, London/Putnams, NY, 1976.

Shoenfeld, Dudley D. *The Crime and the Criminal. A Psychiatric Study of the Lindbergh Case.* Covici-Friede, NY, 1936.

Turrou, Leon G. *Where My Shadow Falls*, Doubleday and Co., NY 1949.

Waller, George. *Kidnap*, Hamish Hamilton, London/Dial Books, NY, 1935.

Whipple, Sidney B. *The Lindbergh Crime*, Blue Ribbon Books, NY, 1935.

-------. *The Trial of Bruno Richard Hauptmann*, Doubleday, Doran, NY, 1937.

Wilson, Frank J. and Day, Beth. *Special Agent: A Quarter Century with the Treasury Department and the Secret Service*, Holt, Rinehart and Winston, NY, 1965.

Vitray, Laura. *The Great Lindbergh Hullabaloo: An Unorthodox Account*, William Faro, NY, 1932.

Wright, Theon. *In Search of the Lindbergh Baby*, Tower Publications, NY, 1981.

Stolen Away, by Max Allan Collins, is a fictionalized story about the Lindbergh case, but is nevertheless well researched and well written. (Bantam Books, NY, 1991)

Several books were used as valuable sources of information about Charles Lindbergh, and the Lindbergh era:

Davis, Kenneth S. *The Hero*, Longmans, London, 1960.

Lees-Milne, James. *Harold Nicholson, A Biography*, Vol II 1930-1968, Chatto and Windus, London/Archon Books, NY, 1981.

Lindbergh, Anne Morrow. *North to the Orient*, Harcourt Brace Jovanovich, NY, 1935.

-----. *Listen! the Wind*, Harcourt Brace Jovanovich, NY, 1938.

-----. *Bring Me A Unicorn: Diaries and Letters of Anne Morrow Lind bergh, 1924-1928*, Harcourt Brace Jovanovich, NY, 1971, 1972.

-----. *Hour of Gold, Hour of Lead: Diaries and Letters of Anne Morrow Lindbergh, 1929-1932*, Harcourt Brace Jovanovich, NY, 1973.

-----. *Locked Rooms and Open Doors: Diaries and Letters of Anne Morrow Lindbergh, 1933-1935*, Harcourt Brace Jovanovich, NY, 1974.

-----. *The Flower and the Nettle: Diaries and Letters of Anne Morrow Lindbergh, 1936-1939*, Harcourt Brace Jovanovich, NY, 1976.

-----. *War Within and War Without: Diaries and Letters of Anne Morrow Lindbergh, 1939-1944*, Harcourt Brace Jovanovich, NY, 1980.

Lindbergh, Charles. *The Spirit of St Louis*, John Murray, London Charles Scribner's Sons, NY, 1953.

-----. *Boyhood on the Upper Mississippi*, Minnesota Historical Society, 1972.

-----. *Autobiography of Values*, Edited by William Jovanovich and Judith A Schiff. Harcourt Brace Jovanovich, NY, 1977.

-----. *The Wartime Journals of Charles A Lindbergh*, Harcourt Brace Jovanovich, NY, 1970.

Mosley, Leonard. *Lindbergh A Biography*, Doubleday & Company, NY, 1976.

Mott, Frank Luther, (ed.). *Headlining America*, Houghton, Mifflin, Boston, 1937. "Hauptmann Execution," by Damon Runyon; and "The Lindberghs Leave America," by Lauren D. Lyman.

Nicolson, Nigel (ed.). *Harold Nicolson, Diaries and Letters 1930-1939,* Collins, London/Atheneum, NY, 1966.
Powers, Richard G. *Secrecy and Power: The Life of J. Edgar Hoover,* The Free Press, NY, 1987.
Ross, Walter S. *The Last Hero,* Harper and Row, NY, 1964.

Hundreds of thousands of words have appeared in magazine articles and periodicals about the Lindberghs, and the Lindbergh Case. These were helpful to the research on this book:

Badin, Michael M. "The Lindbergh Kidnapping: Review of the Autopsy Evidence." *Journal of Forensic Science* October 1983.
Bent, Silas. "Lindbergh and the Press." *Outlook,* April 1932.
Curtin, D. Thomas, and Finn, James J. "How I Captured Hauptmann." *Liberty Magazine,* October 12,19,26; November 2,9,16,23, 1935.
Davidson, David D. "The Story of the Century." *American Heritage,* February 1976.
Fisher, Lloyd C. "The Case New Jersey Would Like to Forget." *Liberty Magazine,* August 1,8,15,29; September 5,12, 1936.
Hauptmann, Bruno Richard. "Hauptmann's Own Story." *New York Daily Mirror,* December 3-10, 1935.
-----. "Why Did You Kill Me?" *Liberty Magazine,* May 2, 1936.
Hoffman, Harold G. "The Crime, The Case, The Challenge." *Liberty Magazine,* January 29; February 5, 12, 19, 26; March 5, 12, 19, 26; April 2, 9, 16, 23, 30, 1938.
-----. "Things I Forgot." *Liberty Magazine,* July 2, 1938.
-----. "More Things I Forgot to Tell." *Liberty Magazine,* July 9, 1938.
Hynd, Alan. "Everyone Wanted to Get Into the Act." *True Magazine,* March 1949. Reprinted in Alan Hynd, Violence in the Night, Fawcett, NY, 1955.
Koehler, Arthur. "Techniques Used in Tracing the Lindbergh Kidnapping Ladder." *Journal of Criminal Law and Criminology,* Vol 27, No 5, 1936-37.
Moseley, Seth H. "The Night the Lindbergh Baby Disappeared."*Yankee Magazine,* March 1982.
Prosser, William. "The Lindbergh Case Revisited: George Waller's 'Kidnap.'" *Minnesota Law Review,* Vol 46, 1962.
Sanders, Paul H. "Scientific and Procedural Aspects of the Hauptmann Trial." *American Bar Association Journal,* May 1935.

Seidman, Louis M. "The Trial and Execution of Bruno Hauptmann: Still Another Case That Will Not Die. *Georgetown Law Journal*, October 1977.

Shaffer, Douglas K. "The Lindbergh Kidnapping: 'Crime of the Century' Still Fascinates After 60 Years." *Hopewell Valley News*, A Five Part Series beginning March 12, 1992.

Thompson, Craig. "Did They Really Solve the Lindbergh Case?" *Saturday Evening Post*, March 8, 1952.

Wedemer, Lou. "50 Unanswered Questions in the Hauptmann Case: A Searching Survey of the Doubts and 'Sinister Suggestions' That Still Shadow the Famous Crime." *Liberty Magazine*, January 4, 1936.

Wendel, Paul H. "Wendel Tells All - 'My 44 Days of Kid-napping, Torture, and Hell in the Lindbergh Case.'" Liberty Magazine, beginning in November 28, 1936.

Wilson, P.W. "The Lindbergh Case." *North American Review*, January 1934.

Yagoda, Ben. "Legacy of a Kidnapping." *New Jersey Monthly*, August 1981.

Yerkes, Peter. "Did Bruno Hauptmann Really Do It?" Today, *The Inquirer Magazine*, April 9, 1978.

Zito, Tom. "Did the Evidence Fit the Crime?" *Life Magazine*, March 1982.

Newspapers devoted entire editions to the Lindbergh crime, and have continued to cover aspects of the story ever since. The *New York Times* put extensive resources into the coverage of the Lindbergh case. Other newspaper sources included:

Boston Globe, Bronx Home News, Chicago Daily Tribune, Detroit News, Hopewell Valley News, Hunterdon County Democrat, Jersey Journal, Manchester Union Leader & Sunday News, New York American, New York Daily News, New York Evening Journal, New York Herald Tribune, Philadelphia Evening Ledger, Philadelphia Record, San Francisco Chronicle, Syracuse Post Standard....

Official Reports, Documents, and Records:
Bronx District Attorney's office
Jersey City Police
Milton, Massachusetts Police
New Jersey State Police
New York City Police

Pawtucket Rhode Island Police
Rhode Island State Police
US Department of Justice - Federal Bureau of Investigation
US Treasury Department - Internal Revenue Service
Trial Transcript of Bruno Richard Hauptmann

Other Sources included various film productions, and transcripts or tapes of interviews of noted authors, witnesses, jurors, or the television productions themselves, to include:

The American Experience - "Lindbergh"
"Reliving the Lindbergh Case" - Hosted by Edwin Newman
Geraldo
Hardcopy
Interviews of Ethel Stockton
Televised interview of Anne Morrow Lindbergh, by Eric Severeid,
    1977.
Taped debate between Anthony Scaduto and Jim Fisher

Index